Robert Godby • Stephanie B. Anderson
Greek Tragedy, European Odyssey:
The Politics and Economics of the Eurozone Crisis

Robert Godby
Stephanie B. Anderson

Greek Tragedy, European Odyssey: The Politics and Economics of the Eurozone Crisis

Barbara Budrich Publishers
Opladen • Berlin • Toronto 2016

The book was in part drafted with the support of a grant by the Kolleg-Forschergruppe (KFG) "The Transformative Power of Europe," hosted at the Freie Universität Berlin. The KFG is funded by the German Research Foundation (DFG) and brings together research on the diffusion of ideas in the EU's internal and external relations. For further information please consult www.transformeurope.eu.

All rights reserved. No part of this publication may be reproduced, stored in or introduced into a retrieval system, or transmitted, in any form, or by any means (electronic, mechanical, photocopying, recording or otherwise) without the prior written permission of Barbara Budrich Publishers. Any person who does any unauthorized act in relation to this publication may be liable to criminal prosecution and civil claims for damages.

You must not circulate this book in any other binding or cover and you must impose this same condition on any acquirer.

A CIP catalogue record for this book is available from

Die Deutsche Bibliothek (The German Library)

© 2016 by Barbara Budrich Publishers, Opladen, Berlin & Toronto
www.barbara-budrich.net

ISBN 978-3-8474-0618-1
eISBN 978-3-8474-0431-6

Das Werk einschließlich aller seiner Teile ist urheberrechtlich geschützt. Jede Verwertung außerhalb der engen Grenzen des Urheberrechtsgesetzes ist ohne Zustimmung des Verlages unzulässig und strafbar. Das gilt insbesondere für Vervielfältigungen, Übersetzungen, Mikroverfilmungen und die Einspeicherung und Verarbeitung in elektronischen Systemen.

Die Deutsche Bibliothek – CIP-Einheitsaufnahme
Ein Titeldatensatz für die Publikation ist bei der Deutschen Bibliothek erhältlich.

Verlag Barbara Budrich Barbara Budrich Publishers
Stauffenbergstr. 7. D-51379 Leverkusen Opladen, Germany
86 Delma Drive. Toronto, ON M8W 4P6 Canada
www.barbara-budrich.net

Jacket illustration by Bettina Lehfeldt, Germany – www.lehfeldtgraphic.de
Editing: Alison Romer, Lancaster, England
Typographical editing: Judith Henning, Hamburg – www.buchfinken.com
Picture credits: photo: wjarek ‚The copy of Troy wooden horse at Canakkale, Turkey, fotolia.com
Printed in Europe on acid-free paper by
paper&tinta, Warsaw

For our European friends

And

For Madeleine and Chloe

Acknowledgements 11

Chapter I: Introduction to the Eurozone Crisis: Where there's smoke, there's fire 13

The European Union: A Model for the World? 15
Understanding the Eurozone Crisis: Layout of Book 20

Chapter II: European Integration: The Road to the EU and the Euro 25

The Origins of European Integration 25
Nationalist versus Federalist Tensions: The Evolution of the European Union (1957-2009) 27
How the EU Works 29
    The EU's Governance Structure 30
The Euro as a Symbol: Creating the Currency of a(n) EUtopia 33
    The Symbolism of the Euro's Design 35
Rationale for the Euro: An Economic House of Cards? 38
Evolution of Monetary Union 39
Conclusions 42

Chapter III: The Flawed Economic and Political Architecture of the Eurozone 45

Why Have a Common Currency at All? 46
    The Structure of Europe's Monetary Union – An Optimal Currency Area? 49
    The EU's Monetary System: The Eurosystem 59
    Banking Instability and Sovereign Risk in the Eurosystem 63
    Why Is There No Political Solution for Economic Integration? 66
    Rodrik's Trilemma 67
Conclusions: The Effects of Europe's Governmental, Economic, and Sociopolitical Flaws 71

Chapter IV: Of 'PIIGS' and 'GIPSIs': Pre-Crisis Structural Imbalances 75

The Ant and the Grasshopper?: A Narrative of the Eurozone Crisis 76
   The 'Ants': Why Does German Policy Often Seem at Odds with Much of Europe's? 78
      Cultural Differences 79
      National Self-Interest...80
      Economic Ideology..81
   The 'Grasshoppers': Why Have They Fared So Much Worse in the Eurozone?..82
      Hours worked: Laziness or Poor Productivity? 84
      The Role of Corruption and Effective Governance 84
   EU Compliance: Did 'Good' Europeans Fare Better than 'Bad' Europeans?..85
      Business Friendliness: Did Red Tape Hurt or Help? 86
      A Culture of Credit..87
Flight of the Bumblebee: Pre-crisis Structural Imbalances and Their Influence in the Eurozone 91
   Structural Imbalances: Trade Imbalances, Productivity Levels and their Influence on the Credit Crisis 91
Private and Public Debt-GDP 103
   Country Specific Structural Imbalances 104
      Greece..104
      Ireland..108
      Portugal..111
      Spain 112
      Italy..114
      Cyprus..116
Conclusions...118

Chapter V: Misperception of European Risk, Market Reactions and Policy Response – A Timeline of the Eurozone Crisis 121

Introduction...121
Timeline of the Crisis..125
   October 2009 to July 2011 – A Period of Denial, Anger, Credit Guarantees, and Bailouts..126

July to December 2011: A Period of Bargaining and
Depression as the Economic Crisis evolves into a Political One 131
December 2011 to March 2013: A Period of Acceptance –
Recognizing the Need for Structural Reforms 140
From Financial Crisis to Political Crisis 151
A Greek Popular Revolt: The 2015 Referendum 154
Conclusions 164

Chapter VI: Counterfactuals, Costs, and Conclusions 167

Where are We Now? Economic and Political Costs 168
    Economic costs 169
    Austerity versus Stimulus 176
    Political Costs 182
Public Attitudes Towards the Euro 184
    Public Attitudes During the Eurozone Crisis 188
    The Rise of Euro-Scepticism 191
    The Eurozone Crisis and Anti-Semitism 193
Reforming The Eurozone's Economic Architecture 195
    The Banking System 195
    How Would the Banking Union Work? 196
    Fiscal Union 198
Conclusions: Economically, the EU needs political union; Politically,
EU leaders cannot afford it. 200

Index 207

Acknowledgements

The inspiration for this book comes out of the experiences of the authors, two University of Wyoming professors, while on sabbatical in Germany in 2011 and 2012. Rob Godby was visiting the Pforzheim University of Applied Sciences in southwest Germany near Frankfurt while Stephanie Anderson was a senior fellow at the KFG or Research College "The Transformative Power of Europe" at the Free University of Berlin. Both authors were in near constant contact while the financial crisis was ongoing. Stephanie would write Rob asking for explanations as to why the euro kept its value despite the financial crisis, and Rob would ask Stephanie about Merkel's policy making within the EU framework. This email correspondence formed the kernel of this book. Both authors have many friends to thank for helping make the effort possible.

From Stephanie: First, I would like to thank Thomas Risse and Tanja Boerzel as well as the other marvelous colleagues at the KFG. Without a doubt, the KFG was the best research environment I have ever worked in. Moreover, their financial support was instrumental in the researching and writing of this book. In Brussels, I would like to give special thanks to Carl Hartzell and Kyriakos Revelas for their years of help and support in my research. I am grateful to my former student, Marit Maidla, who shared some of her insights with me as the crisis went on, and to Nicola Kemp, who took time to explain to me the legal ramifications of the crisis. I also want to recognize Ben Demoret, Janet Constantinides, Nick LaBonde, Peter Stavropoulos, and Ivan Wilson for helping me or providing photos for the book. On a personal note, I would like to thank Elsie Doherty, Julian French, Etienne Mangin, Dave McCall, Susan Nacey, John and Janet O'Hagan, David Rodger, Margaret Rodger, Mary Rodger, Sue Rodger, Astrid Stroh, Emek Ucarer, Sue Wiggins, Lexie and Margaret Wilson, and Ivan and Sharon Wilson who all contributed to a wonderful stay in Europe. I am so lucky to have so many close friends and family in Europe that it feels like a second home.

I would also like to thank the University of Wyoming for their intellectual and financial support, specifically the Political Science department, the Global and Area Studies program, and the International Programs Office. My colleagues in these programs have always been extremely helpful and encouraging. Specifically, I would like to thank Anne Alexander, Gregg Cawley, Andrew Garner, Jean Garrison, David Messenger, and Steve Ropp for the time they gave me to discuss ideas.

I would also like to express my gratitude to my husband Tom Seitz and to my children, Madeleine and Chloe Seitz. They made my time in Berlin unforgettable and have done everything possible to support my research and the writing of my book. We dedicate this book to them and to our European friends.

From Rob: I would like to thank my colleagues at Pforzheim for their support and hospitality during my visit in 2011 and 2012, and in my numerous visits since, including Karl-Heinz Rau, Rudi Kurz, and the staff at Pforz- heim. I would also like to thank Jochen Ebert and Sascha Eichelkraut for their patience and conversation, which, over many coffees and beers, helped frame some of the questions in this book. At the University of Wyoming, both students and faculty deserve a thank you, including Anne Alexander in the International Programs Office, Steve Farkas, and Heather Paterson at the UW MBA program and their faculty, whose continuing partnership with Pforzheim has allowed the conversation begun with this manuscript to continue and broaden among students and instructors in the true spirit of learning. I would also like to thank my own students, who also helped in fleshing out ideas in our classes. A final thanks goes to those people at the European Central Bank and in various EU offices Brussels who will remain nameless only because I fear I will forget someone if I attempt to name them all individually, who also kindly met with me and debated some of the ideas in this book as the research behind it was being done. Thank you everyone. Thanks also to Jessica Post for her help proof-reading and her use of the Oxford comma.

Finally, both co-authors would like to thank one another. We didn't know each other that well when we started this process, but we know each other well now! At the very least, the crisis spawned a beautiful friendship.

Chapter I:
Introduction to the Eurozone Crisis: Where there's smoke, there's fire

As smoke hung heavily over Athens and unforgiving winds blowing out of central Europe spread searing flames toward Greece's ancient capital, residents fled the scorching embers and deadly heat, leaving behind homes and livelihoods. Escaping the late August 2009 wildfires, none could have known that the conflagration pursuing them was only the beginning of a Homeric ordeal that would dash the dreams of millions, ruin personal fortunes, topple governments, and threaten to destroy the aspirations of an entire continent. In the ashes of the pine trees, olive groves and burned foundations, the seeds of an economic and political crisis would soon germinate, with repercussions affecting financial markets across the globe. Athens would enflame again, although desperation and frustration, not tinder-dry woods, would fuel future fires.

In the weeks following the wildfires, perceived failures in the Greek government's response to them, coupled with years of apparent neglect of the firefighting service, and suspicions that the forest fires were the product of unscrupulous land developers using arson to avoid the bureaucracy involved in clearing protected forests, ignited new calls for the ousting of the sitting center-right New Democracy Party. The party, already stung by a string of earlier corruption scandals and holding only a one-seat majority in the Hellenic Parliament, made a strategic blunder. In an attempt to gain greater parliamentary leverage, prime minister Kostas Karamanlis called a snap election in hopes of consolidating his party's power over the main opposition Pan Hellenic Movement (PASOK) and several smaller parties. That early September decision proved disastrous: the voters punished New Democracy, giving it its lowest vote share in party history (up to that time). Unbeknownst to the electorate, however, the returns of the Greek legislative election of October 2009 would set in motion the events of what has since come to be known as the eurozone crisis.

The newly elected center-left PASOK government, led by George Papandreou, assumed office and began to sort through the ledger left by its predecessor. The audit revealed a much larger deficit than expected. For years, previous Greek governments had hidden massive debts from the rest of the European Union (EU), apparently to obscure the fact that Greece had not met the necessary debt and deficit commitments that "eurozone" countries, are required to meet.¹ Countries failing to meet such commitments in the EU were not unusual. Other countries in the recent past, including the largest economies in the bloc, France and Germany, had also failed to meet these targets, especially the deficit target set at three percent of gross domestic product (GDP). More recently, the 2008 global financial crisis and the ensuing government actions across the continent to stabilize markets had also left several other member states outside EU-mandated fiscal guidelines. Deficits were not unusual. What shocked markets was the scale of the revelation: Greece's estimated government deficit for 2009 more than tripled, revised from a previous 3.7 percent of GDP to 12.5 percent shortly after the new government took office. By April 2010, new EU figures suggested the deficit was even larger – nearer to fourteen percent.² The implications of this admission forced investors worldwide to reconsider their faith in the safety of sovereign debt, a faith that had already been tested in rescuing the world financial system in the aftermath of the 2008 global market crash. Questioning the solvency of sovereign debt threatened to undermine the only source of seeming certainty in a still fledgling financial recovery.

Such revisions in official statistics are rare; in Greece, however, such revisions were part of a repeated pattern of obfuscation. Since 2005, the EU had expressed reservations no fewer than five times regarding the biannual reporting of Greek debt and deficit figures. The EU's own statistical agency, Eurostat, had first suggested Greece was guilty of misreporting these numbers in 2004. Following the most recent post-election revelations, on 10 November 2009, the European Economic and Financial Affairs Council (ECOFIN) once more issued a statement imploring the Greek government to rectify the reporting issues and called for an investigation of the ongoing accounting problems in Greece.³ In its August 2010 follow-up report, the

---

1 The eurozone consists of eighteen countries. Greek deficit and debt had been hidden using several tactics for years, including using special financial accounting practices to present misleading government expenditure statistics. See http://www.nytimes.com/2010/02/14/business/global/14debt.html?pagewanted=1&hp (accessed 31 August 2015).

2 These figures come from the European Commission, Report on Greek Government Deficit and Debt Statistics, Brussels, 8 January 2010 COM(2010) 1 Final. Eventually the deficit would be re-estimated to be 15.6 percent of GDP http://ec.europa.eu/eurostat/documents/4187653/6404656/COM_2010_report_greek/c8523cfa-d3c1-4954-8ea1-64bb11e59b3a (accessed 31 August 2015).

3 The ECOFIN statement declared the following: "The Council REGRETS the renewed problems in the Greek fiscal statistics. The Council CALLS ON the Greek government to urgently take measures to restore the confidence of the European Union in Greek statistical information and the related institutional setting. The Council INVITES the Commission to produce a report before the end of 2009. Moreover, the Council INVITES the Commission to propose the appropriate measures to be taken in this situation. In this context, the Council WELCOMES the commitment by the Government to address this issue swiftly and seriously and CONSIDERS the measures announced recently, such as those aiming to make the National Statistical Service fully independent, to be steps in the right direction" p. 4

European Commission identified two primary causes of the repeated pattern of upward debt and deficit revisions: Greece's accounting procedures; and poor governance influencing fiscal reporting. The latter problem was far more troubling than the former as it implied the reported state of Greek finances could be more dependent on electoral and political cycles than on the true state of affairs. While it was stated more diplomatically in official terms, Greece was charged with allowing official agencies to "cook the books" when politically expedient. A quiet suspicion all along, the new deficit revisions in 2009 created a tipping point in financial markets. These problems would no longer be ignored or overlooked. What else had been discounted or misreported in other member states? Was sovereign debt really as safe as credit agencies had rated it?

Just as fraud issues in the US housing crisis led to a loss of investor confidence in what was considered very safe assets, mortgages, and eventually led to the 2008 global financial crisis, Greek reporting of fraudulent numbers led to a loss of confidence in the ultimate safe investment, sovereign debt, that is debt backed by national governments, and eventually led to the eurozone crisis. Unlike in 2008, however, Europe would feel the effects of this crisis for years instead of months. Angela Merkel warned it would be a marathon.[4] According to the EU's Web site, "the inspiration for the € symbol itself came from the Greek epsilon (Є) – a reference to the cradle of European civilization – and the first letter of the word Europe, crossed by two parallel lines to 'certify' the stability of the euro."[5] Ironically, Greece would come to 'certify' the instability of the euro.

The European Union: A Model for the World?

Part of the mystique of the euro is its symbolic power. The euro would allow the EU to displace the United States as the dominant economic superpower. At the turn of the millennium, both T.R. Reid, in his book *The United States of Europe: The New Superpower and the End of American Supremacy* and Mark Leonard in *Why Europe will run the 21st Century* argued that the European model was superior to the American one, and would become the world's new benign hegemon. The euro was the symbol of this new reign:

Council of the European Union, Council conclusions on EU Statistics, 2972nd Economic and Financial Affairs Brussels, 10 November 2009, http://www.consilium.europa.eu/uedocs/cms_data/docs/pressdata/en/ecofin/111007.pdf (accessed 3 August 2015).

4 Euronews "Merkel warns of marathon to solve euro-crisis" 2 December 2011 http://www.euronews.com/2011/12/02/merkel-warns-of-marathon-to-solve-euro-crisis/ (accessed 3 August 2015).

5 http://ec.europa.eu/economy_finance/euro/cash/symbol/index_en.htm.

In pursuit of economic union, Europeans have thrown their marks, francs, lira, escudos, drachma, and so on into history's trash can and replaced them all with the new common currency, the euro, a new currency that has more daily users than the US dollar. ... Europeans want to see the euro replace the dollar as the world's reserve currency..., [b]ut Europe's new money is more than money. It is also a political statement – a daily message in every pocket that cooperation has replaced conflict across the continent.[6]

As a symbol of the EU's success, the euro's image graces more than bills and coins; it has been the ubiquitous emblem of Europe idealized in many art forms, including a neo-classical statue in front of the European Parliament building in Brussels (see image 1-1).

Image 1-1: A neo-classical statue of the euro displayed in front of the European Parliament building in Brussels. Photo by Stephanie Anderson.

Despite hopes that the creation of the euro would allow the EU to rival the US as global hegemon, many observers have worried about the currency's underlying administrative structure. Ultimately, the euro required an economic 'leap of faith' that it would be managed prudently. Skeptics have long worried the euro was vulnerable to crises and economic mismanagement. As

---

6   T. R. Reid, *The United States of Europe: The New Superpower and the End of American Supremacy* (New York: The Penguin Press 2004,) 2.

early as 1997, Martin Feldstein, a Harvard economist, argued "there is no doubt that the real rationale for EMU is political and not economic. Indeed, the adverse economic effects of a single currency on unemployment and inflation would outweigh any gains from facilitating trade and the capital flows among the EMU members."[7]

Once trouble began, the structure of the currency union would not create the incentives necessary for union members to take corrective action to avoid ever worsening outcomes. In a 2005 HSBC report called "European Meltdown?", Robert Prior-Wandesforde and Gwyn Hacche warned:

> The eurozone's current path is unsustainable. We believe the single currency has helped create significant economic strains which look set to become more and more extreme if nothing is done. In particular, it is probably only a matter of time before Germany and the Netherlands are dragged into deflation, while Italy seems destined to move in and out of recession for years to come.[8]

Some even doubted the ability of the common currency to survive, being used by so many different countries, each with potentially different goals and objectives and likely most concerned with their own self-interests. In 2006, Frits Bolkestein, the former EU internal market commissioner, questioned the chances of survival for the euro in the long term as he thought leaders would put short term political interests ahead of the long term interests of the union. He argued that states "will be forced by political pressure to borrow more and increase their budget deficit, with consequences for interest rates and inflation," so "the real test for the euro is not now, but in ten years time."[9] Not incurring a deficit requires reducing spending, politically an unpopular decision that could cost an election. Deficits among countries would, however, threaten the currency union. This chain of events is exactly what happened and resulted in the European financial crisis.

As long as the eurozone continued to show good growth, however, the early naysayers were ignored, that is until the eurozone crisis gave the cynics their day in the sun. Feldstein almost gleefully said 'I told you so' in his article titled, "The Failure of the Euro: The Little Currency that Couldn't".[10] Rather than becoming a model for the world, Europe, in the months – and

---

7   Martin Feldstein, "EMU and International Conflict," *Foreign Affairs* (1997): 60.
8   Robert Prior-Wandesforde and Gwyn Hacche, "European meltdown? Europe fiddles as Rome burns" HSBC Global Research, July 2005, http://quantlabs.net/academy/download/free_quant_instituitional_books_/%5BHSBC%5D%20European%20Meltdown%20-%20Europe%20Fiddles%20as%20Rome%20Burns.pdf (accessed 3 August 2015).
9   Mark Beunderman, "Ex-commissioner questions survival of euro" *EUObserver.com*, 26 January 2006.
10 Martin Feldstein, "The Failure of the Euro: The Little Currency that Couldn't" *Foreign Affairs* (January/February 2012): 91:1, 105-116.

now years – since the crisis began, has seemed in decline. In 2014, almost a full five years after the crisis began, European Council President Herman Van Rompuy went so far as to say the EU was in "a survival crisis!"[11]

The crisis, apparently caused by one of the monetary union's smallest member states, has had dramatic effects, not only on the economies of Europe, but also on human lives. While other countries, for example the United States, have been able to find the path to economic recovery relatively quickly after the financial crisis, the EU has unfortunately not. The International Federation of Red Cross and Red Crescent Societies (IFRC) published a report in 2013 stating that the humanitarian impact of the crisis had only begun to rear its ugly head. The report chastised the EU: "Whilst other continents successfully reduce poverty, Europe adds to it."[12]

This long-lasting economic crisis surrounding the euro has had inevitable political consequences too, ones that have undermined the very reason for its existence. As unemployment and even suicide rates increased across the most affected by the crisis, the extreme right, including neo-Nazi parties, the antithesis of European integration, has increased in popularity and with it calls for a return to national currencies and a rollback of the European Union. In France, in May 2012, the National Front took eighteen percent in the presidential elections, the best results the party has ever received. In the same month, Golden Dawn, an extreme nationalist party, which some have accused of being openly racist, won a seven percent share of votes in Greek legislative elections. In recent polling, the anti-immigrant Freedom Party is the third largest party in the Netherlands, as is the Danish People's Party in Denmark. Austria's Freedom Party has similarly been running second in opinion polls. Jobbik, currently polling second, is the fastest growing party in Hungary. Its leader, Gabor Vona, has accused the EU of colonizing its nation; its MPs removed the EU flag from the Representatives' office building.

The widespread suffering caused by economic conditions, coupled with political opportunism by parties hoping to gain from the general dissatisfaction of the electorate, has generated a great deal of negative press and cast a pall on the idea of European integration. According to the Pew research center, many Europeans are second-guessing whether EU membership is a "good thing" for their country.[13] Eurobarometer, the EU polling organization, notes

---

11 Herman Van Rompuy, Speech by President Herman Van Rompuy at the Brussels Economic Forum 2014 – 4th Annual Tommaso Padoa-Schioppa Lecture, Brussels, 10 June 2014 EUCO 127/14, 5 http://www.consilium.europa.eu/uedocs/cms_data/docs/pressdata/en/ec/143160.pdf (accessed 3 August 2015).

12 The International Federation of Red Cross and Red Crescent Societies (IFRC), *Think Differently: Humanitarian Impacts of the Economic Crisis in Europe*, (Geneva: IFRC, 2013) 10, http://www.ifrc.org/PageFiles/134339/1260300-Economic%20crisis%20Report_EN_LR.pdf.

13 Pew Research Center, "European Union: The Latest Casualty of the Eurozone Crisis" http://www.pewglobal.org/european-union-the-latest-casualty-of-the-euro-crisis/.

that a majority of Europeans are worried about the effects of the crisis on their personal finances, and are pessimistic about the future. Such feelings are reflected in numerous political cartoons where the EU is sometimes depicted as a sinking ship.

Is the EU really sinking? Hope for the union is not completely lost. Truth be told, polling data and electoral results still indicate a majority of Europeans, even within the eurozone, support the ideals of European integration, the EU, and the common currency. Despite the growth of fringe parties and people's worries, the European Union has still maintained support, even in the worst days of the crisis. For example, in October 2011, Eurobarometer reported that a majority of Europeans, fifty-five percent, believed that coordinated economic action within the EU would provide better protection in the current crisis. Moreover, the Europeans are willing to put their money where their mouth is: according to one poll, fifty percent considered it "desirable" for their countries to give financial help to other EU member states.[14] According to polls in 2012, a majority of people in eurozone countries thought the euro was good for their country and two-thirds thought it good for the EU.[15] Europeans in the eurozone do not want to abandon the currency, at least not yet. In other words, in the very short period of ten years, the euro may have succeeded in its political goal of creating a sense of unity among Europeans, but the crisis has certainly tested that unity. Subsequently, support for the EU, the euro and other EU institutions has fallen, and in the worst affected countries such as Greece, it may be the case that a majority no longer supports these ideas.

Extreme right and populist parties very often increase their support during times of uncertainty and crisis. The question is whether such political changes will result in an undoing of what has been over fifty years of integrative effort. If EU presidents and prime ministers can demonstrate coordinated leadership on the issue and return economic stability to Europe, the EU model could still prove itself. German chancellor Angela Merkel has declared that, in response to the eurocrisis, the EU is on the inevitable path of political union. Perhaps; however, if Europe's leadership cannot find the political will and resources to make difficult decisions, the euro could still fail, and with it, the European ideal could become bankrupt as well. Understanding these issues is the purpose of this book.

---

14 http://ec.europa.eu/public_opinion/topics/eb76_europeans__and__the__crisis_analytical__summary_en.pdf.
15 http://ec.europa.eu/public_opinion/flash/fl_362_sum_en.pdf.

Understanding the Eurozone Crisis: Layout of Book

The eurozone crisis is particularly difficult to follow because of the intertwining of economics and politics among the now nineteen countries sharing the euro in not-quite-confederal European Union, against the backdrop of the international financial system. The book focuses on three key questions:

1. Why has the eurocrisis been so severe?;
2. Why did Europeans choose the sets of policies they did in reaction to the crisis?; and
3. Why not abandon the euro altogether?

First, why has the eurozone crisis been so long and so severe? After the 2008 global financial crisis began in the US, Europe and most of the developed world, fell into recession. In the US and Europe, the financial crisis-induced recessions officially ended in the second quarter of 2009, with economic contraction lasting six quarters in the US and five in the EU and eurozone. Afterward, stronger growth occurred in Europe relative to the United States, until the European financial crisis started in late 2009.

The structure of the monetary system left the eurozone sharing a common currency, but not a common treasury, allowing excessive debts to build up within the currency union that eventually led to the crisis. Once the crisis began, the common currency that tied member states together also allowed the crisis to spread more easily to other countries. By the last quarter of 2011, European economies began to contract as the crisis worsened, and its contagion spread to most of the economies on the continent. Europe would not emerge from recession until 2013.

"Emerge" might be too strong a term. As of 2015, this lack of growth has produced high unemployment across most of the continent, leaving some countries with Great-Depression-like conditions. Youth unemployment has hovered around fifty percent in Greece and Spain, while general unemployment rates are double or more what they were before the crisis, with the worst affected countries experiencing unemployment rates for the entire population in excess of twenty percent.

Why has this crisis lingered for so long? In part, the answer lies in the cause, a financial crisis, which, when one occurs, results in worse conditions than the usual recession. There is also a strong case to be made that the policies European leaders chose to counteract the crisis actually exacerbated it. Given the severity of the eurozone crisis, policymaking would have been difficult under any circumstance, requiring difficult political and economic choices. The structure of the EU, however, made effective policy-making more difficult, as it created incentives within countries to act in their own interests and not necessarily in those of the entire Union's.

Why did the eurozone member state governments choose the policies they did? Economics has typically provided an orthodox toolkit for use during crises: Keynesianism. Keynesianism prescribes increased government expenditure to offset the drops in private sector spending that occurs during recessions, plus an expansion of the money supply to create growth in the economy through greater lending. The financial crisis, however, left crisis countries unable to borrow to finance the deficits Keynesianism requires. Moreover, eurozone countries were initially unable to come to agreement regarding expansion of the money supply for fear it would touch off inflation in those countries not yet affected by economic contraction. As a result, the only policy choice left was "austerity", i.e., cutting government spending in an effort to reduce deficits and balance the books. This policy choice, unfortunately, led to even greater economic contraction as economies now saw more reduction in economic activity and worsening unemployment.

Such outcomes appear to have worsened the crisis, or at best prolonged it, as well as resulting in the deterioration of political support for the Union. The following chapters explain these issues in more detail.

Second, why did the European Union member states, whose economic policies, in the past, have been much more interventionist than those of the US, now reject these policies? Because many attributed the crisis to a case of poor Greek management rather than to structural problems within the eurozone. To many in Europe, the narrative of the European financial crisis began with Greece accumulating excessive debt and deficits prior to the crisis, making the government dependent on borrowing to maintain government operations, social entitlements, and to finance interest payments. When the crisis hit, lenders were no longer willing to support such a situation with more loans. The clear solution was to reduce the debt through government cutbacks; however, doing so required massive cuts to spending and entitlements. Such cuts were both massively unpopular and insufficient to balance the books. Without borrowing, interest payments could not be met and a Greek national default loomed. Avoiding this would require Europe bailing out Greece, but who should pay?

The question of "who should pay" led to issues of morality, sovereignty, and national pride: Should Germans and Finns pay for what many in these countries perceived were caused by a corrupt government of Greece? Would bailing out Greece only encourage such behavior in the future, undermining a long-term solution to the real problem – excessive debt? Understandably, countries in Europe, especially those in the richer north, did not want to pay for the mistakes of Greece, or, later, of other southern countries. Rather, some leaders and EU citizens felt these countries needed to learn the true costs of profligate spending and to reform in order to regain the confidence of credit markets. At the same time, the other member states had to save their own financial systems, which were deeply intertwined with those of Greece and the rest of Europe.

The result was limited bailouts in return for austerity in aided countries. Fearing default, the markets cut off access to credit leaving the governments of the affected economies high and dry. To qualify for bailouts, the governments had to adhere to austerity measures causing these economies to contract, thereby reducing tax revenues and worsening deficits, instead of correcting them. Instead of improving the crisis, Europe's reaction actually led to a death spiral in many troubled economies. Was this result inevitable or would other policies have avoided such a situation? While this book argues in the affirmative, it also attempts to equip readers with the tools to draw their own conclusions.

Finally, considering all the economic problems, why does the euro continue to exist? Why has the euro been able to withstand the stress? Why has it not broken? European Central Bank president Mario Draghi once likened the euro to the bumblebee: it should not have been able to fly.[16] Why did it, and does it still? Did the very idea of the euro, that is this new symbol of European unity, contribute both to its ability to defy gravity and its tensile strength in withstanding all the economic pressures of the international financial markets? This book analyzes and evaluates the political power of the euro as a symbol to rally people and governments to withstand severe austerity measures. However, can this symbolic power sustain the euro indefinitely? The rise of anti-euro and anti-Europe parties across the continent as well the disunity and dissension among member states begs the question of whether the eurozone crisis will breed so much mistrust among the peoples that popular support for the European project will decline or possibly even evaporate completely.

This book explores the crisis in detail. Chapter two provides an historical background and explains how the European Union itself functions. Next, it explains the economic, political, and symbolic importance of the euro as well as the evolution of economic and monetary union.

Chapter three discusses the economic theory behind the single currency. It compares the requirements necessary for a perfect currency union to those existing in the European Union.

Chapter four delves into the specific economic, political and cultural differences that make up the eurozone member countries. By comparing the so-called PIIGS (Portugal, Ireland, Italy, Greece & Spain) or GIPSI (Greece, Ireland, Portugal, Spain & Italy), both offensive acronyms, countries with each other and with the wealthier countries in the eurozone, the authors

---

16 Speech by Mario Draghi, President of the European Central Bank at the Global Investment Conference in London, 26 July 2012, https://www.ecb.europa.eu/press/key/date/2012/html/sp120726.en.html.

demonstrate that all countries bear some of the blame; the eurozone crisis is a product of an intricate economic minuet between the north and the south. This chapter also pays particular attention to Germany as the main actor in policy formation.

In chapter five, the authors create a timeline of the crisis explaining how each event led to the next, from the discovery of Greece's 'cooked books' to the European Central Bank's decision to launch its "big bazooka".

Finally, in the conclusion, the authors provide counterfactuals: what would have happened economically and politically had the euro split up? Next, the authors assess the economic and political costs of the crisis. Interestingly, the economic costs far outweigh the political; in some ways, the European Union may be stronger today politically than it was before the crisis. In the end, the authors conclude that, in light of the weak leadership seen during the crisis, there is an inverse relationship between comfort and cooperation.[17] It is possible that only through the crucible of a crisis will the European project be able to achieve the integration that Europe has aspired to for over half a century.

---

17 The authors are indebted to Thomas R. Seitz for this observation.

Chapter II:
European Integration: The Road to the EU and the Euro

The Origins of European Integration

The road to a common European currency began during the aftermath of World War II in a drive to integrate the continent. The idea of a united Europe became increasingly popular in the 1940s when resistance groups preached unity to combat the nationalism that had started two world wars. Jean Monnet, who would later be called the "father of Europe," was a leading advocate of this school of thinking:

> There will be no peace in Europe if the States are reconstituted on the basis of national sovereignty, with all that that entails in terms of prestige politics and economic protectionism. ... The countries of Europe are too small to guarantee their peoples the prosperity that modern conditions make possible and consequently necessary. They need larger markets. ... Prosperity for the States of Europe and the social developments that must go with it will only be possible if they form a federation or a 'European entity' that makes them into a common economic unit...[18]

In his address on 19 September 1946 at the University of Zurich, UK statesman Winston Churchill agreed calling for the creation of a United States of Europe:

> We must build a kind of United States of Europe. In this way only will hundreds of millions of toilers be able to regain the simple joys and hopes, which make life worth living. The process is simple. All that is needed is the resolve of hundreds of millions of men and women to do right instead of wrong and to gain as their reward blessing instead of cursing...
>
> The structure of the United States of Europe, if well and truly built, will be such as to make the material strength of a single state less important. Small nations will count as much as large ones and gain their honour by their contribution to the common cause.[19]

---

18 Jean Monnet, *Speech to the National Liberation Committee*, 1943, http://www.cvce.eu/content/publication/1997/10/13/b61a8924-57bf-4890-9e4b-73bf4d882549/publishable_en.pdf (accessed 28 July 2015).
19 Winston Churchill, Speech to the Academic Youth in Zurich, University of Zurich, September 9, 1946.

Such a construction sounds straightforward enough, but how does one gain "the resolve of hundreds of millions of men and women"? In the case of the United States, a multinational state of immigrants, identity is woven around a civil religion[20] and a creed rather than the traditional glue of race or language.[21] To construct a 'European', that is to graft a new affiliation and loyalty atop the long-existing national ones, Monnet proposed: "Make men work together. Show them that beyond their differences and geographical boundaries there lies a common interest."[22]

As the first step, French statesmen Robert Schuman and Monnet collaborated on a revolutionary proposal to pool Europe's coal and steel resources under a European government:

> By pooling basic production and by instituting a new High Authority, whose decisions will bind France, Germany and other member countries, this proposal will lead to the realization of the first concrete foundation of a European federation indispensable to the preservation of peace.[23]

The Treaty of Paris, signed on 18 April 1951 created the European Coal and Steel Community (ECSC) among France, Germany, Italy and the Benelux countries (Belgium, the Netherlands and Luxembourg) and established the first supranational European governmental institution. Its purpose was to coordinate and consolidate the economic interests of member states to achieve war-time reconstruction quickly, raise living standards, and ensure European peace by pooling the coal and steel production capability of all six nations, which had historically been central to national munitions production.

Governance of the ECSC was directed by several institutions, each a forerunner of similar institutions functioning today in the European Union. The executive body governing the ECSC, the High Authority, would eventually evolve into the European Commission. Its charge was to work in the interest of the community of nations as opposed to national interests. The ECSC also had a Common Assembly with consultative power to the High Authority, but no direct legislative power. Originally made up of seventy-eight members appointed or elected by their constituent states, this body was the forerunner of the modern European Parliament. The Special Council of Ministers included representatives from the member states' national govern-

---

20 Jürgen Habermas, Ciaran Cronin, and Pablo De Greiff, *The Inclusion of the Other: Studies in Political Theory* (Cambridge, Mass: MIT Press, 1998), 113.
21 Benedict Anderson, Imagined Communities: Reflections on the Origin and Spread of Nationalism (New York: Verso Books, 2006), 47.
22 Tim Lister, "Britain, Germany and France – Europe's reluctant dance partners," *CNN.com*, December 11, 2011, http://www.cnn.com/2011/12/09/world/europe/europe-triangular-relationship.
23 The Schuman Declaration, 9 May 1950 http://europa.eu/about-eu/basic-information/symbols/europe-day/schuman-declaration/index_en.htm (accessed 25 July 2015).

ments. This group evolved into the EU's Council, also known as the Council of Ministers. The High Authority required the consent of the Special Council in all areas of executive action except coal and steel, where the Council of Ministers only advised the High Authority. In this way, national interests were represented in non-coal and steel decisions as Council rules requiring unanimity in decision-making allowed members to veto actions not in their country's interest. Other institutions governing the ECSC included the Court of Justice, which adjudicated disputes and ensured ECSC laws were observed, as well as the Consultative Community. The Court continues today as the European Court of Justice (ECJ). The Consultative Community, an advisory group to the High Authority representing coal and steel consumers and dealers, workers (unions), and employers, was a precursor to today's Economic and Social Committee of the EU.

Nationalist versus Federalist Tensions: The Evolution of the European Union (1957-2009)

One year after the signing of the Treaty of Rome, in 1958, nationalist sentiments in the European Economic Community (EEC) began to grow, particularly in France, with the election of Charles De Gaulle as President of the newborn Fifth Republic. De Gaulle disapproved of France's status in the EEC as one among six rather than as leader. He believed the fragile governments of the previous Fourth Republic had negotiated the Treaty of Rome from a position of weakness. De Gaulle eschewed supranational integration efforts, instead envisioning *"l'Europe des patries"* or a "Europe of states", with France as its *de facto* head. In 1960, when Denmark, Norway, Ireland and the United Kingdom applied for membership, France, fearing its foreign policy interests could be undermined by this wider expansion, particularly the addition of the United Kingdom, vetoed British admission to the EEC, resulting in the suspension of the remaining countries' membership processes and a victory for France's nationalist interests.

The conflict between nationalist and federalist efforts came to a head in 1965, when French concerns regarding its sovereignty over agricultural policy resulted in "the empty chair" crisis. As a protest over the use of majority voting in the Council, which had undermined the principle of national vetoes, the French withdrew representation from the Council, effectively halting proceedings. The Luxembourg Compromise of 1966 resulted, which instituted the practice of vetoes in matters of national interest. This practice continues to this day and has, thus, limited the formation of a strong, federal, European governance system.

De Gaulle's opposition to the supranational authority of EEC institutions also resulted in the first informal European leaders' summits in 1961 as an attempt to offset the growing power of the EEC's supranational authority.

Although these early meetings did not initially create a permanent nationalist counterweight to federal EC power, they eventually resulted in the creation of a new European institution in 1975 – the European Council. This body, now the preeminent decision-making body, is made up of member state chief executives, and takes decisions by consensus, i.e., all members retain a veto, except where the treaties provide otherwise.[24]

Although the United Kingdom, Denmark and Ireland were formally admitted to the EEC in 1973 after De Gaulle's death, the European project had lost much of its momentum and entered a period called "Eurosclerosis". Despite the establishment of a common market in 1958, interstate trade remained stymied by a host of non-tariff barriers and customs regulations. Federalists demonstrated to remove customs and border controls altogether. To revive the European integration process, the 1986 Single European Act (SEA), the first major revision of the original Treaties of Rome, sought "to improve the economic and social situation by extending common policies and pursuing new objectives" and "to ensure a smoother functioning of the Communities."

A common currency seemed the natural accompaniment to the newly completed single market. The Delors Report (1989) established the stages and processes by which monetary union should occur, and in 1992, the Maastricht treaty set the ball in motion. It also changed the EU's governing structure to one based on 'three pillars:' the European Community pillar; the Common Foreign and Security Policy pillar; and the Justice and Home Affairs pillar. Although the first pillar served largely as an extension of existing institutional structures, the latter two pillars were established to keep these areas purely intergovernmental, that is, firmly in the grasp of the member states and out of the hands of the EU institutions. Forty years after Churchill's speech in Zurich, the political and economic integration of Europe was well underway, yet the balancing of nationalist and supranational interests continued to define the Union's governance.

In 2009, the Lisbon treaty, a less ambitious version of the failed Constitutional treaty of 2005, replaced the rotating member state presidency with a permanent president of the European Council in order to provide continuity of leadership. In addition, it augmented the power of the High Representative for Foreign and Security Policy by making him/her a Vice President of the European Commission, changed the system of qualified majority voting in the Council, and boosted the power of the European Parliament by forcing the European Council to nominate a Commission president in line with EP election results and by increasing its legislative mandate. It also removed the pillar system. The euro was named the official currency of the EU, and the European

---

24 Treaty on European Union, article 15(4).

Central Bank became an official EU institution. However, these changes had little impact on the governance of the eurozone crisis.

Image 2-1: Demonstration for a common currency outside the Berlaymont, 12 May 1978, © EC P-001974/04-07, http://ec.europa.eu/avservices/photo/photoDetails.cfm?sitelang=en&mgid=64#2 (accessed 31 July 2015).

How the EU Works

The nationalist versus federalist tensions visible in the governing structures of the EU make it difficult to label. It is not a federation, like the United States, where each of the states has signed a constitution and agreed to submit to the federal authority. In general, the member states run the show in the EU. There is no federal government with the power to tax and spend. The lion's share of financing comes from member state contributions as a percentage of their Gross National Income (GNI). In other words, Brussels is dependent on the member states for money; the EU's independent sources of income, from customs duties on imports and through VAT, only covers roughly a third of expenditure. The member states also retain their powers over foreign, security, and defense policy; were these policies to shift to Brussels, the member states would have to agree explicitly in a treaty. The power to amend the treaties resides exclusively among the member states. Nevertheless, there are supranational or federal elements to the European Union. All member states are bound by the European Court of Justice, as well as by Commission regulations and directives. The member states have surrendered all competence in certain areas to the European Commission, for example, in commercial and fisheries policies.

This odd set of governing structures with supranational (where there is an authority higher than the state governing state behavior) and intergovernmental qualities (where decisions are made by consensus among the states) has led to the label of *sui generis* – basically, a species unto itself. Neither fish nor fowl, the EU is in a class of its own.

Yet, this designation is unsatisfying. Being neither here nor there, numerous academics, politicians, and European citizens want the EU to become a real federation. However, federalism is also known as the 'F-word', and many, especially on the right side of the political spectrum, desire to move away from federalism, placing authority back in the national capitals. Such tension is visible throughout the history of the EU as each treaty bringing "ever closer union" is actually a compromise among the states where, superficially, it appears that the Union is inching towards federation, yet the member states preserve key competences. For example, the official name of the Maastricht treaty, which changed the name of the European Community to the European Union, was the Treaty *on* European Union, rather than the Treaty *of* European Union. In other words, it did not create a union, but only discussed it. The euro is a perfect example of such a compromise with the introduction of a common currency and a central bank, but without the corresponding banking union or fiscal union and where national capitals retain crucial powers.

Intergovernmental decision-making has defined Europe's reaction to the eurozone crisis. Some governments have been unwilling to consider EU policies that might undermine their strength domestically or cost them an election, thus constraining a strong EU-wide response to the crisis. Specifically, any policy that might imply an intergovernmental transfer of wealth to other nations has been especially difficult to agree upon, thereby undermining aid to the most troubled countries in the crisis, or the creation of new institutions that could strengthen the Union. Simply put, the structure of the EU system implies that domestic politics in individual states can have important implications on EU-wide decision-making.

The EU's Governance Structure

Promising "ever closer union", the founding 1957 Treaty of Rome created a governing structure akin to a presidential-parliamentary system[25] with a

---

25 In the presidential-parliamentary or semi-presidential system, the cabinet, or in this case, the College of Commissioners, can be dismissed by either the European Commission president or by the European Parliament in a vote of no confidence. Although the European Parliament may dismiss the College of Commissioners as a whole, the Parliament may neither appoint a new one nor remove individual Commissioners. The Commission President may remove individual Commissioners.

separate, bicameral legislative branch made up of a Council, composed of member state representatives, and a parliament to represent the people, an executive branch headed by the Commission to implement legislation, and a judicial branch in the form of the European Court of Justice. Although separate, the powers of the different institutions were far from equal; the Council dominated. Until 1979, the parliament was indirectly elected with almost no powers. The power of legislative initiative lay solely in the Commission, and, yet, the member states in the European Council set the agenda for Europe. Each member state nominated a justice to sit on the Court. No decisions could be made without member state approval.

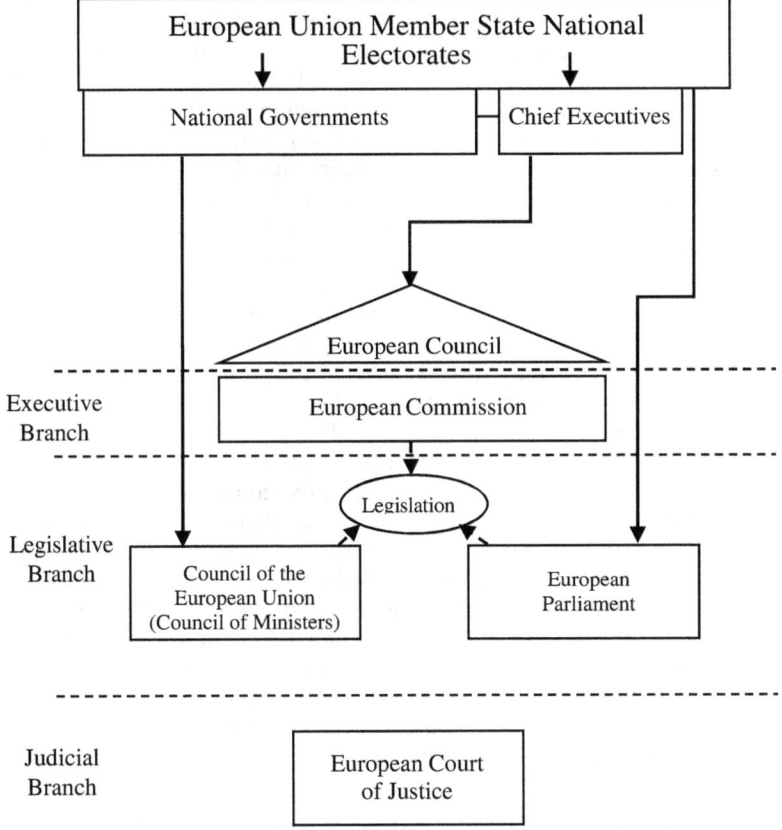

Figure 2-1: A chart of EU governance. Solid arrows in the diagram identify who is responsible for appointing/electing the members of each body. Broken arrows denote legislative action.

As a rule of thumb, "The Commission proposes, the Council disposes." In other words, the Commission has the exclusive right of initiative: only the Commission can propose legislation because the Commission represents Community interests rather than national interests. Nevertheless, individual member states can suggest legislation for the Commission to propose. The Commission is made up of the College of Commissioners, one from each member state, who, although member state appointees, promise to work in the Union's interest only. In general, the Commission is composed of former or defeated politicians, for example, José Manuel Barroso, European Commission president during the eurozone crisis, was a former prime minister of Portugal; Joaquín Almunia Amann, Commissioner for Competition, was the defeated socialist party candidate for prime minister of Spain.

The Council of the European Union, often referred to simply as "the Council" or by its old name, "the Council of Ministers", represents the governments of the member states (MS). The Council meets in different configurations of ministers. For example, the General Affairs Council (GAC) is composed of MS European Affairs ministers; the Economic and Finance Committee (EcoFin) is made up of economic and finance ministers from all member states. Each representative acts solely in the national interest. "The Council disposes" means that, typically, the member states have the final say over any proposed legislation.

Depending on the competence involved, for example, customs union or security policy, the EU has different procedures in place to guide legislative decisions. Despite being the only directly elected institution, the European Parliament was customarily shut out of the legislative process until the 1990's. Legislative decisions often by-passed the EP entirely, or only gave them a ceremonial nod. Under consultation (formerly assent) procedure, the Council 'consults' with Parliament, but is under no obligation to incorporate its suggestions. Such was the disdain for the Parliament that the EP took the Council to the European Court of Justice – and won – demanding that the Council at least restrain from enacting a decision before the EP could render an opinion. Consent procedure gives the EP the power of an up-or-down vote without the ability to amend. Today, the European Parliament has increased clout as added competences have been shifted to what was called "co-decision", now the ordinary legislative procedure. Under this procedure, the European Parliament is given equal power to the Council. With regards to the eurozone crisis, the European Parliament has played a marginal role. Article 133 of the Lisbon Treaty states,

> Without prejudice to the powers of the European Central Bank, the European Parliament and the Council, acting in accordance with the ordinary legislative procedure, shall lay down the measures necessary for the use of the euro as the single currency. Such measures shall be adopted after consultation of the European Central Bank.

Nevertheless, questions regarding breach of excessive deficit or external monetary agreements remain exclusively in the Council's hands.

The Euro as a Symbol: Creating the Currency of a(n) EUtopia

The integration process may be losing steam. Decisions regarding the European Union are mainly addressed by national parliaments, i.e., the educated elites, with whom the idea of Europe has been highly popular.[26] However, among the people, more than seventy-five percent of Europeans polled could not say how many member states there were.[27] Such ignorance can be taken as an indication of apathy. When treaty ratification has been put to a popular vote, the results have been rather underwhelming. The Danes voted no in the first referendum on Maastricht. The French voted yes only by the narrowest of margins.[28] The Irish rejected both the Treaty of Nice and the Treaty of Lisbon. Sweden, the UK, and Denmark have refused to join the single currency. The European Parliament elections of June 2004 reflected this public dissatisfaction with and skepticism towards the EU with a turnout of just 45.3 percent; at the time, the lowest turnout in the history of the assembly. Moreover, in the new ten EU members, whose populace overwhelmingly voted to join, only twenty-six percent voted. To quote Parliament spokesman David Harley, it was a "disappointing and pathetically low turnout."[29] In 2009 and 2014, turnout decreased further to 43 percent and 42.54 percent respectively.[30] Significantly, the Euro-skeptic and right-wing nationalist parties achieved their best results to date across the continent.[31] Altogether, this public skepticism represents a significant 'speed bump' on the road to European integration.

In the words of Raymond Aron, a sympathetic critic of European unity efforts,

> the name Europe distinguished a continent or a civilisation, not an economic or political unit.... The European idea is empty; it has neither the transcendence of Messianic ideologies nor the immanence of concrete

---

26 Standard *Eurobarometer* 57 (2002), 12-15.
27 Andrew Rettman, "Most Europeans don't know their union has 25 states," *EUObserver.com*, 11 October 2006.
28 The Maastricht treaty passed in France 50.5 percent "yes" and 49.5 percent "no".
29 Paul Taylor, "Europe's Voters Turn Backs on EU, Governments," *Reuters*, 14 June 2004.
30 "Results of the 2014 European Elections," European Parliament, http://www.results-elections2014.eu/en/turnout.html (accessed 3 August 2015).
31 William Horsley, "Euro-skeptics storm the citadel," *BBC News*, 14 June 2004. See also *Economist*, "The Eurosceptic Union," 31 May 2014, http://www.economist.com/news/europe/21603034-impact-rise-anti-establishment-parties-europe-and-abroad-euroscepticunion?zid=309&ah=80dcf288b8561b012f603b9fd9577f0e (accessed 3 August 2015).

patriotism. It was created by intellectuals, and that fact accounts at once for its genuine appeal to the mind and its feeble echo in the heart.[32]

Benedict Anderson argued, "*in themselves*, market-zones, 'natural'-geographic or politico-administrative, do not create attachments. Who will willingly die for the Comecon or the EEC?"[33] Jacques Delors recognized the problem when he warned that "you can't fall in love with a single market." Economic advantages of integration do not sway public opinion. Rather, according to Liesbet Hooghe and Gary Marks, identity does: "Citizens do indeed take into account the economic consequences of European integration, but conceptions of group membership appear to be more powerful."[34]

Therefore, to encourage a feeling of togetherness and 'Europeaness', the EU has sought to create both a narrative and symbols, that is, a story around which the citizens could identify:

> To put it in a nutshell, the identity narrative channels political emotions so that they can fuel efforts to modify a balance of power; it transforms the perceptions of the past and of the present; it changes the organization of human groups and creates new ones; it alters cultures by emphasizing certain traits and skewing their meanings and logic. The identity narrative brings forth a new interpretation of the world in order to modify it.[35]

This identity narrative is clearly spelled out on the EU's Web page:

> The EU was created in the aftermath of the Second World War. The first steps were to foster economic cooperation: the idea being that countries who trade with one another become economically interdependent and so more likely to avoid conflict. The result was the European Economic Community (EEC), created in 1958, and initially increasing economic cooperation between six countries: Belgium, Germany, France, Italy, Luxembourg and the Netherlands. ... The EU has delivered half a century of peace, stability and prosperity, helped raise living standards, and launched a single European currency, the euro.[36]

32　Ernst B. Haas, *The Uniting of Europe: Political, Economic and Social Forces, 1950–1957* (London: Stevens & Sons 1958), 28-29.
33　Anderson, *Imagined Communities*, 53.
34　Liesbet Hooghe and Gary Marks, "Does Identity or Economic Rationality Drive Public Opinion on European Integration?," *Political Science and Politics* 37:03 (2004): 415.
35　Denis-Constant Martin "The Choices of Identity" *Social Identities* 1:1 (1995): 7. For more on the importance and role of narrative in identity building, see Paul Ricoeur *Oneself as Another* (Chicago: University of Chicago Press, 1995).
36　The European Union, "How the EU Works," http://europa.eu/about-eu/index_en.htm (accessed 3 May 2015).

Through the hardship of war, the Europeans have learned how to create a(n) EUtopia.³⁷ This is the basic narrative of the European Union, the story told and retold to remind its citizens what they have in common and what they have accomplished through cooperation.

As a constant reminder of this group identity, the EU has adopted certain symbols. For example, the EU has a flag with a blue background with twelve yellow stars and a 'national' anthem (Beethoven's Ode to Joy). Peter van Ham remarked, "The EU's striking logo – a blue flag with a circle of 12 stars – is already omnipresent. The application of 'euro' to everything from trains and soccer championships to a unit of currency will make it one of the most frequently used names across the continent and one of the world's most popular brands."³⁸

Michael Billig explained, in his book *Banal Nationalism*, that the mundane day-to-day identity of 'national' symbols such as flags, anthems, money, EU passports, etc., is what causes the people to recognize themselves as a particular group out of habit.³⁹ According to the EU Website, the euro is the ultimate symbol of European integration: "The euro – used every day by some 338.6 million Europeans – is the most tangible proof of cooperation between EU countries."⁴⁰

The Symbolism of the Euro's Design

In 1993, the European Parliament sponsored a competition to get people excited about the introduction of the euro. It asked individuals to choose among ten different designs for the new common currency, the most amusing of which was a coin that said in Dutch, "money only stinks when it's in another man's pocket." Explaining the rationale, Egon Klepsch, EP president wrote "I am convinced that this competition to produce a design for the ECU and this consultation of the citizens can play an important role in spreading information and knowledge about the European Economic and Monetary Union ... We must make it clear that there is no alternative to the European Community, the sole guarantor of peace and security in Europe."⁴¹ In 2008,

---

37 Borrowed from Kalypso Nicolaidis and Robert Howse, "'This is my EUtopia ...': Narrative as Power," *Journal of Common Market Studies* 40:4 (2002): 767.
38 Peter Van Ham, "The Rise of the Brand State," *Foreign Affairs* (2001): 5-6.
39 Michael Billig, *Banal Nationalism* (London: Sage, 1995), 8.
40 "Money and the EU," European Union, http://europa.eu/about-eu/basic-information/money/index_en.htm (accessed 3 May 2015).
41 Letter from Egon A. Klepsch, European Parliament president on the poster for the Graphic ECU Competition, European Parliament, 1993.

the European Commission sponsored a similar competition to commemorate the tenth anniversary of the euro.⁴²

Image 2-2: Euro notes

In the end, none of the proposed designs from the 1993 competition were chosen. Instead, the euro was designed with depictions of nondescript bridges, tunnels and arches that could be found in any EU member state with Roman ruins. The goal was to put something common and familiar on the currency that would symbolize the linking together of Europe:

> On the front of both series of euro banknotes, windows and doorways are shown. They symbolise the European spirit of openness and cooperation. The bridges on the back symbolise communication between the people of Europe and between Europe and the rest of the world.⁴³

In doing so, the euro became both the figurative and literal currency of the Union. In the pockets of all Europeans, the euro was the concrete symbol of peace and prosperity on the continent.

---

42 "Design the New Euro," European Commission, formerly at http://ec.europa.eu/news/economy/080208_1_en.htm. While this Web site no longer works, on 14 March 2008, the winner of the competition was announced: http://ec.europa.eu/economy_finance/articles/euro/article12315_en.htm (accessed 31 July 2015).
43 "Banknotes," European Central Bank, http://www.ecb.europa.eu/euro/banknotes/html/index.en.html (accessed 31 July 2015).

Image 2-3: Captain Euro, see www.captaineuro.com.

Image 2-4: "Happy Birthday euro!" Celebration poster of the euro's one year anniversary by Constatin (2002). http://bookshop.europa.eu/en/happy-birthday-euro-pbKC4902151/

Image 2-5: The European Central Bank in Frankfurt.

Image 2-6: An introductory packet of euro coins from France during the changeover. Photo by Stephanie Anderson.

To further cement the euro in the hearts of the people, in the 1990's, European Parliament President Enrique Barón Crespo supported the creation of a new comic book hero for Europe: Captain Euro (see image 2-3). Working against his archenemy, Dr. D. Vider, he protects Europe from division within. In 2002, one year after the 'birth' of the euro, the Commission commissioned an artist, Constatin, to commemorate the anniversary. The image is of twelve star parents greeting their toddler (see image 2-4).

The euro has become a symbol for the people to rally around. In front of the European Parliament stands a neo-classical statue of the euro. In front of the European Central Bank is another, more modern and cartoonish depiction of the euro symbol (see image 2-5). In 2002, the New Year heralded the advent of the euro; people gave the introductory packages of coins as gifts (see image 2-6), and huge state-sponsored celebrations filled the streets and the airways. In contrast, the United States would likely come under a great deal of criticism if it placed such statues and art depicting the dollar sign in front of the US Capitol or the US Federal Reserve buildings around the country.

Rationale for the Euro: An Economic House of Cards?

In the United States, fifty states have close to completely free trade and share the same currency. Upon casual inspection, the economic fundamentals are broadly similar across the EU and US. Each has an approximately comparable population and gross domestic product (GDP).[44] Both include only developed economies. Socially, European ancestry in the United States is still obvious in its laws, institutions, and cultures. There are, however, important differences. Fundamentally, a united Europe is still an unfinished project. In economic matters affecting the entire eurozone or the whole EU, it is still a confederation, one that approaches difficult decisions slowly based on consensus of the member nations.[45] The emergence of "Merkozy", that is Angela Merkel, chancellor of Germany, and Nicholas Sarkozy, the president of France as the primary decision-makers during the eurozone crisis from 2009 until 2012, is in itself indicative of the vast difference in governance between the two unions. Europe's governance, dominated by these two leaders pre-

---

44　In 2012, the eurozone had a population of 331 million people, while the United States had a population of 312 million. US GDP at current prices in 2012 was $15.1 trillion and eurozone GDP across countries at current prices converted to US dollars was $12.2 trillion, IMF April 2013 World Economic Outlook Database, www.imf.org.

45　The description of a confederation is meant narrowly here, and is focused on the decision-making apparatus of major policy initiatives. The EU should not be generalized as a confederation in all issues. The EU has elements and institutions that reflect everything from intergovernmentalism (where national governments are the primary actors in the process of decision-making) to federalism, depending on the policy area.

siding over the eurozone's two largest economies, would be comparable to the governors of New York and California dominating the political debate rather than the president of the United States. In the US, strong federal governance has ensured this does not occur. In Europe, however, regional interests dominate as healthier and wealthier economies have the greatest power in dictating policy. How did this system of economic governance evolve?

Evolution of Monetary Union

Efforts to achieve closer economic integration began in the late 1960s. At The Hague Summit of 1969, the European Council delegated Pierre Werner, then Prime Minister of Luxembourg, the task of reporting on how the European Community might avoid exchange rate volatility among its member states. The result was the 1970 Werner Plan, which recommended a common currency or irrevocably fixed exchange rates among member currencies to occur over a period of ten years in three stages. The first stage would lay the groundwork for the transfer of economic policy across the EC from national governments to a single centralized, community-wide body. In effect, the report called for greater political integration to achieve economic goals. In light of the 1966 Luxembourg compromise, establishing the dominance of national governments over European policy making, the plan was not adopted.

In 1972, after the breakdown of the Bretton Woods fixed exchange rate system, concerns mounted in the European Community regarding exchange rate volatility and the negative impacts such risk implied for closer economic integration and trade in the EC. The Six co-opted an idea from the Werner Plan establishing a cooperative semi-pegged exchange rate system, referred to as "the snake in the tunnel", in which currencies would be allowed to fluctuate by only +/- 2.25 percent between countries. However, the arrangement failed to reduce exchange rate fluctuations. In his 1975 Report on European Union, Belgian Prime Minister Leo Tindemans criticized the lack of progress in this area and stated categorically that that "unless it [progresses] European Union will be meaningless."[46]

In 1979, the EC made another attempt based on a new reference currency referred to as the European Currency Unit or ECU, which, in turn, was based on the values of the participating countries' currencies in the newly created European Monetary System (EMS). Again, exchange rates of individual countries were pegged within a range of +/- 2.25 percent of the ECU value,

---

46 Report on European Union in *Bulletin of the European Communities*, 1976, supplement 1, 11-35, http://www.cvce.eu/content/publication/1997/10/13/284c9784-9bd2-472b-b704-ba4bb1f3122d/publishable_en.pdf (accessed 31 July 2015).

with a wider band of +/- 6 percent allowed for the Italian lira. The EMS also proved volatile. Over time, because of the German Bundesbank's (the German central bank) strict anti-inflation policies, the Deutsche Mark became the central currency within this system and other currencies had to follow the Bundesbank's lead to maintain their exchange rates.

By the late 1980s, member countries were primarily using national interest rates to maintain their EMS exchange rate targets. Differences in economic conditions and policy priorities across member states led to a crisis in the system in September 1992 as speculators recognized several countries would not be able to maintain their exchange rates given domestic economic conditions. What is referred to as a "time inconsistency" problem occurred: that is, countries that had committed to a fixed exchange rate regime earlier now found it optimal to renege on that commitment.[47] On "Black Wednesday," 16 September 1992, under intense pressure from currency speculators in international exchange markets, Britain was forced to withdraw from the EMS. The conflict between dreadfully weak domestic economic conditions and the high interest rates (over ten percent) necessary to maintain exchange rate targets proved unworkable. The following day, Italy, unable to maintain exchange rate targets, also withdrew from the EMS. When the French franc came under speculative pressure the following year, EMS target ranges were widened to fifteen percent to accommodate it. While in principle, the EMS still functioned, in practice, the system had completely broken down and no longer provided the exchange rate stability it was meant to create. The hope was that the eventual introduction of the single currency would eliminate such crises in the future.

In 1988, European Commission President Jacques Delors pushed for an economic and monetary union to accompany the plans for a single market. Although the gears were already set in motion by the time of the June 1988 European Council with fundamental French and German consent, the fall of the Berlin Wall in the next year and the dissolution of the Eastern Bloc has-

---

47 This problem of commitment to a fixed exchange rate is referred to as a "time inconsistency" problem. Initially, a country sees it as optimal to adopt a specific exchange rate; however, doing so then limits the monetary policy options in that country as interest rates must be held at levels that support the target exchange rate. If the country's domestic economy later falls into a recession, for example, it then faces a conflict between maintaining higher interest rates to protect the exchange rate or lowering them to assist domestic recovery, which is inconsistent with the commitment to maintain the fixed exchange rate. Since internal politics usually trump a government's priorities, currency speculators will also recognize that higher interest rate policies needed to maintain exchange rates will eventually be abandoned. They then begin to sell these currencies in anticipation, adding further pressure for an exchange rate devaluation, which makes the conflict the government faces more intense and usually hastens the abandonment of the country's exchange rate policy. This is what happened in Europe, in 1992 and 1993, with George Soros being the most famous of the currency speculators involved.

tened EMU. To allay fears of a 'German Europe', Kohl promised to pursue unification in the framework of the European Union, thereby assuring a 'European Germany'. Germany would give up the Deutsche Mark (DM) for the common European currency.

EMU occurred in three stages. Stage I, beginning on 1 July 1990, eliminated many exchange rate controls and restrictions on capital movement while working on the criteria necessary for the transition to irrevocably fixed exchange rates. Stage II, beginning on 1 January 1994, created the European Monetary Institute (EMI), predecessor to the European Central Bank.

The strength of the Deutsche Mark forced other member states to follow German economic monetary policy if they were to maintain their exchange rates. Effectively, German economic policy had become European policy, much to the dissatisfaction of several other European Community member states. Some saw the single currency as a way to minimize Germany's excessive influence. Adopting such a system would commit countries to exchange rate parity and allow Europe-wide monetary policy to be determined for all of Europe, avoiding the problems the EMS experienced. Following the outline recommended in the 1989 Delors Report, the Maastricht Treaty of 1992 defined the new European Union and conditions under which a new single currency would be adopted: the euro.

The euro first came into existence in 1999 as a virtual currency, used only as a unit of account among the original eleven participating EU countries. In 2001, Greece received approval to become part of the euro at the start of the following year, joining France, Germany, Luxembourg, Spain, Italy, Portugal, Belgium, the Netherlands, Finland, Ireland and Austria, now often referred to collectively as the eurozone or "Eurogroup". At the beginning of 2002, the euro replaced national currencies in participating countries to great fanfare. The euro's introduction as the single currency of the monetary union fueled optimism that it would replace the US dollar as the world reserve currency. The following decade never lived up to such hopes; nevertheless, the euro has emerged as the only major alternative to the dollar in international finance.

To coordinate economic policies more closely, the Eurogroup of finance ministers meet on a regular basis, typically a day before EU-wide meetings of the Economic and Financial Affairs Council (ECOFIN).[48] Since the euro-crisis began, it has also been common for Eurogroup chief executives to convene "euro-summits" to decide crisis policy in a manner similar to the European Council. Again, these meetings have been unofficial, but have served to ensure policy coordination across eurozone countries.

---

48 The Council of Ministers is often referred to as Ecofin when finance ministers meet to decide economic and financial issues.

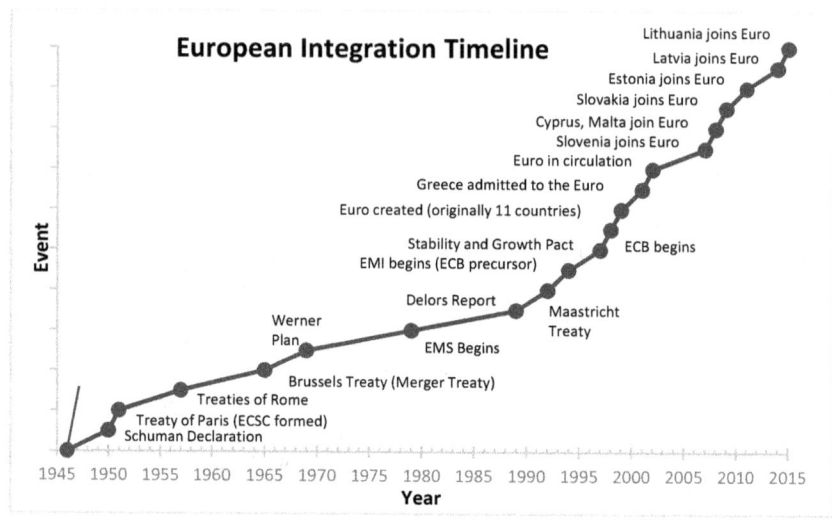

Figure 2-2: The Process of European economic integration over time. Efforts to stabilize currency exchange rates among member countries in the European Community began in the 1970s and led directly to the creation of the euro in 1999. More and more countries have joined the eurozone for a total of 19 as of 2015.

The implementation of the euro as a common currency was a critical political achievement, one that had been decades in the making. Ideally, the creation of the eurozone would ensure significant economic benefits for those countries participating. In some quarters, specifically Germany and northern Europe, it was thought the euro would mitigate the threat of inflation through the enshrining of a sound continent-wide monetary policy. Other countries saw the creation of the euro as a spur to growth, easing trade and creating better access to credit markets, particularly those countries in the south. In general, the euro was expected to create the conditions for "economic convergence," the condition in which all member economies' standards of living converge to a common outcome, bringing greater prosperity to the entire union. This promise has since led to additional countries joining the currency, including Slovenia in 2007, Cyprus and Malta in 2008, Slovakia in 2009, Estonia in 2011, Latvia in 2014, and Lithuania in 2015.

Conclusions

Despite the hopes of the original visionaries, a "United States of Europe" has not yet emerged. Instead the EU, and the eurozone in particular, represent hybrid governmental institutions that are far more economically than politically integrated. The eurozone is a supranational economic government. However, politically, the institution could be considered to behave more often like a confederation, with intergovernmental relationships defining its political direction. Without political consensus on a stronger federal union, discussions on a common fiscal or banking union have been sidestepped throughout the evolution of the current eurozone.

As a result, one can draw the following conclusions about the European Union:

1) The governing structure is skewed towards the Council; Brussels is hostage to member state capitals in all areas except those few where it has exclusive competence: customs union; competition rules; common fisheries policy; common commercial policy; the conclusion of certain international agreements; and monetary policy for eurozone countries;
2) Member states are reluctant to give up more power to Brussels.
3) The EU appears to be more federal than it truly is; and
4) Many question whether Brussels has been given too much or not enough power from the member states.

The above issues are all in play in the eurozone crisis. Despite the fact that monetary policy is decided by the ECB, it is the member states that dominated during the crisis.

Chapter III:
The Flawed Economic and Political Architecture of the Eurozone

As noted in the previous chapter, the structure of the EU is the consequence of attempting to accommodate two different visions of European integration over decades of negotiation. One vision, personified in the ideas of Jean Monnet and Robert Schuman, would prefer to see Europe evolve into a federation wherein European integration would create a "United States of Europe" with full political and economic integration. An opposing nationalist view, personified by leaders such as Charles De Gaulle, envisioned that integration would create a "Europe of States" ("L'Europe des patries"), resulting in a confederation of sovereign states. Over time, these visions have alternated in their ascendency as the driving influence in the process of European integration, resulting in the governance system now in place.

Jean Monnet reportedly predicted, "The fusion [of economic functions] would compel nations to fuse their sovereignty into that of a single European State."[49] This federalist vision gained traction with the 1989 Delors Report that provided a blueprint for adoption of a single currency. Hans Tietmeyer, President of the Deutsche Bundesbank from 1993 to 1999, recognized the implications of such a move writing in 1991, "A European currency will lead to member nations transferring their sovereignty over financial and wage policy as well as monetary affairs. It is an illusion to think that states can hold on to their autonomy over taxation policies."[50]

However, a federation was not forthcoming. The implementation of the euro created an economic union designed to fit the political structures of the EU, and not vice versa. Whereas many currency unions occur in the context of a common economic union, the euro-system had to fit the intergovernmental nature of the European Union and be adopted without a strong political, fiscal, or banking union. These structural omissions have fueled many criticisms and much skepticism towards monetary union, especially in Germany. In 1992, sixty-two German economists signed a document warning against the implementation of the common currency. The adoption of the euro and Maastricht Treaty were challenged in the country's constitutional

---

[49] This quotation was reportedly penned by Jean Monnet in a memo on April 3, 1952 as found in Thierry Baudet, *The Significance of Borders: Why Representative Government and the Rule of Law Require Nation States* (Boston, MA: Brill Publishing, 2012), 148.

[50] Peter Shore, "Fighting Against Federalism," in *Implications of the Euro: A Critical Perspective from the Left*, edited by Philip Whyman, Mark Baimbridge, and Brian Burkitt, (Bodmin, Great Britain: MPG Books Ltd, 2006) 148.

court in 1997.⁵¹ In addition, many US economists, in both the Federal Reserve and academia, voiced skepticism regarding the euro's potential success.⁵²

This chapter explains why the economic structure of the eurozone may have been doomed to experience an eventual crisis, why attempts to address the economic shortcomings of the currency union's structure have prolonged its economic cost, and why a political solution is not possible in light of Rodrik's trilemma of globalization.

Why Have a Common Currency at All?

Consider the benefits of a common currency among several countries. In a world with only one currency, countries would never again have to worry about the uncertainties that render international trade and investment unsure today. A common currency removes *exchange rate risk*, the uncertainty that investors and traders, not to mention foreign travelers, often experience as they conduct economic transactions in foreign currencies. Eliminating different currencies eliminates the need for exchange rates and having to first exchange one currency for another in order to buy foreign goods or services, making it easier to trade. Second, a common currency makes price differences between foreign goods, relative to domestic ones, transparent, thereby facilitating competition and better functioning of the free market.

After World War II, Bretton Woods, an agreement meant to help aid post-war recovery in the developed world, named after the town in New Hampshire where the conference took place, created a set of fixed exchange rates among nations, as well as two of the most important international financial institutions we have today: the International Monetary Fund (IMF), and the International Bank for Reconstruction and Development, more commonly called the World Bank. The conventional wisdom of the time was that to avoid the problems the international financial system experienced between the wars, a system of fixed exchange rates was needed.⁵³ The Bretton Woods

---

51 "Leitsatz," Entscheidungen, http://www.bundesverfassungsgericht.de/entscheidungen/rs19980331_2bvr187797.html (accessed 31 July 2015).
52 For a detailed history of these criticisms, see: Lars Jonung and Eoin Drae, "The Euro: It can't Happen. It's a Bad Idea. It won't Last: US Economists on the EMU 1989-2002," *European Economy* Economic Papers 395 European Commission, December 2009, http://ec.europa.eu/economy_finance/publications/publication16345_en.pdf (accessed 31 July 2015).
53 In the post-war period, an understanding developed that the Treaty of Versailles, and, in particular, reparations payments required of Germany, created significant political and economic instability in the post-World War I period. The debt Germany owed following the war led to the printing of German currency and the hyper-inflation that the country experienced in the 1920s. These economic troubles then contributed to Hitler's rise to

system, as the post-war organization of exchange rates was called, would rely on regulated sets of market economies within states and strict controls on the values of currencies between states. This system would remove the potential for speculative financial flows between countries that had disrupted national economies and international relations between the wars, and ensure that financial flows instead funded the reconstruction of war-torn economies. Such a liberal economic system in which economies relied on competitive forces, with an integrated international economic system relying on competitive trade and investment, would deepen international economic ties, thereby increasing the likelihood of peace. The motive to use economic ties to promote peace was also a driving force in the movement for greater European integration.

A system of fixed exchange rates provided considerable benefits during the process of European integration. Having a fixed exchange rate system ensured that trade patterns between countries were determined by their abilities to produce goods more cheaply. As a result, countries specialized in what they could produce at relatively lowest cost, and then traded for goods that other countries produced more economically. Compared to a common currency, a system of fixed exchange rates only incurs the additional costs of currency exchange. All the other benefits of a common currency remain; the prices of goods and assets between countries do not fluctuate in unpredictable ways as they had before the wars, thereby facilitating trade. Put simply, a common currency fixes all participating countries' exchange rates at parity (1:1).

In the late 1960s and early 1970s, however, the Bretton Woods Agreement broke down, and countries resorted to allowing their exchange rates to "float", i.e., to be determined in international exchange markets. The result was much greater uncertainty in international trade, which threatened to limit greater European integration from occurring. To avoid this problem and to allow deeper economic integration among European Community member states, Europe attempted to restore fixed exchange rates in two ways. First, in the 1970s, the EC used the "snake in the tunnel" mechanism wherein exchange rates (the snake) were allowed to only fluctuate within a narrow band of values (the tunnel) relative to the US dollar, which had been the reference currency during the Bretton Woods period. As noted in the last chapter, this

---

power. Simultaneously, during the 1920s, a significant increase in the flow of speculative financial capital across countries led to additional international financial instability. Finally, in the 1930s, increasingly isolationist trade policies and the formation of trade blocs meant to reduce imports, coupled with competitive exchange rate devaluations – "beggar thy neighbour" policies meant to increase exports – led to a breakdown of the international financial system. In 1945, the understanding was that many of these problems could have been avoided had countries coordinated their exchange rates in the interwar period and that failure to do so had led in part to the political tensions that caused World War II.

attempt failed by the end of that decade. A second attempt, in the 1980's, called the European Monetary System (EMS) fixed exchange rates within a range around a basket of their own currencies (called the European Currency Unit), but failed in the nineties.

Why did Europe's fixed exchange rates fail? Very simply, the reason was national interests. While a country can potentially benefit from greater trade when the costs of trading are reduced, for example, by fixing exchange rates to reduce uncertainty in the costs of goods and services traded, they are costly in the sense that they eliminate a country's ability to use monetary policy. A country controlling its own currency can change its interest rates and exchange rate to manage its economy. In the early 1990s, maintaining the fixed exchange rates among European countries became very difficult as economic conditions began to diverge among member states. Germany, absorbing the costs of reunification, experienced a relatively weaker economy than other European states, some of which had experienced significant housing booms in the late 1980s. Despite its own weak conditions, Germany decided to set relatively higher interest rates by reducing its money supply within its economy to counteract the inflationary effects of its reunification expenditures. These higher interest rates drove its exchange rate higher relative to other European currencies as international investors attempted to take advantage of the higher interest rates paid on German assets. Under the EMS, Britain and Italy, along with many of the other countries in Europe, were forced to follow, hiking interest rates to protect their exchange rates with Germany.

The problem, however, is that higher interest rates within a country reduce economic activity and can lead to recessions as the costs of borrowing to finance consumption and investment increases. Less expenditure due to the higher costs of borrowing first leads to reduced employment, then greater decreases in borrowing and lending as business conditions weaken, and finally, further job losses and recession. As exchange rate conditions became strained, weak domestic economic conditions caused by the end of the housing boom in Britain and Italy, recessionary conditions elsewhere in the world depressing trade, and the high interest rates necessary to maintain their exchange rate with Germany resulted in currency speculators expecting many European countries, particularly Britain, eventually to abandon their high interest rate policies due to the poor economic conditions these were creating in each country. The reasoning was simple: they deduced that Britain, in particular, and other countries such as Italy, would not sacrifice their own economies to maintain a commitment to European economic integration and the fixed exchange rates the European Monetary System required. The political costs of doing so within each country were simply too high.

Acting on this expectation, they began selling the currencies of the countries they believed would have to break away from the EMS, resulting in further declines in these countries' exchange rates. These countries were forced to raise interest rates to offset the decline in their exchange rate, worsening domestic economic conditions and tipping their own economies into worse recessions. Finally, the speculators' expectations were self-fulfilling, and domestic pressures led to Britain and other EMS countries succumbing to conditions and abandoning the EMS on Black Wednesday, 16 September 1992. The lesson learned was simple: When the cost of maintaining them becomes too high, countries will abandon their commitment to fixed exchange rates. Domestic interests will prevail over international commitments under such circumstances. Such currency speculation in part led to the abandonment of the Bretton Woods system. After several failures at fixing exchange rates among European countries, Europe chose a common currency as the solution.

A common currency creates commitment and adherence by allowing no alternative. While leaving a currency union is possible, such a departure would incur considerable risk and uncertainty that could result in greater costs than those borne by staying. If a country were to leave a common currency, what currency would be used instead, and how much would it be worth? Further, a common currency is also symbolic, and committing to one creates a difficult process to reverse not only economically, but also politically. Additionally, creating a common currency requires the creation of a single central bank setting monetary policy over the entire currency area, thereby taking the interest rate decisions out of the hands of individual governments. Therefore, "leaving" is much more difficult to do than it is under fixed exchange rates where "leaving" only requires a change in monetary policy. In this way, the decision to commit Europe to a common currency area was meant to achieve what the fixed exchange rate systems could not: a long-lasting system in which exchange rate uncertainty would be eliminated between countries. The cost of doing so, however, would be eliminating a degree of state sovereignty. A single currency requires that a "one-size-fits-all" monetary policy across the currency area be used regardless of differences in individual countries' preferences, or perhaps in spite of them.

The Structure of Europe's Monetary Union – An Optimal Currency Area?

Economists have studied the idea of common currency areas, specifically, when they will work and what causes them to break down. A common currency area that has no tendency to break down and does not lead to countries leaving the common currency or set of fixed exchange rates is called an "optimal currency area." Such an area describes one in which conditions ensure the benefits of leaving the currency union are outweighed by the benefits of staying.[54] Canadian economist Robert Mundell, winner of the Nobel Memorial Prize in Economics in 1999, first developed the theory of an optimal currency area in 1961.

Table 3-1: Optimal Currency Area Characteristics of the Eurozone

Optimal Currency Area Criteria	Eurozone Area Conditions
Economic criteria	
Degree of trade openness and integration	High
Product diversification	High
Labour mobility	Low
Wage flexibility	Low
Level of debt	Varies from low to high
Fiscal transfers possible	Officially limited
Social criteria	
Homogeneous policy preferences	Regional/limited
High degree of solidarity with other nations	Regional/limited

The adoption of a common currency, however, like the adoption of fixed exchange rates, comes at a cost: the loss of the country's ability to utilize independent monetary policy to manage its economy or to adjust to a country-specific economic shock, such as a natural disaster or economic crisis within the country. In the absence of a currency union, if a negative or "recessionary" economic shock were to occur, a country could lower its exchange rate by lowering its interest rate. Increasing the money supply, or "expansionary monetary policy" to stimulate growth through lower interest rates by encouraging greater investment, simultaneously causes depreciation in the country's exchange rate, stimulating trade with the rest of the world. If, when a currency union is in place, other options exist to adjust to the shock or stimulate the economy and reduce the costs of the shock, then the member state is less likely to leave. The characteristics and conditions that might allow such options are described in table 3-1[55], as are eurozone conditions with respect to these qualities.

The optimal currency area literature suggests that common currency areas will be better served if they include the economic and social criteria shown. With respect to economic criteria, trade openness and product diversi-

---

54 Economists call such a situation "incentive compatible" in that the commitment to enter a currency union is compatible with incentives to stay.
55 The sources for the table are Zuzana Gáková and Lewis Dijkstra, "Labour mobility between the regions of the EU-27 and a comparison with the USA" European Union Regional Policy, 02/2008 http://ec.europa.eu/regional_policy/sources/docgener/focus/2008_02_labour.pdf (accessed 31 August 2015), Richard and Charles Wyplosz. The Economics of the European Integration (New York: McGraw Hill, 2009) and www.OECD.org.

fication allow economies to better integrate and benefit from a common currency area, increasing the benefits of such a union. Labour mobility and wage flexibility are necessary to allow the union to adjust more quickly to severe country-specific shocks. The final two conditions – lower levels of debt and the ability to create fiscal transfers across member states – increase the number of options a country has to react to such a shock, in light of the loss of an independent monetary policy.

With regard to the social criteria, a high degree of solidarity or "common identity" among the union's populations could ease the political tensions a common currency generates. Specifically, if populations have similar values and policy preferences, it is less likely that the "one-size-fits-all" monetary policy will be considered disadvantageous to one country over another, and, thus, will lead to fewer economic or political conflicts over which monetary policy should be implemented in the union.

In Europe, as the table notes, both qualities are somewhat regional. The eurozone spans both northern and southern European countries with significant cultural and historical differences. These differences, not to mention differences over economic policy preferences, have played a role in the European financial crisis. Furthermore, the crisis has exacerbated these differences, potentially increasing the perceived cost of the monetary union within the member states most affected, especially those in the south, particularly Greece. In the current crisis, bailouts to southern periphery countries have been widely unpopular in the other countries that have financed them, potentially undermining support for the currency union overall. Significantly, the idea of eurobonds, that is, bonds that allow the joint liability for debt to support countries cut off from credit markets, has also been soundly rejected, especially by northern countries, most vocally Germany, while supported by the most negatively affected states.[56]

Successful monetary unions have historically had three common characteristics that have allowed them to succeed. Each requires states to give up a degree of sovereignty over monetary and fiscal policy for the good of the currency: 1) economic integration and the ability to manage and react to external and internal shocks (a political union); 2) a common fiscal framework allowing collective transfers and if necessary, collective debt (fiscal union); and 3) a strong central bank able to oversee the banking sector and

---

56 Differences in preferences also led to the failure of the EMS system. In Germany, political and public preferences typically prioritize concerns about inflation above those regarding unemployment and economic activity levels. In the 1990s, Germany's decision to focus on inflation despite the economic cost of such actions led to their monetary policy decision to increase interest rates and impose contractionary monetary policy. In Britain and other countries that eventually had to leave the EMS after failing to maintain their exchange rates due to the domestic cost, these decisions reflected a political and public preference to protect employment and economic activity over inflation.

act as a lender of last resort in the common currency (a banking union). The European monetary union, however, was critically lacking in several of these features when it was launched. The first two conditions are consistent with the conditions necessary to form an "optimal currency area." The lack of a political and fiscal union can be blamed in part for both the conditions that led to the European financial crisis and leaders' inability to act once it began. The third characteristic, the presence of a banking union – a strong central bank that can act as a union-wide lender of last resort – has proven invaluable in financial crises for over a century. The design of the European monetary union's economic architecture has contributed to the severity of the eurozone crisis, and has hindered its recovery. Much of the effort to address the crisis has therefore focused on trying to establish these missing elements, specifically, fiscal and banking unions.

With the loss of monetary policy, governments can only use expansionary fiscal policy to address macroeconomic shocks: i.e., expansion of government expenditures; lower taxes to stimulate growth; or both. Outside aid or changes in union-wide monetary policy could be possible, but only if such changes were acceptable to all other member states. Further, it would be advantageous if such policies were coordinated, timely and effective. Without political union to streamline decision-making, such changes would most likely be disjointed, slow, and, therefore, less effective. As noted in the last chapter, EU-wide decision making requires unanimity over serious policy matters, and individual member state interests constrain the options available. Policy made at the union level will likely be slow in coming and weaker than needed for the most affected countries. In the European financial crisis, policy responses by the EU and eurozone collectively have often been characterized as "too little, too late".

For countries in a currency union, using expansionary fiscal policy to counter a recessionary shock may require governments to borrow as tax revenues could decline. Such borrowing may be checked if a country lacks a significant stock of savings in the country, or cannot borrow at reasonable rates from international financial markets. The credit may come from other member states in the union in the form of transfers, or from international lenders and financial markets. Such rates require that a country maintains a sustainable debt load, facilitated by a strong "fiscal union". A fiscal union refers to a set of rules that ensures all countries follow similar policies to ensure their access to credit, if necessary, is maintained. In the EU, the structure of the fiscal union backing the euro was described in the Maastricht Treaty.

With the implementation of the euro in 1999, fiscal policies regulating government expenditures and taxation by country were left effectively independent, but limited. The "Maastricht Criteria" stipulated critical fiscal requirements that all countries using the euro had to meet before they could officially adopt the euro, specifically:

1) Limiting annual government deficit levels to no more than 3% of GDP;
2) Limiting their ratio of national debt to GDP to no more than 60%; and
3) Maintaining an annual average inflation rate no greater than 1.5% more than the average rate of the three lowest inflation states in the eurozone.[57]

The debt and deficit limits were meant to ensure debt brakes existed within the currency union so that individual countries would be able to access international credit markets at affordable interest rates should a severe economic shock occur. The third was to ensure that no country embarked on inflationary policies that caused it to become uncompetitive; otherwise, if the price of one member state's goods increased with respect to the others', it would create an incentive for the state to leave the union to devalue its exchange rate. Overall, these conditions aimed to control the costs of joining the common currency and to encourage countries to remain in the union by preserving the ability to use fiscal policy if faced with a severe economic shock.

To limit members' liability vis-à-vis other members, the Treaty prohibited bailouts of one country by another. Such a ban removed domestic incentives to maintain high levels of public expenditure and accumulate higher debts with the thought of passing those debts onto the union as a whole, an incentive referred to as moral hazard. Transfers between countries, if one country found it could not access credit, were also prohibited, as was the use of joint-liability, that is, having other countries back a troubled country's debt to allow it access to international credit. The structure of the fiscal union implied by the Maastricht Treaty was clear: countries that faced shocks were expected to remedy the situation only by utilizing their own resources and access to credit.

The criteria were to be enforced by rules described in the European Stability and Growth Pact (SGP), adopted at the original urging of Germany, to encourage members to adopt the 'golden rule' or balanced budgets. Otherwise, moral hazard might lead to countries pursuing otherwise imprudent fiscal policies leading to higher debts and deficits, without thought to the destabilizing effects on the currency union. As a result, the SGP specified sanctions for the failure to meet the Maastricht conditions, including fines and even the suspension of EU expenditures within the country.

---

57 The three states considered cannot be ones in economic distress or experiencing abnormal economic conditions, for example a severe recession.

Consider why the Maastricht conditions might be necessary to avoid a country exiting the common currency and triggering the potential for the currency to unravel as previous European fixed exchange rate mechanisms had. In the face of a severe economic shock affecting one country, but not the entire union, a country without the ability to borrow from international credit markets to finance expansionary fiscal policy would have no choice but to suffer through the recessionary effects of the negative shock to its economy.[58] Eventually, the lack of demand in the economy will drive down prices and wages as unemployment mounts, allowing it to expand its exports within the currency union. The eventual recovery through lower wages and prices is referred to as "internal devaluation", as it has the same effect that lowering the exchange rate would have had if the country had been able to pursue such a policy. The process of recovery, however, can be long and drawn out, and the costs of such outcomes fall directly on the people of the country, making the effects very politically costly to sitting governments.

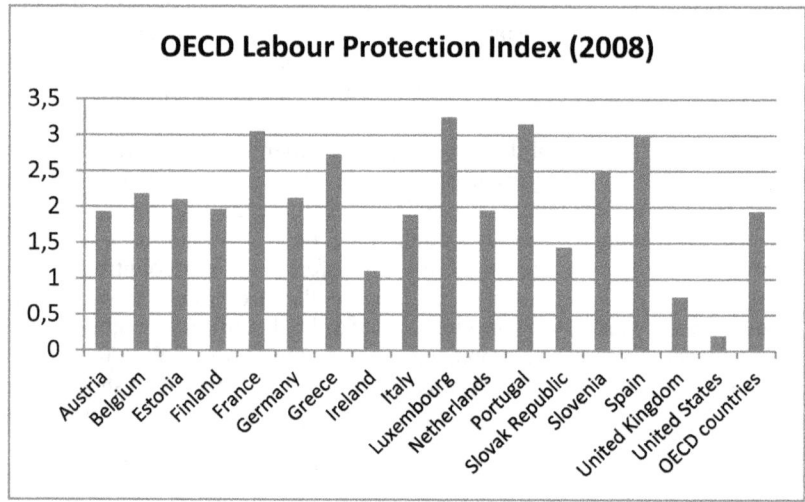

Figure 3-1: OECD strictness of overall employment protection index. The high index scores of EU countries relative to the United States indicate how difficult it is to use labour market adjustment to adapt to economic conditions. In a currency area, internal devaluation becomes very difficult for countries to achieve. Source: OECD.

This costly process will be even more prolonged if wage flexibility is low in a nation, due to, for example, excessive labour protections that limit wage ad-

---

58 If a severe shock affected the entire union, expansionary monetary policy could be used to devalue the currency and relieve conditions across the union.

justment. In Europe, such protections are relatively high compared to other developed economies, such as the United States, as shown in figure 3-1, and were especially high in 2008 at the beginning of the European financial crisis.

One means of reducing the potential political costs of such a shock is labour migration, as displaced workers look for employment elsewhere. This migration can occur inside and outside the country and, while not optimal for workers, can reduce the cost that a state experiences in adjusting to such a severe economic shock. For example, in the United States, unemployed workers in Oklahoma famously migrated to California during the Great Depression, allowing internal economic adjustment among US states affected differently during the period.[59] Similarly, economic migrants are commonplace among countries around the world, and their existence is part of global adjustment to country-specific shocks. As such, migration can ease unemployment within a state by rebalancing the demand and supply of available labour as well as providing an option for the unemployed.

Nevertheless, the labour mobility option – having people move to other regions or countries with better economic conditions – may well be limited by cultural and linguistic factors or immigration restrictions between countries. Such restrictions may include outright laws against such movement or, as in the case of Europe, differences in social programs, language, or culture that create disincentives to move, or that make such relocation difficult. For example, a Greek worker might have trouble finding a job in Finland because the languages are so different. Despite the promise of freedom of movement of workers in the 1957 Treaty of Rome, language and cultural differences across countries have limited this goal in practice. The situation is so problematic that the European Commission declared 2006 the "European Year of Workers' Mobility" to find ways to overcome obstacles to free movement of people.[60] Compared to US labour mobility, the levels found in the eurozone have been estimated to be two and a half times lower.[61] Wage inflexibility, coupled with limited labour mobility, implies adjustment to a country-specific shock would be slow and costly without other policy interventions. Clearly, labour migration and internal devaluation impose the costs of adjustment to a macroeconomic shock on the people within the country, and if adjustment requires either to occur, political pressure may build to rethink currency membership.

---

59 John Steinbeck's famous novel *The Grapes of Wrath* depicts this migration.
60 http://europa.eu/legislation_summaries/internal_market/living_and_working_in_the_internal_market/c11333_en.htm (accessed 31 July 2015).
61 See Economist "Europe's debt crisis: At a bursting point?" 27 January 2012, retrieved 8 June 2013 from http://www.economist.com/blogs/charlemagne/2012/01/europes-debt-crisis, and Zuzana Gakova and Lewis Kijkstra, "Labour mobility between the regions of the EU-27 and a comparison with the USA" European Population Conference, Vienna, Austria, 1-4 September 2010, http://epc2010.princeton.edu/abstracts/100976 (accessed 31 July 2015).

One means to offset a negative economic shock is the use of fiscal policy. However, to do so requires adequate "fiscal space", defined as lower levels of debt, which allows countries better access to the financing necessary to implement expansionary fiscal policy. The Maastricht criteria were meant to ensure such conditions; however, once the common currency was adopted, political incentives led to some countries to ignore or weaken them.

Almost immediately after the euro replaced national currencies, some countries violated the Maastricht and SGP rules. As image 3 illustrates, debt–GDP levels across the original twelve eurozone countries have varied significantly, but, in general, have grown over time. This growth occurred even before the world financial crisis of 2008 and the eurozone crisis in 2009, and has continued since. With respect to violations of treaty requirements, first Portugal was found to be in violation in 2002, and then Greece in 2005, but sanctions were not imposed. In 2002 and 2003, France and Germany, the two largest countries in the eurozone accounting for fifty percent of eurozone output, had both exceeded the three percent deficit rule. In 2003, France and Germany also exceeded the sixty percent debt–GDP rule, which they have broken every year since. Germany's failure to achieve Maastricht targets was primarily due to the costs of reunification with former East Germany. France had missed the targets after a severe economic slowdown in the early 2000s. In each case, the Commission began sanction proceedings as directed under SGP, but both countries successfully lobbied against any punitive action being taken against them. More importantly, they also lobbied for a reinterpretation of the SGP rules,[62] which was to have significant influence on the future course of events in the eurozone.

At the European Council meeting of 22-23 March 2005, the member states agreed to German–French proposals that would change rules defined in the SGP regarding violations of the accord. Their proposals allowed the inclusion of special circumstances under which the Maastricht convergence requirements need not be strictly met; specifically, if debt–GDP requirements were met, deficit rules could be loosened. By implication, the structural deficit limits (the deficit adjusted for the business cycle) could now also be loosened when economies slowed, allowing counter-cyclical fiscal expenditures to expand when necessary. Furthermore, deficit limits would also be waived if deemed necessary by the severity of an economic downturn, or if expenditures were undertaken to enhance future productivity, and "all other relevant factors." These ideas had merit from an economic perspective. They allowed for large-scale public infrastructure investment, like that occurring in former East Germany. Relaxing the Maastricht limits also safeguarded against increased austerity measures exactly when the opposite type of fiscal

---

62 See European Council Presidency Conclusions, Brussels, 22-23 March 2005, http://www.consilium.europa.eu/uedocs/cms_data/docs/pressdata/en/ec/84335.pdf (accessed 31 July 2015).

policy might be called for in the event of an economic slowdown. Ironically, the Germany of the mid-2000's, with the help of France, undermined the strict rules the Germany of the 1990's had adopted to protect the eurozone.

Unfortunately, the loosening of Maastricht and SGP requirements made any type of fiscal controls nearly impossible, should a government wish to avoid them for economic or political reasons. As a result, the member states had wider variations in fiscal stance than beforehand. As shown by the rise in debt–GDP across countries in image 3, the French–German effort to avoid sanctions set a standard and practice that was to continue. Deficits and debt limits began to be missed repeatedly by several countries in the eurozone, each time justified on the wider grounds now available to governments to waive Maastricht limits.[63] The net result of the rising debt-GDP levels was to reduce the potential fiscal space, i.e., the ability countries had to borrow on international financial markets. Such a move was also potentially destabilizing to the currency union, as it increased the possibility countries could face a debt crisis if borrowing as a means of servicing debt obligations became difficult.

Overall, from an economic perspective, the implementation of the euro as a single currency was potentially flawed and prone to instability. While trade integration and diversification suggested that the benefits of a currency union could be significant and that country-specific shocks should not occur often, much of the eurozone lacked the ability to deal with such shocks. Therefore, if they were to occur, the economic and political costs could be large. Since the treaty structure of the eurozone intentionally limits transfers among union members, countercyclical aid to offset the costs of such events would not be available from the rest of the eurozone. In these circumstances, if countries found they could not finance a fiscal expansion to offset the shock, country-specific shocks would inflict greater costs on affected countries, potentially resulting in countries reconsidering currency membership.

---

63 After the currency union was created in Europe, some countries, specifically Greece, exceeded Maastricht debt and deficit limits by reporting misleading economic statistics, thereby causing a severe understatement of their actual debt and deficit levels. Still others began or continued to miss these targets claiming excesses were due to special economic circumstances such as changes in the business cycle. Often, however, excessive deficits and resulting increases in debt levels were due to domestic political pressures to maintain politically popular spending. Sanctions in all cases were neither levied nor seriously considered once the SGP rules were changed in March 2005. Political expediency forced the Maastricht limits to be ignored after the precedent set by Germany and France.

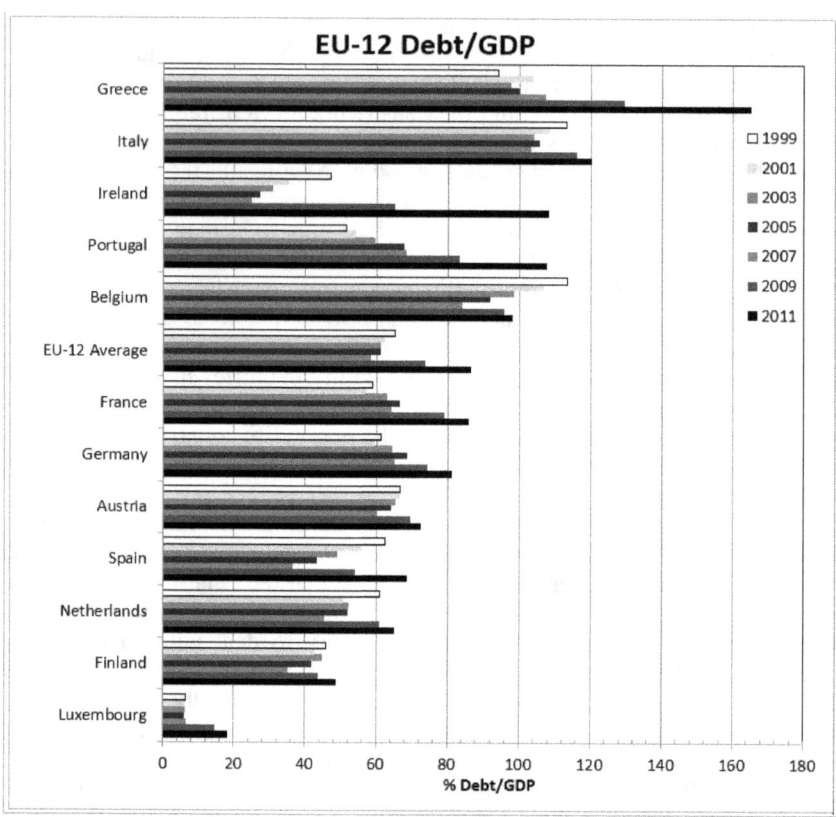

Figure 3-2: Debt-GDP levels for the original twelve eurozone countries. Since the inception of the euro, some countries have had relatively higher debt-GDP ratios, indicating that access to financial markets could potentially become problematic. Several also saw debt loads rise as a proportion of national income after the euro was implemented, despite the Maastricht criteria meant to limit such debt growth. By 2007 and the beginning of the eurozone crisis, a majority of countries had debt-GDP ratios greater than the 60 percent specified in the Maastricht Treaty (dashed line). Source: Eurostat.

This, in fact, is what happened during the European financial crisis. The 2008 US financial crisis and its repercussions around the world led to increased debt and deficit levels in European countries to stabilize the recessionary effects in their economies. The accounting irregularities uncovered after the Greek elections in 2009 led to that country losing access to international borrowing, except at exorbitant interest rates that reflected doubt that Greece could support its recently discovered debt obligations. Unable to borrow to meet its debt obligations, a default on its sovereign debt loomed, which would likely require an exit from the currency union. A bailout eventually arrived from other eurozone and EU states, but it turned out to be too small, and the costs it imposed on Greece too high, to resolve the crisis.

The uncertainty created subsequently affected Ireland and Portugal, both of which found access to international credit markets similarly restricted and only at excessive interest rates. They quickly found their domestic resources too small to overcome a potential default and the possibility of leaving the union. This process threatened to create, like tipping dominoes, a chain reaction across the continent that would eventually result in the failure of the common currency.

In general, the structure of the fiscal union backing Europe's common currency was not necessarily optimal and could be potentially destabilized by regional or country-specific shocks, both due to the original design and the evolution of the rules following the euro's adoption. Furthermore, differences in social attitudes across nations also likely undermined its stability. Lack of labour market flexibility would aggravate the costs of any shock as well. Since the crisis, redefining the fiscal union has focused on structural adjustment – that is, removing impediments to the labour market adjusting, as well as rule changes to ensure countries would, in the future, maintain greater fiscal space. In 2012, the SGP rules were strengthened through the implementation of "the fiscal compact" to allow greater scrutiny by the EU over states' debts and deficits, and stronger economic sanctions if these were deemed excessive. Rules were also adopted recognizing that some transfers might be necessary between states in special circumstances. In 2010, the creation of bailout actions and facilities to aid Greece, then Ireland and Portugal and any future countries in trouble, increased the ability to allow transfers in the currency area among countries. These changes have strengthened the fiscal union beyond that originally implemented in the eurozone.

Such changes, however, required consensus among EU and eurozone states and were generally implemented too late to avoid undermining faith in the survival of the euro. This uncertainty and the prolonged period required to make policy has also worsened the recessionary effects of the crisis across the union. In addition to a flawed, fiscal union, the central banking architecture of the monetary union also made the financial sectors of each country more prone to destabilizing shocks.

The EU's Monetary System: The Eurosystem

Currency union requires the creation of a single central bank responsible for monetary policy. In a two-stage process begun in 1994, the European Monetary Institute (EMI) took over the administration of the European Exchange Rate Mechanism (ERM) and oversaw the coordination and convergence of member state monetary policies in preparation for the adoption of the euro. In May 1998, the original eleven members of the euro met the convergence conditions defined by the Maastricht Treaty necessary to form the currency union, and, in June 1998, the second stage of the process began with the adoption of the ECB and the European System of Central Banks (ESCB), which consists of the central banks of all EU members and the ECB, replacing the EMI.[64]

The "Eurosystem" forms the central banking architecture of the eurozone and refers to a subset of the ESCB banks consisting of the ECB and the national central banks of the eurozone countries as shown in figure 3-3. The ECB is overseen by a president, vice-president, and four directors who make up the Executive Board, with appointments staggered and lasting eight years. Appointments to the ECB's Executive Board are recommended by the EU Council of Ministers and approved by heads of state or EU member governments. During the European financial crisis, two presidents have governed the ECB, Jean-Claude Trichet of France until 31 October 2011, and Mario Draghi of Italy from 1 November 2011 to the present. The Executive Board and the governors of each of the nineteen eurozone national central banks meet as the Governing Council, making all monetary policy decisions in the currency area by majority vote every two weeks. Monetary policy, once determined, is implemented by the ECB, which issues instructions to the national central banks of the eurozone, who carry it out.

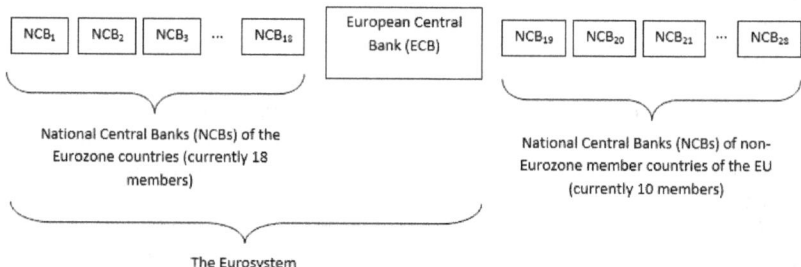

Figure 3-3: Structure of the ESCB.

A central bank has three inter-related functions: 1) ensuring the stability of the financial system; 2) acting as a lender of last resort to ensure that banks and states have access to credit when necessary; and 3) controlling monetary policy, the availability of money in the economic system for transactions and private lending. To maintain stability in a currency, the bank's conduct should be independent and free from outside political influence.

---

64 Luxembourg had to create a central bank, as it had previously been part of a currency union with Belgium.

For example, in the United States, the Federal Reserve or "Fed" serves as the politically independent entity performing all three of these tasks. It determines US monetary policy to achieve two – sometimes conflicting – mandates: to maintain employment by sustaining conditions for growth and to maintain price stability. By controlling monetary policy and, indirectly, the levels of interest and underlying credit conditions across all fifty states, the Fed attempts to achieve both of these goals, but it can often face tradeoffs. The Fed can loosen policy and create better conditions for growth in some areas while causing inflation in others. As part of monetary policy, it can also intervene in bond markets and take other actions to soothe conditions if they become turbulent. The Fed can also act as a lender of last resort by loaning directly to banks if they are cut off from credit. The Fed can also use this lender of last resort function to provide credit to the Federal government through bond market purchases. The ability of the Federal Reserve to use each of these actions proved vital during the financial crisis of 2008 and its aftermath. While controversial, many economists and other observers credit the swift and effective use of these instruments with helping to quell the US crisis by early 2009.

By comparison, the sole purpose of the Eurosystem is to ensure price stability through the ECB as defined in the treaty articles. As a result, the Eurosystem's greatest concern with respect to monetary policy has been inflation. In practice, price stability has been interpreted to mean an inflation rate across the eurozone of less than two percent. The ECB even put out a video with the catchphrase "how low can you go?" with the euro symbol dancing the limbo. Unlike the Federal Reserve, the ECB is mandated only to maintain price stability; therefore, its ability to use monetary policy to stimulate growth is very limited. If one country or region faces recession, it will likely not see monetary policy relief if such action threatens inflationary conditions in other countries. During the eurozone crisis, credit relief to all states in the form of expansionary monetary policy, causing lower interest rates, could have reduced the economic damage to the afflicted, mostly southern, countries by providing additional support to employment and output conditions. Monetary policy, however, did not loosen during this period, but, in fact, tightened in mid-2011 as concern escalated regarding potential inflationary conditions in stronger northern states.

Like the German banking system where strong bank independence is preferred and upon which much of the Eurosystem design was based, separation of regulatory authority from the actual central bank is assumed to enhance the central bank's political independence. Bank regulations are therefore not under ECB supervision, but instead remain the responsibility of the individual member states. National authorities are also responsible for the stability of banks within their jurisdictions, including deposit insurance, which, across the EU, must insure the first 100,000 euro in bank deposits from loss in the event of bank failure. If a national banking crisis arose, the national treasury, and by extension the taxpayers of that country only, are responsible for any costs incurred to support the banking system.

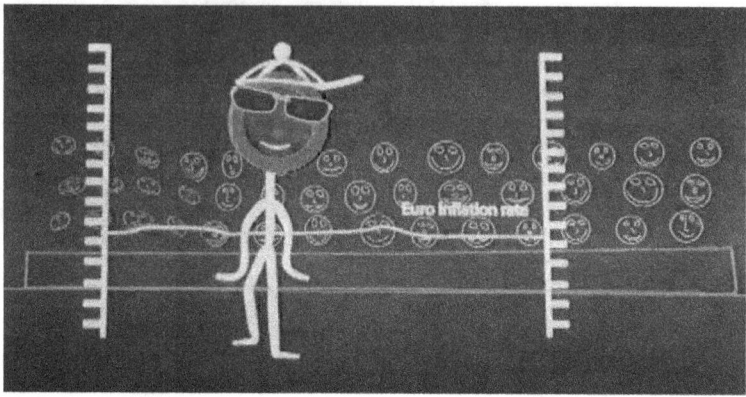

Image 3-1: From the European Commission video "Low inflation with a limbo-dancing euro!" (2010) https://www.youtube.com/watch?v=FxiPqsUE0hc (accessed 31 July 2015).

Within the EU framework, the ECB cannot act as a lender of last resort. Specifically, common interpretation of treaty rules prohibits the ECB from acting directly as a lender of last resort to sovereign states as such actions would violate the EU's "no-bailout" policy.[65] Furthermore, by being unable to purchase national debt directly, the ECB largely refrained from entering into global financial markets to maintain lower sovereign debt rates of member countries at the start of the eurozone crisis, and since has done so only under very specific conditions. The intent of the policy was to eliminate moral hazard and to create a debt brake for states; otherwise, states might not perceive that they faced the discipline of private markets to control their fiscal decisions. Within countries, national central banks may engage in emergency lending as a lender of last resort only to institutions within their jurisdiction. Nevertheless, such actions must be coordinated with the ECB and other central banks to ensure such actions do not undermine overall monetary policy. Private institutions, however, can use funds to purchase national debt in bond

---

65 Controversially, the ECB did begin more significant interventions in sovereign debt markets in August 2011, but only a year and a half after the bailout of Greece and almost two years after the start of the crisis. Notably, Germany's representative to the Governing Council argued vociferously that such support was illegal.

markets; thus, an indirect channel exists to finance government debt in the banking system.

Since national central banks police their own banking systems, in the event of a banking failure, each has different practices and procedures governing bank resolution or shut down. During the eurozone crisis, remarkably few banks have closed despite its seriousness. Instead, bank rescues have occurred, typically protecting bank creditors at taxpayers' expense. The lack of a common set of procedures means that regulators in some countries may be unwilling to impose losses on creditors and "resolve" illiquid institutions. Such reticence could occur if a regulator feared a credit market backlash at other institutions in their country, potentially worsening a banking crisis in their country, or for fear of political repercussions. This self-restraint potentially creates weaker banks in some countries versus others and an increased chance that a country-specific banking crisis could occur, destabilizing the monetary union, as eventually occurred, in Ireland, Portugal, Spain and Cyprus. The solution is a common set of regulatory rules and procedures across the eurozone or a so-called "banking union" to generate more certainty and avoid the propping up of illiquid banks, thereby stabilizing the system.

Banking Instability and Sovereign Risk in the Eurosystem

Monetary unions are most successful when they are least likely to experience country-specific shocks, whether on the goods producing side of the economy or in financial markets. After the Greek revelations regarding their public debt in 2009, however, markets quickly came to the realization that financial markets in the eurozone were, in fact, quite susceptible to financial crisis, in large part because of the currency union's structure. While eurozone members adopted a common currency, the evolution of rules governing fiscal discipline had not created a convergence in fiscal discipline. The Eurosystem and its distribution of responsibilities created a seriously destabilizing Achilles heel: the problem posed by national banking systems.

In a nutshell, national banking systems generated country-specific liabilities that created sovereign debt crises. In Greece, Ireland, Italy, Spain, and Cyprus, real-estate bubbles led to highly leveraged banks, much as it did in the United States in the mid-2000s. Furthermore, across Europe, exposure to now-questionable Greek debt, in addition to the price decline in world securities after the 2008 US financial crisis and ensuing global recession, created more bank weakness. Ireland, for example, was forced to take a national bailout in 2010 after the costs of a banking system rescue were so high that international finance markets effectively cut off credit to the nation. The sudden increase in sovereign debt caused by the combined effects of a recession and bank rescues increased public debt from 24.8 percent in 2007 to over 108 percent by 2011 as shown in figure 3-2. World financial markets reacted to the sudden risk in Ireland's apparent ability to service its debt sustainably, by more than doubling sovereign interest rates to levels approaching nine percent in 2010. The result was an unsustainable debt level, leaving Ireland with what appeared only two inevitable choices: it could leave the euro and default on its sovereign debt; or request outside aid – a "bailout." Ireland chose the latter, requesting a bailout in November 2010. Portugal, with similar experiences, also requested a bailout early the following year.

The relationship of bank failures to sovereign debt has sometimes been referred to as the "Doom Loop." Within the EU framework, the Eurosystem can act as a lender of last resort, but only to banks. If a financial institution finds credit is unavailable as might occur in a financial crisis, the national central bank can provide temporary emergency assistance in return for collateral, as a stopgap measure, until private credit for the bank is reestablished, or it is shut down. The collateral eligible to be used for such actions includes that country's sovereign bonds. In the event such a bailout is deemed necessary, the treasury of the country involved assumes the costs of the bailout, financing them through sovereign debt. The doom loop occurs as a consequence of the following chain of events:

1. Bank asset values fall as a consequence of a financial shock, for example, the effect the financial crisis of 2008 had on real-estate market loans.
2. Banks, then, experience illiquidity – the inability to borrow – as markets become concerned about their solvency and cut-off credit. A bank crisis, or "run", occurs as depositors rush to withdraw their funds, fearing that if the bank fails, they could suffer a loss of some, or all, of their balances.
3. National governments step in to stabilize their financial systems by providing liquidity (loans) to banks. If the bank system requires a large bailout, countries must increase their debt, often substantially.
4. Concerns regarding the country's sovereign debt sustainability and solvency in reaction to bailout costs drive sovereign bond interest rates up.
5. Banks, as large holders of domestic bonds, see their asset values fall further as bond prices are inversely related to interest rates, returning the loop to step 1. Self-fulfilling bank illiquidity and sovereign debt crises emerge as the negative feedback loop worsens until either national default or an external bailout of the country occurs.

This process allows a state in the eurozone potentially to be forced into crisis by the weakness of its banking system. In other jurisdictions, such as the United States, a federal banking union guarantees that the failure of a local bank cannot result in the insolvency of the individual state where the bank is located. For example, New York State cannot be bankrupted by its own banks because its lender of last resort is not the New York State government, but the Federal Reserve, which serves all fifty states and, crucially, has the ability to 'print' money.[66] Considering that the Federal Reserve can 'print' money, such bailouts do not require loans. As part of a larger banking union in 2008, failing banks in New York and across the United States were bailed out by the federal system, and the banking crisis did not trigger a series of state debt crises.[67] Member states in the European monetary union cannot print euros; that ability lies with the ECB. Instead, member states must borrow, and, therefore, the structure of the European banking system can lead to destabilizing shocks and a cut-off of credit to member countries if, in bailing out their banks, financial markets begin to worry about the country's ability to cover its debts. The result is a crisis in which the costs rapidly escalate into conditions where the country could default, leading to its departure from the currency union.

To avoid this problem, an improved banking union could be structured in two ways. First, the ECB, which has control of money printing and, therefore, borrows in the currency it creates, could be the lender of last resort. Second, should a bank get into trouble and threaten default, bank runs – the condition in which customers, fearing a bank failure, rush to withdraw their money and cause the bank to fail[68] – could be avoided if bank deposits were insured in such a way that customers never worried about losing their deposits. Under the pre-crisis rules of the Eurosystem, each country had to insure its banking system, up to €100,000 per bank depositor, and pay out any such insurance in a banking crisis if the bank involved failed. This requirement, however, could force the country to borrow to meet such obligations, with unintended consequences. Such borrowing, in turn, could cause concern in international financial markets and result in credit being cut off except at unaffordable interest rates. Under these circumstances, depositors, fearing the insurance on their deposits might not be honored, might then rush to withdraw funds, thereby undermining the stabilizing effect the insurance is supposed to have. A larger insurance pool across all the member states in the monetary union could avoid this situation, minimizing bank runs and breaking the doom loop. The prohibition on joint-liability, however, has also been interpreted as prohibiting such a system.

---

66 Technically in the United States the Federal Reserve prints money by creating reserve deposits for the banks it lends to. It does not actually print money and deliver it to banks.
67 The Troubled Asset Relief Program (TARP) provided a form of Federal bailout in the United States in October 2008. With authorization to use as much as $700 billion, funds were provided to recapitalize the banking system.
68 This type of event is depicted in the film *It's a Wonderful Life* (1946), https://www.youtube.com/watch?v=lbwjS9iJ2Sw.

In a unilateral action, the European Central Bank stemmed the crisis by promising to "do whatever it takes": offering unlimited credit to troubled economies. In effect, the central bank took over the powers of a lender of last resort, something that was controversial across the union, but was effective in stopping the spread of the crisis and preserving the euro, which appeared to be facing an imminent breakdown. Since the announcement in 2012, this policy, while unused, has increased the power of the bank and installed a missing element: a central bank with the power to lend as needed to ensure necessary liquidity.

Since 2014, the Eurosystem has been reformed to create a better banking union. The ECB has been put in charge of regulating most large banks across the union under a common set of rules. Furthermore, plans are now underway to increase the value of the insurance pool backing depositor insurance in each country, although a single multi-national pool has yet to be created. While new rules have been implemented, agreement across the eurozone and EU countries to create a single deposit insurance pool has been difficult to reach, primarily due to resistance from Germany on the grounds that it violates the joint-liability rule of the Maastricht Treaty.

Why Is There No Political Solution for Economic Integration?

The implementation of the euro, combined with a set of national sovereign governments, was at best only an intermediate step toward the greater political integration of Europe. Stabilizing the currency union would require further changes in EU governance and, more generally, a change in the balance regarding state versus supranational sovereignty, tipping the scales toward a more federal system. For example, bailout mechanisms put in place during the European financial crisis have required repudiation of the Maastricht ban on national transfers between countries. Efforts to strengthen the stability and growth pact weakened in the mid-2000s have also reduced the flexibility of individual nations to determine their own fiscal policies. Similarly, to strengthen the banking union, national discretion over bank closures has been reduced as the European Central Bank has taken over the responsibility of regulation and resolution for major banks in the monetary union.

These steps, however, have not gone far enough. Creating a deposit insurance pool, with the requisite repeal of the Maastricht ban on joint credit liability, will cost the member states more sovereignty. Germany, especially, has resisted such moves. Additionally, if more binding limits on fiscal policy are to be achieved, member states will have to cede national sovereignty to the interests of the greater union, but, at this time, countries such as France, Greece, Italy, and other countries oppose such changes. Given the political dissatisfactions that have developed within parts of the European electorate during the European financial crisis, especially in reaction to such crisis policymaking and to changes in the structure of the union's economic system, Europe's own governance system may need to evolve. The EU's major political institutions should consider allowing greater electoral participation to address the alienation large portions of the population apparently feel in being unable to affect directly union-wide decision-making. Currently, some policy decisions are driven, not by the will of the entire continent, but, instead, by a majority within the largest economies in the European Union, specifically Germany and France.

After the implementation of the euro, political and economic theorists eventually realized that the European process of integration had fallen into a trap. The euro's creation attempted to maintain sovereignty and the cost of doing so was currency area economic instability. The fundamental problem facing Europe's integration was that to design a system that could achieve deep economic integration, while simultaneously protecting national sovereignty, and maintaining direct political democracy over the supranational governance of Europe, invokes a sociopolitical impossibility, first described by Dani Rodrik as the "international trilemma of globalization."

Rodrik's Trilemma

Dani Rodrik first penned his trilemma to describe the political and economic challenge of globalization.[69] His insight recognized that deeper global integration cannot be achieved while preserving national sovereignty in policymaking and involving democratic politics that allow domestic preferences to determine overall governmental policy. Diagrammatically, the trilemma is shown in figure 3-4.

Rodrik noted that deeper international economic integration, allowing free flow of trade and capital, would require a tradeoff. Countries that wished to be open and to compete for international trade and capital could not interfere with economic transactions. For this reason, greater economic integration among countries would reduce the political space from which policies could be drawn, decreasing the role of democracy in the formation of economic policy.

In describing the trilemma, Rodrik noted that a compromise is necessary. Deep economic integration cannot occur simultaneously with sovereign state policy-making and democratic politics. At best, only two of these goals can be achieved. For example, in the early stages of European integration, the Bretton Woods compromise could not result in truly deep economic integration. The reason was that the fixed exchange rate system of Bretton Woods

---

69 Dani Rodrik, "How far will international economic integration go?" *The Journal of Economic Perspectives* (2000): 177-186.

was maintained by direct interference with economic markets. Countries often resorted to financial capital flow limits and strict bank regulation in order to maintain their exchange rates and domestic economic policies. Such activities allowed countries to preserve some independence in their economic policies while keeping domestic input as decision-makers were accountable to their own electorates.

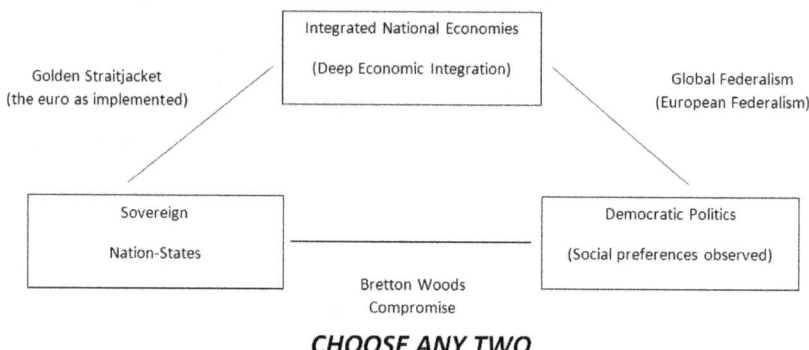

CHOOSE ANY TWO

Figure 3-4: Rodrik's international trilemma applied to Europe. Source: Rodrik, p. 181, with authors' notations regarding the euro.

Worldwide, Rodrik noted, states remained in control of economic policy consistent with the preferences of their electorates and routinely used capital controls and trade restrictions throughout the postwar period until the early 1970s when the Bretton Woods Agreement finally broke down. This breakdown led to a movement toward greater globalization and a suspension of those institutions that had allowed countries to maintain sovereign economic policies. The world economy began to move toward deeper economic integration. Specifically, individual countries' capital flow rules and the General Agreement on Tariffs and Trade (GATT) were both used to limit trade flows consistent with national democratic preferences, while maintaining exchange rates. The existence of these limits, however, ensured deeper economic integration across countries did not transpire.

The GATT was superseded by the World Trade Organization, which has worked to limit trade and capital controls, leading towards international trade liberalization and a narrowing of political options, which Rodrik defined as the Golden Straitjacket. This term reflects Rodrik's observation that maintaining states with fully independent policies determined by domestic political preferences cannot occur if deep economic integration allowing the free flow of capital and goods is desired. Deep economic integration requires that governments not interfere with the free markets. Therefore, open economies have little ability to impose control over economic outcomes regardless of electoral preferences. Should electoral preferences prefer protections or other interferences with deeper economic integration, for example, to preserve economic sectors or avoid outside trade competition, the result would require some withdrawal from deeper economic integration.

Worldwide, greater competition among states requires that policies become harmonized to international norms regardless of domestic preferences, if deep economic integration were to be achieved. Using monetary policy to affect the terms of trade can allow a country to protect sectors of the economy or worker wages, but participating in a common currency area removes this option. In such a case, labour protections or other independent policies cannot be maintained if they adversely affect competition and differ from those of trade partners: the more similar political preferences, the more stable the currency union.

In Europe, greater efforts toward closer integration in the 1970s moved the continent slowly toward the straitjacket outcome as those efforts narrowed the potential set of national economic policy choices countries had. The breakdown of the ERM and fixed exchange rate regimes exemplified the political tradeoff member states faced when they imposed conditions on their economies necessary to support integration. This conflict led to Britain's withdrawal from the ERM in the early 1990s. Faced with an electorate that demanded policies that were not consistent with those necessary to support its fixed exchange rate, the government withdrew from the ERM. The implementation of the euro, with its lack of an exit method, does not offer states an easy exit option. When policy preferences of a national electorate diverge from the policies necessary to maintain currency union membership, the social frustration can generate political instability.

With respect to the euro, adopting it necessitated giving up national monetary policy and transferring this power to the European Central Bank, while limiting fiscal policy to the convergence criteria defined in the Maastricht Treaty. Governments moved toward becoming technocratic entities in these areas, administering economic and social policies consistent with maintenance of the common currency regardless of public opinion. The costs of adhering to 'Golden Straitjacket' policies were high because governments have been unable to find the political will to reduce labour market and wage rigidities within their borders. In Rodrik's trilemma, the need to balance the requirements of deep integration across countries as implied by the euro, combined with the governance structure adopted for the EU, leaves no room for contrary social preferences expressed in democratic politics to be incorporated. Elected member state governments are locked into those policies necessary to maintain the currency irrespective of electoral preferences. As noted in the last chapter, reducing the instability in the current common currency arrangement in Europe will require additional reduction in sovereign discretion over more economic policy, thereby further alienating electorates from control over economic policy unless changes are made to its system of democratic governance.

If opinion polling and election outcomes are any indicator, the adoption of the euro created a technocratic role for national governments in implementing economic policy that may now have undermined people's trust in Europe-wide institutions and their willingness to move toward the political integration necessary to politically stabilize the currency union.[70] A populist backlash has resulted in unstable political environments across the eurozone, especially in Greece and Italy, where anti-European parties, whose platforms include leaving the euro, have often received the most votes in recent national elections. This political backlash has been in part fed and made worse by the perception among citizens that their votes have no impact on the policies their countries have taken, and is an "on the ground" example of the type of alienation Rodrik described that could occur in his straitjacket outcome. Reliance on technocratic solutions imposed by recent bailouts during the eurozone crisis (described in more detail in later chapters), and the imposition of technocratic governments in Italy and Spain, and EU-mandated austerity plans across the eurozone during the euro crisis have only worsened people's perceived alienation from the European political process. Such alienation threatens to compound the political instability currently present in the eurozone and, ironically, threatens to undermine support for greater economic and political integration across Europe at exactly the time when needed most.

Alternatively, Rodrik suggested deep global economic integration and democratic politics could occur simultaneously, evolving into a kind of "global federalism," but this would necessitate the eclipse of the state as the primary economic policy maker. In Europe, this outcome might be referred to as European federalism, a situation in which deeper economic and political integration would take place simultaneously. Such an economic and political union could be achieved by the creation of supranational European governance, electorally accountable directly to the people of Europe. States would

---

70 See Eurobarometer polling regarding support for European-wide institutions including the ECB. From spring of 2008 through spring 2012 support for the ECB had dropped by 47 percent across the eurozone, support for the EU dropped by 46 percent, and support dropped for the European Parliament, the European Commission and the euro by 34 percent, 32 percent, and 7 percent, respectively. See Flash Eurobarometer 335, July 2012, and Felix Roth, Lars Jonung, and Felicitas Nowak-Lehmann, *Public support for the single European currency, the Euro, 1990 to 2011. Does the financial crisis matter?* Working Paper 2012: 20 July 2012 http://www.researchgate. net/profile/Lars_Jonung2/publication/239807580_Public_Support_for_the_Single_European_Currency_the_Euro_1990_to_2011._Does_the_Financial_Crisis_Matter/links/0f31753366da33b8e8000000.pdf (accessed 31 July 2015). Despite these significant declines in support, consistent with economic downturns, support for the European project as a whole remained. For more discussion of opinion polls during the crisis, see chapter 4.

then only administer their territories within this framework with some differences in taxation and regulation possible among jurisdictions as long as they did not interfere with economic activity.

Conclusions: The Effects of Europe's Governmental, Economic, and Sociopolitical Flaws

The effects of the three architectural design flaws present in the eurozone: governmental, economic, and sociopolitical flaws, undercut the three characteristics successful monetary unions usually have, that is, the ability to manage and react to external and internal shocks; a common fiscal framework allowing collective transfers and, if necessary, collective debt; and a strong central bank able to act as a lender of last resort in the common currency. The inability of Europe to achieve a greater political union resulted in a currency union that has become technocratic in nature and seemingly removed from the people, especially since the crisis began.

The structure of the EU's currency union was the logical outcome of the decades-long process of European integration. As such, the design of the currency union was made to fit within the philosophical and organizational constraints of a European governance system that was, itself, a compromise between nationalist and federalist visions of 'Europe'. With regard to the theory of Optimal Currency Areas, the EU's common currency was not optimally designed. Efforts to preserve national sovereignty resulted in a less stable monetary union.

As noted at the beginning of the chapter, some of the currency union's designers hoped that changes over time would lead to deeper fiscal and banking integration as well as deeper political integration. Ironically, not only did these reforms not occur, but the relatively fragile fiscal union in the form of the Stability and Growth Pact was also weakened. Stronger fiscal and banking governance could have avoided or, at least mitigated, the eurozone crisis. A stronger banking union with greater powers could have avoided the bank failures that triggered the country-specific shocks that destabilized the monetary union. A stronger fiscal union might have avoided the cut-off of credit, the fear of default, and the possible exit from the currency union debtor countries faced.

To avoid the chaotic exits of countries from the common currency during the eurozone crisis, the rest of the eurozone, the EU, and the IMF, had to finance a series of bailouts, something never intended in the original design of the monetary union. The terms of these bailouts have been very protective of the financing countries' contributions as creditors, and required recipient countries to institute very painful, dramatic, and politically unpopular reforms. The public backlash to these reforms, in turn, has highlighted the final architectural flaw in the eurozone: the lack of a political union.

Together, the economic design of monetary union and the Eurosystem, combined with the lack of a federal system to coordinate broad, effective, and timely continent-wide economic policies have contributed to conditions in the union that helped precipitate and then worsen the crisis, as well as cripple the EU's policy response. By adopting the euro and giving up their sovereign currencies, eurozone members adopted a common currency without a sovereign. The European monetary union's ability to solve the current crisis was then hamstrung by its economic and monetary architecture and lack of a federal system to move toward solutions that were in the best interest of the currency area as a whole. Without the waiving of long-standing policy stances regarding joint fiscal actions and the role of the ECB, finding policy solutions that reduced pressures in markets proved very difficult, and policy reaction took too long, undermining market confidence in policy-makers' ability to address the situation.

Only when the ECB acted independently and unilaterally, offering its resources as a lender of last resort, was the crisis brought under control in 2012. As an independent entity, the ECB does not need the support of governmental institutions to act. Still, recognizing that such actions would create political dissension among the currency union member governments, such actions were not taken until almost three years after the crisis began. Once taken though, these actions then created time for the European Union and the eurozone to address internal political conflicts and structural changes necessary in the banking and fiscal union. They also demonstrated how necessary it is to have a centralized governance system capable of acting in the union's interest regardless of any individual country preferences. In the longer term, the European Union will not only have to address the shortcomings in its currency union architecture, but also the democratic deficit present in the system by adopting a wider federal governance system, one that creates a system of decision-making in the common interest of the entire union and without deference to the preferences of particular countries.

In order to save the euro, "more Europe" appears necessary. In a very important speech in July 2012, when the European Central Bank pledged to "do whatever it takes" to preserve the euro, Mario Draghi, the president of the ECB compared European monetary union to a bumblebee.[71] He remarked that, like the bee, the monetary union should not have been able to fly; yet, it did for almost a decade before the shortcomings in its design caught up with it. To continue flying, Europe will have to ensure it has a stronger fiscal and banking union than in the euro's original design. Such changes will require more supranational governance, not less. In other words, states will have to cede additional sovereignty to support the long-term stability of monetary

---

71 Mario Draghi, speech to the Global Investment Conference, London, 26 July 2012, http://www.ecb.int/press/key/date/2012/html/sp120726.en.html (accessed 31 July 2015).

union. In adopting a more supranational approach with common fiscal and banking policies, the eurozone will also have to become more democratic and less technocratic, allowing European governance to be more responsive to the will of the people.

As is often the case with unstable structures, unexpected tremors can lead to their imminent collapse without immediate remedial work to repair them. The financial crisis of 2008 provided such a tremor, and the damage resulting was the European financial crisis that began in Greece in 2009. Since then, the eurozone has struggled to repair the foundations of economic and political integration the post-war generations of Europe built, but this reconstruction will have to occur while the structure is occupied, with predictable political distress, anxiety, conflict and costs.

Chapter IV:
Of 'PIIGS' and 'GIPSIs': Pre-Crisis Structural Imbalances

To join the European Union, all member states must be democracies with functioning free market systems, adopt the *acquis communautaire*, that is, all the EU legislation to date, and be on the European continent. Aside from these commonalities, the countries all have different political systems, political cultures, and economic structures. As established in the previous chapter, for a currency union to function properly, the participants must be similar enough in competitiveness and productivity, and yet, the EU member states are not. Much of the explanation of the eurozone crisis and its popular narrative are based on these differences.

In the popular narrative of the eurozone crisis, i.e., the story surrounding the event, the rich, hard-working north had to bail out the lazy, corrupt south in order to save the euro. The Greeks bristle at the charge. How true is it? Of all the countries, Greece, with its relative poverty, poor governance and compliance, as well as corruption, has long been viewed as "Europe's Basket Case"[72]. This reputation may have blinded politicians and pundits to what was really going on in the eurozone crisis. Jean Pisani-Ferry, in his book *The Euro crisis and its aftermath*, argued that, had the financial crisis begun in Ireland, with its good reputation for compliance and governance, politicians might have seen it for what it was: economic imbalances and faulty banking regulations. Instead, the original narrative focused on falsified data, corruption, and poor governance.

This chapter examines structural imbalances that led to the crisis. In fact, both the north and south are to blame, if 'blame' is the correct word. Economic pressures led to a cycle of the 'north' lending to the 'south' so these countries could buy 'northern' products. Through a series of case studies, this chapter establishes how the political and economic differences among the member states set the stage for the eurozone crisis.

---

[72] Joanna Kakissis, "Europe's Basket Case" *Foreign Policy*, 24 June 2013. However, Greece was so labeled long before the Eurozone crisis. In a speech by Lucas Papademos of the Bank of Greece, "Greece and the Euro" to the Ninth Frankfurt European Banking Congress, 19 November 1999, he stated "the Greek economy had been described by a leading financial newspaper as the basket case of western Europe." http://www.bankofgreece.gr/Pages/en/Bank/News/Speeches/DispItem.aspx?Item_ID=242&List_ID=b2e9402e-db05-4166-9f09-e1b26a1c6f1b (accessed 3 August 2015).

The Ant and the Grasshopper?: A Narrative of the Eurozone Crisis

The common narrative of the eurozone crisis has often laid blame at the feet of the so-called PIIGS countries, Portugal, Italy, Ireland, Greece, and Spain. In the 1990's, PIGS referred to countries with a great deal of debt or to the southern countries of Schengen: Portugal, Italy, Greece and Spain, but not Ireland. However, before the 2004 expansion, Spain, Portugal, Ireland and Greece were known as "the poor four", that is the weakest economies of the EU. During the eurozone crisis, PIGS was changed to PIIGS to include both Ireland and Italy.[73]

The term PIIGS was deemed offensive with negative impacts on the narrative of the eurozone crisis. Samuel Brazys and Niamh Hardiman went so far as to argue that the use of the term PIIGS as a heuristic affected the behaviour of market actors and consequently Irish bond yields.[74] Carlos X. Alexandre took credit for coining a "new, and logical, acronym – GIPSI – that actually reflects the credit risk by order of magnitude (from high to low)."[75] Although GIPSI sounds very close to Gypsy, a slur against the Roma people, from which the verb "to gyp"[76] is derived, GIPSI has become the accepted acronym for these countries. Nevertheless, the use of either term has very negative connotations and characterizes the countries as either weak, spendthrift, or corrupt. We, the authors, chose to refer to Spain, Portugal, Italy, Greece, and Ireland as SPIGI as suggested by Erik Bleich.[77]

Although they have been among the weakest economies of the EU, the SPIGI countries have little in common. Italy, one of the founding members and one of the largest EU members, is usually ranked among the world's top ten economies. Spain, Portugal and Greece saw the EU as a way to stabilize their regimes after dictatorships, as well as gaining other advantages; Ireland joined, in part, to get out from under the shadow of its former colonial overlord, Great Britain.

---

73 See "Europe's PIGS country by country" *BBC News*, 11 February 2010 http://news.bbc.co.uk/2/hi/8510603.stm (accessed 3 August 2015).
74 Samuel Brazys, and Niamh Hardiman. "From 'Tiger' to 'PIIGS': Ireland and the use of heuristics in comparative political economy," *European Journal of Political Research* 54.1 (2015): 23-42.
75 Carlos X. Alexandre, "2011: Year of the European GIPSI?" http://seekingalpha.com/article/236784-2011-the-year-of-the-european-gipsi (accessed 3 August 2015).
76 Merriam-Webster defines gyp as a fraud or a swindle, http://www.merriam-webster.com/dictionary/gyp (accessed 15 August 2015).
77 Erik Bleich, "Say Goodbye to PIGS and GIPSIs" Opinion: *Al Jazeera*, 3 December 2012, http://www.aljazeera.com/indepth/opinion/2012/12/201212392653337846.html (accessed 3 August 2015).

In general, the narrative follows the storyline of the Greek slave Aesop's fable, "The Ant and the Grasshopper". As the morality tale goes, the grasshopper plays all summer while the ant toils to store food for winter. In the end, the grasshopper has nothing, while the ant is safe during the cold months. In the eurozone crisis storyline, the Germans are the hard-working ants whereas the Greeks are the Mediterranean grasshoppers who squandered their opportunity for saving. In the fable, the grasshopper only recognized the error of his ways when he was cold and hungry. By the same token, the question of "moral hazard" frequently makes its way into the eurozone crisis lexicon: if the hard working northerners give their hard-earned cash to the lazy, corrupt southerners, won't the cycle continue? Won't the lessons have been lost? Will the lazy south have any incentive to fix their corrupt governments and their business-unfriendly environments? Won't the ants in the north be subsidizing the grasshoppers' devil-may-care lifestyle?

In June 2013, Greek prime minister George Papandreou admitted his mistakes in handling the eurozone crisis, and said that the people, who had unduly suffered, were "in the main, not to blame for the crisis." He did blame Brussels and its "orthodoxy of austerity":

> Small Greece, he argued, had been made the scapegoat for a larger political and economic failure. As Mr. Papandreou mockingly put it, Europe chose to point the finger at "those profligate, idle, ouzo-swilling, Zorba-dancing Greeks." Instead of addressing the harder, underlying issues, the impulse was to say: "They are the problem! Punish them!"[78]

So convinced are some by this tale that the *New York Times* printed an op-ed piece by Todd Buchholz, which argued that the Germans were so hard working, they had lost part of their very soul and envied the Greeks theirs:

> No, Germany's real motivation to help Greece is not cash; it's culture. Germans struggle with a national envy. For over 200 years, they have been searching for a missing part of their soul: passion. They find it in the south and covet the loosey-goosey, sun-filled days of their freewheeling Mediterranean neighbors.[79]

Such analysis, based on stereotypes, add little to an understanding of the eurozone crisis. 'National envy' aside, the Greeks work the most hours and the Germans the least. After the introduction of the euro, the SPIGI countries

---

[78] Chrystia Freeland, "Economic worries and the global elite," *Reuters*, 13 June 2013 http://www.reuters.com/article/2013/06/13/column-freeland-idUSL2N0EP1B420130613 (accessed 15 August 2015).

[79] Todd Buchholz, "Germany's Mediterranean Envy," *The New York Times*, 25 September 2011 http://www.nytimes.com/2011/09/26/opinion/germanys-love-for-greece.html (accessed 15 August 2015).

far outpaced the north in terms of economic growth. France and Germany were the first to break the Stability and Growth Pact (SGP) in 2003. Structural imbalances in the eurozone explain these seemingly contradictory realities.

Nevertheless, the characterization of the SPIGI countries as 'grasshoppers' does explain some of the tension between the 'north' and the 'south'. The issue of moral hazard continually rears its ugly head: the profligate Mediterraneans must learn a lesson from the crisis lest the cycle be repeated. The Germans especially, informed by Lutheranism, as well as their history with inflation, the rise of Hitler, and rebirth via the *Wirtschaftwunder*, or economic miracle, believe they have a universal solution for economic growth: the application of Ordoliberalism or austerity measures.

The 'Ants': Why Does German Policy Often Seem at Odds with Much of Europe's?

The press, particularly the English-speaking press, has frequently labelled Germany as obstinate in its opposition to many of the proposals meant to stabilize the crisis. For example, Germany officially resisted the European Central Bank's intervention in Spanish and Italian bond markets in late summer of 2011.[80] The country also opposed the consideration of Euro-bond proposals to create joint liability across states in the currency union as a means to support the sovereign bond markets of troubled countries. German representatives to the ECB have also opposed allowing the bank to act as a lender of last resort.[81] Some German politicians and academics have vehemently opposed crisis bailout programs and the EU mechanisms created to back them, going so far as to take them to the Constitutional Court in in Karlsruhe in an effort to avoid German participation. Germany has also strenuously advocated tough austerity measures for bailed-out countries in spite of the fact that these policies threatened to worsen their recessionary conditions. These austerity demands have resulted in a political backlash that has caused some to question sovereign democracy in the EU.

---

80 The European Central Bank's intervention in Spanish and Italian bond markets in August 2011 was strongly resisted by German delegates to the ECB, and led to Jürgen Stark resigning in protest from its Executive Board as a signal of German opposition to the policy. This action and open antagonism of ECB efforts occurred in spite of strong support elsewhere in Europe.

81 Although in 2012, the German government appeared tacitly to support Mario Draghi's declaration to do "whatever it takes" to save the euro, a policy that was eventually unveiled as the ECB's Outright Monetary Transactions (OMT) Program in August 2012 and one credited with stabilizing sovereign bond markets, the euro exchange rate, and finally ending the European Financial crisis, many German politicians attacked the program and also challenged its legality in court.

Why has Germany been so often at odds with significant portions of the eurozone over so many crisis policies? In ECB matters, Germany has regularly appeared to stand alone as the most vehement opponent to expansionary monetary policy. In other cases, particularly in meetings of the European Council, Germany has frequently been cast as the leader of a group of northern European countries including Finland, The Netherlands, Austria, Slovakia, and the Baltic states, which have advocated stricter policies for troubled countries. German politicians have habitually been the most vocal in Europe regarding the need for other member states to impose greater austerity on their national budgets and the necessity to introduce greater wage and labour reforms across EU economies. Elsewhere in Europe, the German viewpoint has been far less popular. While Germany was able to use its economic might to ensure its concerns were considered in EU policymaking throughout the first years of the crisis, as recessionary conditions have worsened across the continent, German policy stances have come under greater scrutiny. Some have even called the backlash to German economic orthodoxy a "revolt".[82] Reasons for this divide range from cultural differences to national interests to economic ideology.

Cultural Differences

Cultural dissimilarities between Germany (and northern European countries) and those of western and southern Europe stem from historical religious and cultural differences and recent economic experience in the twentieth century. A common theme in the press regarding distinctions between the north and the south has been the influence of religious history among these countries. Popular German opposition to allowing greater aid and latitude to crisis countries regarding fiscal austerity has often been attributed to the influence of Lutheranism, focusing on the acceptability of suffering and the importance of frugality as moral lessons during the eurozone crisis. Angela Merkel, herself the daughter of a Lutheran pastor, has used the example of the thrifty Swabian housewife[83] as an illustration of German thinking regarding good fiscal management. German narratives regarding their own willingness to accept self-sacrifice and discipline, the importance of saving, eschewing the use of credit, and the expectation of self-reliance as a means of dealing with

---

82 See, for example, *New York Times*, "Germany's insistence on Austerity meets with Revolt in the Eurozone," 8 October 2014, p. B4. http://www.nytimes.com/2014/10/08/business/rift-opens-among-eurozone-leaders-over-germanys-insistence-on-austerity.html?emc=eta1 (accessed 3 August 2015).
83 See, for example, "Hail, the Swabian housewife" *The Economist*, 1 February 2014, http://www.economist.com/news/europe/21595503-views-economics-euro-and-much-else-draw-cultural-archetype-hail-swabian, (accessed 3 August 2015).

problems all play into popular explanations of German opposition to programs aimed at easing crisis conditions in debt markets and stimulating economic growth in troubled countries. This so-called Protestant work ethic has been contrasted to supposed Roman Catholic attitudes as a possible explanation of why the crisis has afflicted mainly Catholic countries.[84]

The hyperinflation Germany experienced during the Weimar Republic in the 1920's that led to the rise of the Third Reich has often been held up as a reason why Germans oppose expansionary monetary policy. In addition, inflation has a negative effect on savings. As a result, Germans regard inflation as a much more serious problem than a general lack of economic growth.[85] While cultural differences may play a role in national populations' viewpoints regarding the crisis, some have argued that such reasoning is too simplistic and relies on unreasonable and negative national stereotypes. Instead, a far simpler argument can be made: self-interest.

National Self-Interest

An obvious reason for German opposition to softer bailout policies could be attributed to national self-interest. As the primary creditor country in the eurozone, Germany has the most to fear from a troubled country's default as it would absorb the greatest proportion of losses should such an event occur. Moreover, permitting the ECB to support sovereign debt purchases and act as a lender of last resort could reduce the urgency and necessity of reform. Easier monetary policy and actions that decrease the pressure on a country both to reduce its debt and reform its economy could be seen as creating moral hazard by diminishing the cost of imprudent behaviour that may have led to the crisis in the first place. In addition, such a policy could make a country more likely to renege on its financial commitments. Any creditor could be forgiven for preferring policies that make a country more likely to focus on debt reduction and less likely to default. Germany would also see such interests as in the best interest of the eurozone too, as reduced debt and greater competitiveness would also make the currency union more stable in the long run.

Furthermore, expansion of the money supply, like that necessary to support expanded bond purchases by the bank, is usually presumed to be inflationary. Above normal inflation would also undermine the value of the loans

---

84   CNN, "Catholic vs. Protestant: European Debt Crisis," 9 December 2011, http://ireport.cnn.com/docs/DOC-715376 (accessed 3 August 2015).
85   See for example Nicholas Kulish, "German Fears about Inflation Stall Bold Steps in Debt Crisis," *New York Times* 2 December 2011, http://www.nytimes.com/2011/12/02/world/europe/haunted-by-20s-hyperinflation-germans-balk-at-euro-aid.html?pagewanted=all (accessed 3 August 2015).

indebted countries owe to Germany and the rest of the union. Since interest rates are fixed on bailout debt, any increase in inflation rates reduces the expected return on the loans made to help bailed out countries, while decreasing their real cost to borrowing countries. The latter effect could again be seen as causing moral hazard by reducing the cost of the financial crisis on those countries thought to have been its cause from a German perspective.

Economic Ideology

Academics also point to economic ideology for Germany's stance during the crisis. In an effort to avoid the economic errors that led to World War II, since 1946, ordoliberalism, or *Ordnungspolitik*, developed in the 1930s at the Freiberg School, has heavily influenced post-war German economic policy This line of thought is an offshoot of classical liberalism that focuses on free markets and minimal governmental influence or interference in the economy. *Ordnungspolitik* defines several principles to be adhered to in a well-functioning free market economy. Specifically, it argues that: (i) politics should avoid any activity that distorts prices in the economy and, thereby, distorts free market outcomes; (ii) monetary policy should focus only on price stability; (iii) the government should ensure markets are as competitive as possible by controlling restraints of trade or monopolies; (iv) property rights be respected and that individuals be free to conduct any contracts as long as they do not undermine competition; (v) individual liability be maintained (agents are held accountable for economic decisions) in markets as an incentive to ensure moral hazard does not lead to irresponsible behavior; and (vi) policy should be steady to avoid economic uncertainty.[86]

The general idea of these principles and the ideas of ordoliberalism is that the government should support the economy and only regulate anti-competitive practices. The role of government is not to affect market outcomes, but to support the market and to ensure competitiveness. To the degree that macroeconomic management is necessary, it should be accomplished through redistribution policies and not activist fiscal policies. *Ordnungspolitik* opposes the Keynesian policies that shaped much of the rest of the western world after World War II in which fiscal and monetary policy is used to manage macroeconomic outcomes. The government should also minimize its impact on the economy through the maintenance of a balanced budget, with expenditures limited to those necessary to provide public goods and services such as education, security, and defence.

---

86 See Tim Stuchtey, "Miracles are Possible – or a Classic German Approach to the Current Crisis," American Institute for Contemporary German Studies (AICGS) Transatlantic Perspectives, June 2009.

As these principles have dominated German economic policy making since World War II, all German economists will, at some time, have been exposed to these ideas. Given that the German government, the Bundesbank and German institutions heavily recruit from their own universities, and the fact that there are relatively few scholars espousing alternative viewpoints such as Keynesianism in German academia, ordoliberalism has become the prevailing economic orthodoxy in Germany.[87] German orthodox economics simply does not recognize Keynesian economics as a viable alternative. Correspondingly, it focuses on long-term solutions and undervalues policies intended to stimulate affected economies in the short term. The Keynesian perspective, with its concern for the demand side of the economy, is far more prevalent in the rest of Europe. As a result, other countries' economists instead call for economic stimulus to reduce unemployment in the short term and to ease credit market conditions to encourage greater economic activity.[88]

The 'Grasshoppers': Why Have They Fared So Much Worse in the Eurozone?

In many ways, the SPIGI countries look like stronger economies than the north's. The south works more than the north, many of the SPIGI countries have extremely favourable business environments as well as effective governments, and, while corruption is certainly a problem in countries such as Italy and Greece, the problem is more nuanced than one might think. Moreover, the SPIGI countries outpaced the north in growth from 1999 until the housing crisis hit in 2006 and 2007. Ireland's growth was extremely high with very low debt to GDP ratios; as an outlier, it artificially raises the SPIGI growth rates. However, taking an average of Greece, Spain, Italy, and Portugal's growth rate from the same period, the south's growth still outpaced the north's, Germany, Finland, Austria, and The Netherlands (see figure 4-1).

On the other hand, a closer look at the statistics reveals that structural imbalances in the eurozone set the stage for the crisis. In the end, the growth the SPIGI countries exhibited was not real growth, but the product of housing bubbles inflated by the easier credit available to them as members of the eurozone. Moreover, the corruption and less effective governments in Greece, Italy and Spain weakened their response to the crisis.

---

87   See Sebastian Dullien and Ulrike Guerot, "The Long Shadow of Ordoliberalism: Germany's Approach to the Euro-Crisis," European Council on Foreign Relations Policy Brief (ECFR) 49, February 2012 http://www.ecfr.eu/page/-/ECFR49_GERMANY_BRIEF.pdf (accessed 3 August 2015).
88   Ibid.

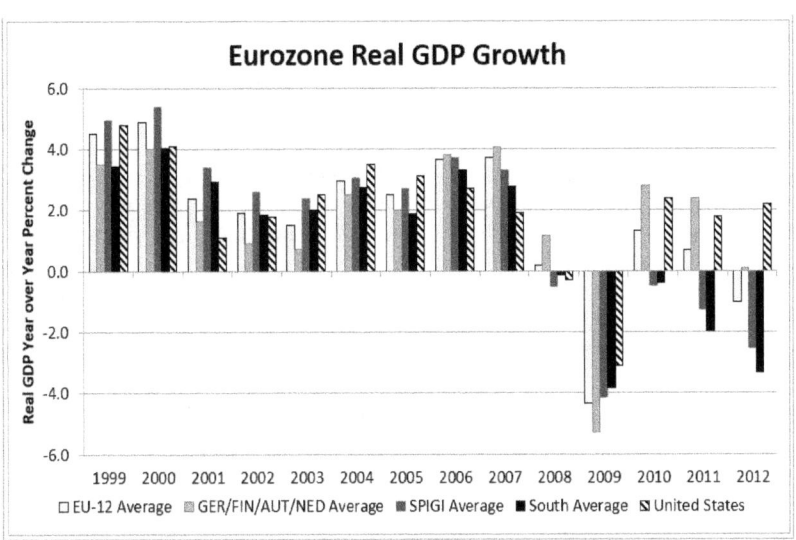

Figure 4-1: Real GDP growth rates in the eurozone were relatively high over the first nine years of the euro's introduction (1999-2007) with the original twelve eurozone countries (EU-12) averaging better growth than the United States. Performance, however, varied by region with northern economies (Germany/Finland/Austria/Netherlands) lagging behind the rest of the eurozone until 2006 when Germany began to overcome the malaise caused by reunification. In 2008, SPIGI (Spain, Portugal, Ireland, Greece and Italy) and southern (Greece, Italy, Spain and Portugal) countries experienced contraction similar to the United States, while northern countries still experienced some growth, causing the EU-12 overall to average a positive although near-zero growth rate. In 2009, most European countries experienced recessions, but, following that year, northern countries, the EU-12 as a whole, and the United States returned to positive growth rates. In contrast, SPIGI) and southern countries continued to experience contraction five years after the US financial crisis began in 2008. Source data: Eurostat.

The following section documents the differences in key economic areas: hours worked; corruption; effectiveness of governments; EU compliance; business-friendly environments; the degree to which the member state has benefited from integration; and attitudes towards credit. The statistics do not support the black-and-white grasshopper/ant stereotypes. In only three areas are there significant versus-the-rest differences. These are hours worked, the degree to which EU integration has benefited them, and attitudes toward credit. These three factors hold the answer in a nutshell: people in poorer countries work longer hours, making them more vulnerable to austerity measures, and Mediterranean and Anglo-Saxon cultures take a more permissive approach towards credit, making them more likely to have taken advantage of the credit offered by membership in the eurozone.

Hours Worked: Laziness or Poor Productivity?

One of the most pervasive stereotypes of the SPIGI countries is that their inhabitants are lazy. Whether it is the Spanish with their siestas or the Guinness-swilling Irish, these people have supposedly reaped what they have sown. According to OECD statistics, in general, the SPIGI countries work more hours per year than the north. Greeks work the most; Germans work the least. Since the poorer countries work longer hours than their richer counterparts, the cause of the eurozone crisis cannot be attributed to laziness. In any case, 'laziness' is a red herring: Why do the poorer countries' inhabitants work more hours, and yet are poorer? The answer lies in productivity; in other words, the north's workers can produce more in fewer hours. Differences in productivity were a significant cause of the structural imbalances that caused the crisis, and will be addressed later in this chapter.

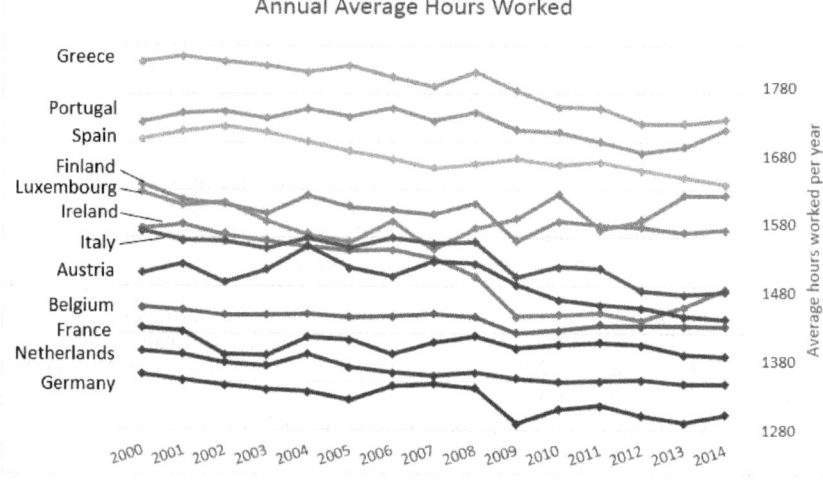

Figure 4-2: Hours worked per capita per year among the twelve eurozone countries.[89]

The Role of Corruption and Effective Governance

Another likely reason why the people in poorer countries work harder is because their governments are more likely to be corrupt or ineffective. In general, corruption varies a great deal in Europe from Denmark, which Transparency International ranks as the least corrupt government on earth, to

---

89   OECD.stat http://stats.oecd.org/index.aspx?DataSetCode=ANHRS (accessed 3 August 2015).

Greece, which ranks as the most corrupt in Europe, although with a rating of 80 out of 177 countries, it still ranks in the top half of the world. Ireland is very clean, while Portugal and Cyprus are in the same league as Austria. Italy, Spain and Greece are the most corrupt, which partially explains the ineffectiveness of these governments as well as their poor EU compliance records. In other words, corruption is a contributing factor, although not the deciding one.

All the governments in the European Union and the eurozone are "effective". The World Bank charts the people's perception of "the quality of public and civil services and their degree of independence from political pressures, the quality of policy formulation and implementation, and the credibility of the government's commitment to such policies."[90] All EU countries fall into the top two categories. The Irish, Cypriots and Portuguese rank their governments highly. Spain, Italy and Greece have less support, and yet still fall in the good governance grouping. Interestingly, these are the same three countries that are marked the most corrupt of the original euro-twelve on the previous chart. In addition, since the World Bank uses people's perceptions of the governments for their index, it is possible that the people will score more highly governments that do not impose reforms or that continue with popular profligate spending. That said, effective governance is most likely only a contributing factor and not a deciding one in the eurozone crisis.

EU Compliance: Did 'Good' Europeans Fare Better than 'Bad' Europeans?

Are the SPIGI countries less likely to implement EU directives, i.e., do what the EU says? Is that why the eurozone crisis affected them more than others? Tanja Börzel established in her 2000 research into environmental compliance that there was "no southern problem".[91] Her more recent research on the subject confirms her previous assessment. A 2012 chart of all infringement proceedings against the first fifteen member states for non-compliance ranks Italy, France, Greece, Belgium and Germany as the worst, Portugal, Ireland, Luxembourg, Spain and the UK as being in the middle, and The Netherlands, Austria, Denmark, Sweden and Finland as being the best. Granted, these numbers are skewed by the amount of time a country has been a member: the longer in the EU, the more likely not to have complied. Nevertheless, the numbers demonstrate that the issue is not a question of wealth or support for

---

90 See http://www.eea.europa.eu/data-and-maps/figures/world-bank-government-effectiveness-index-2010 (accessed 3 August 2015).
91 Tanja A. Börzel, "Why there is no 'Southern Problem': On Environmental Leaders and Laggards in the European Union," *Journal of European Public Policy* 7:1 (March 2000): 141-62.

the EU; France, Belgium and Germany are among the worst and Portugal, Ireland, and Spain are in the middle. Italy and Greece have some of the worst compliance records, most likely due to less effective governments, and yet they sandwich France, which was ranked as both one of the least corrupt and most effective governments. In addition, both France and Germany were among the first to violate the original Growth and Stability Pact in the early 2000's and to advocate for laxer regulations, which arguably contributed to the eurozone crisis a few years later.

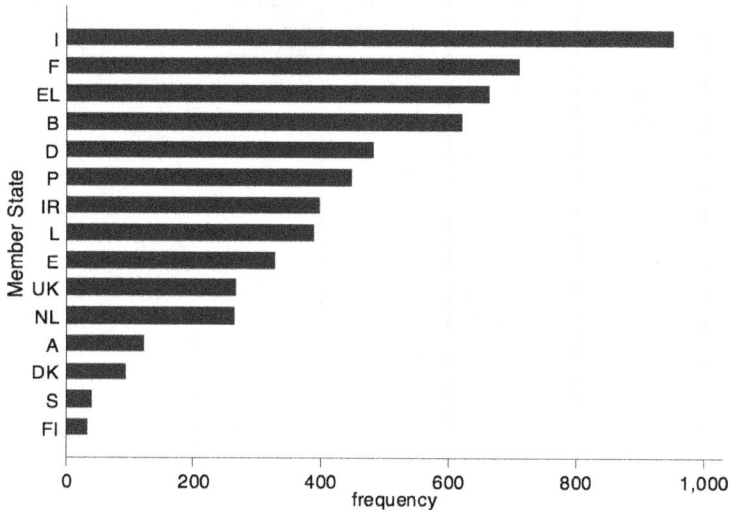

Figure 4-3: Sum of infringement proceedings by member state as of 2012.[92]

Business Friendliness: Did Red Tape Hurt or Help?

Are the SPIGI countries less open to business with too much red tape? Did overregulation weaken SPIGI economies and exacerbate their exposure to the eurozone crisis? The answer is no; there is no pattern in this area that would explain why the SPIGI countries felt the brunt of the crisis. *Forbes* magazine ranks countries on their favourable business environment based on eleven different factors including: property rights; innovation; taxes; technology;

---

92 Tanja A. Börzel and Moritz Knoll, "Quantifying Non- Compliance in the EU," *Freie Universität Berlin* http://www.polsoz.fu-berlin.de/polwiss/forschung/international/europa/arbeitspapiere/2012-15_BoerzelKnoll_Non-Compliance.pdf?1367709772. (accessed 3 August 2015).

corruption; freedom (personal, trade and monetary); red tape; investor protection; and stock market performance. Two of the SPIGI countries make the top twenty-five: Ireland ranks number one; Portugal is twenty, just below France. Among other countries in this list of 145: Finland is number six; Germany is twenty-four; Cyprus is twenty-seven; Spain is thirty-three; Italy is thirty-seven just above South Korea, and Greece is forty-six. Again, there is no stark difference between the SPIGI countries and the north.[93] Nevertheless, Greece is one of the worst countries in the EU for red tape. It is notorious for its rigid labour markets where it is almost impossible to fire workers. On the other hand, business friendliness may really be a measure of a lack of regulation, which might make some countries, such as Ireland, fertile soil for housing bubbles and bank failures. Countries, such as Germany, can afford to be less business friendly and to regulate to a higher degree because corporations will still flock to the thriving German economy.

A Culture of Credit

Where the SPIGI countries differ significantly from other member states is in their view of credit. *The Economist* deemed credit human kind's greatest invention, but also argued it was a two-edged sword:

> At its core, finance does just two simple things. It can act as an economic time machine, helping savers transport today's surplus income into the future, or giving borrowers access to future earnings now. It can also act as a safety net, insuring against floods, fires or illness. By providing these two kinds of service, a well-tuned financial system smooths away life's sharpest ups and downs, making an uncertain world more predictable. In addition, as investors seek out people and companies with the best ideas, finance acts as an engine of growth.
>
> Yet finance can also terrorise. When bubbles burst and markets crash, plans paved years into the future can be destroyed.[94]

---

93 Kurt Badenhausen, "Map: The Best and Worst Countries for Business," *Forbes Magazine* http://www.forbes.com/sites/kurtbadenhausn/2013/12/04/map-the-best-and-worst-countries-for-business/ (accessed 3 August 2015).

94 *The Economist*, "The Slumps that Shaped Modern Finance" Digital Highlights, 10 April 2014, http://www.economist.com/news/essays/21600451-finance-not-merely-prone-crises-it-shaped-them-five-historical-crises-show-how-aspects-today-s-fina (accessed 3 August 2015).

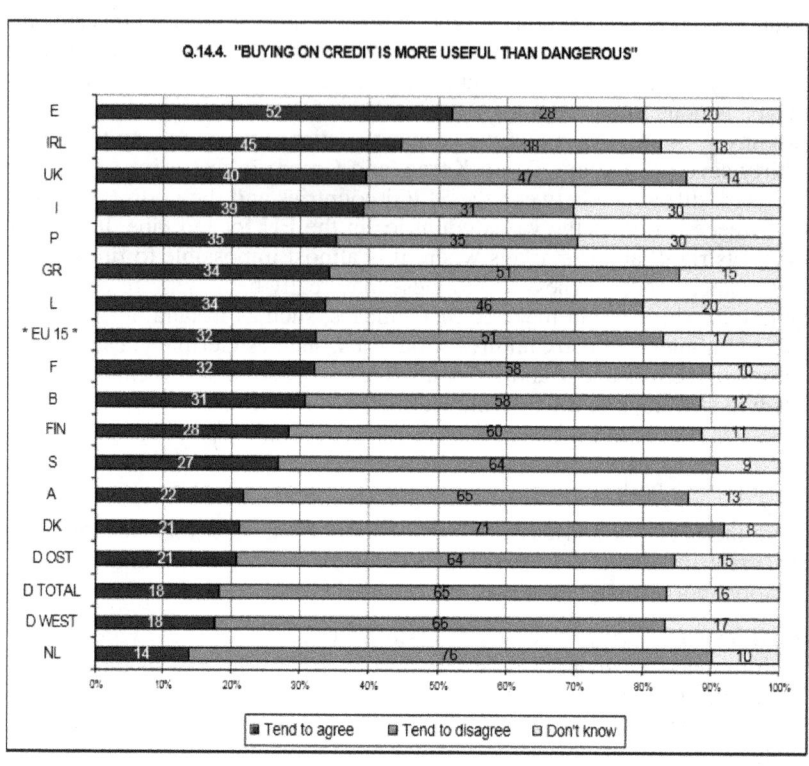

http://ec.europa.eu/public_opinion/archives/ebs/ebs_160_en.pdf page 13

Figure 4-4: Mediterranean countries and Anglo-Saxon countries have a much more favourable view of credit than other EU members.

This Eurobarometer poll from 2001 shows that the English-speaking and Southern countries see buying on credit as useful whereas Nordic and Germanic countries have a strong cultural aversion to it. Adyen, an Internet payments company, estimates that fewer than thirty percent of Germans have credit cards. The Netherlands also has very low credit card penetration.[95] This cultural split explains part of the mistrust and miscommunication that has characterized the political side of the crisis.

A second interesting split, albeit not as stark as the credit divide, is in how much a member state has benefited economically from European inte-

---

95 "Overview Supported Payment Methods," Adyen http://www.adyen.com/wp-content/uploads/2011/03/overview-payment-methods.pdf (accessed 3 August 2015).

gration. In 2014, the Bertelsmann Stiftung did an assessment of how the single European market affected each member state over the twenty-year period from 1992-2012. In calculating the cumulative gains of GDP per capital, the following table shows that, in general, the creditor countries are in the top half of those who gained the most, and the SPIGI countries are in the bottom half. Interestingly, Greece is the only loser in the group. That said, all the countries did benefit absolutely from integration, and even Greece, when one compares the GDP per capita using 2014 rather than 2012 figures (see table 4-1).[96]

This chart reflects the structural imbalances that allowed some countries to benefit more from integration than others, in large part because of the euro. Economic benefits (costs) of integration include the internal market in Europe and the external impacts for trade outside of Europe. Since the D-Mark would have traded on the open market at a value higher than the euro, Germany received an economic boost from integration and monetary union since its goods were cheaper when traded in euros. In other words, if a Canadian were to buy a Braun coffee maker, it would be cheaper for him or her to buy when priced in euros than it would have been in D-Marks because the euro reflected a basket or average of European currencies and not just the most expensive one – the D-Mark. For Greece, the effects were the opposite; the euro is higher than the Greek drachma would have been if traded on the open market. Therefore from Greece's perspective, European integration inflicted a sort of double-whammy: not only was it less competitive in the internal market, on the external market, its goods were more expensive than they would have been if the drachma had floated.[97]

---

96 Thieß Petersen, Michael Böhmer, and Johannes Weisser, "20 years of the European single market: growth effects of EU Integration," Policy Brief 2014/02 Bertelsmann Stiftung, 1.
97 The value of integration was not just limited to the impacts caused by the adoption of a common currency. As can be seen, countries that were members of the EU and its common market system, but that did not adopt the euro, were also affected (note Sweden, the United Kingdom and Denmark). The degree to which they were affected depended on many factors, including their degree of labour market openness, and cultural, geographic and economic factors. Trade imbalances within the set of countries adopting the common currency are evident, however, and these particularly impacted SPIGI countries, reducing the benefits to Italy, Spain, Portugal and most of all Greece where integration appears to have reduced economic outcomes, particularly after the European financial crisis began. The impact to Ireland was worsened by having adopted the common currency after the financial crisis occurred, but prior to this time this country saw significant benefits from integration that were in part reversed after events after 2008.

Table 4-1: Comparison of gross domestic product per capital in 2012 with and without increased European integration. In general, the SPIGI countries benefited less from integration than the north. Source: Prognos AG/Bertelsmann Stiftung.

	Difference in Percent	Difference in euros
Germany	2.3%	680
Denmark	2%	720
Belgium	1.6%	470
Austria	1.4%	450
Finland	1.2%	360
United Kingdom	1%	310
Ireland	0.9%	330
Italy	0.9%	200
France	0.8%	230
Spain	0.7%	150
Netherlands	0.6%	190
Portugal	0.4%	60
Sweden	0.4%	140
Greece	-1.3%	-190

While all the factors discussed contributed to the crisis, the main cause was structural imbalances among eurozone countries. In fact, the eurozone crisis began as an intricate minuet between the north and the south; countries with higher worker productivity will produce goods at lower cost that require markets in order to be sold. These productivity imbalances can create economic pressures for trade deficits, and, when combined with different attitudes towards credit, allowed the SPIGI countries to buy BMW cars based on the rapidly increasing values of their homes. One analogy describes the relationship as one between a bartender and a regular customer with a tab. The bartender keeps selling beer to the customer who keeps putting the cost on his tab. The bartender should stop selling beer on credit, and the customer should stop drinking. However, the bartender makes money off of each transaction, and the customer enjoys spending the money. In the end, if the customer cannot afford to pay his bill, the bartender will lose out, so he keeps extending the credit. The relationship is symbiotic.

Flight of the Bumblebee: Pre-crisis Structural Imbalances and Their Influence in the Eurozone

According to currency union theory, the eurozone was not supposed to be able to fly; nonetheless, like a bumblebee, it did. From 2001 to 2007, the original twelve countries of the eurozone experienced average annual real GDP growth rates of over 2.7 percent with the average EU rate outpacing that of the US, and the southern countries (Greece, Italy, Spain, and Portugal) outpacing the northern economies (Germany, Finland, Austria, and The Netherlands). The house looked sound, but it lacked the structure needed to withstand an ill wind. The world financial crisis of 2008 and 2009 that burst the US housing bubble also burst similar bubbles throughout much of Europe. What had appeared to be a successful integration of eurozone economies had actually masked structural imbalances that now challenged the eurozone's recovery.

The structural imbalances meant that the financial crisis had different impacts in different regions. Northern countries, particularly Germany, Austria, Finland and The Netherlands, which had lagged behind southern and eurozone economies as a whole in the euro's first five years, now accounted for the majority of eurozone growth post 2009. In contrast, the southern periphery, Greece, Portugal, Spain and Italy, plus Ireland, all fell into what might be called a depression. As of 2014, levels of unemployment in SPIGI countries ranged from nearly twelve percent to over twenty-seven percent,[98] with unemployment rates for youth under twenty-five years of age ranging from twenty-three percent to over fifty-three percent.[99] The following section details the economic imbalances in labour productivity and trade, and how the single currency aggravated them leading to housing bubbles, high interest rates, credit crunches, unemployment and severe recessions.

Structural Imbalances: Trade Imbalances, Productivity Levels and their Influence on the Credit Crisis

Like a ship in difficulty far from shore, any repairs to the eurozone will have to be made while the ship sails on. The primary challenge to overhauling the eurozone is two-fold. First, the original twelve euro countries always varied immensely with regard to competitiveness. Second, the most affected countries do not have the internal resources necessary to address current economic

---

[98] "Unemployment Rate in Member States of the European Union in May 2014," Statista: The Statistics Portal, http://www.statista.com/statistics/268830/unemployment-rate-in-eu-countries/ (accessed 3 August 2015).

[99] "Unemployment Rate by Sex and Age Groups," Eurostat, http://ec.europa.eu/eurostat/en/web/products-datasets/-/UNE_RT_M (accessed 3 August 2015).

conditions; therefore, they need the aid of other eurozone countries if they are to remain in the currency union.

The creation of the eurozone exacerbated competitiveness differences by increasing access to credit markets. In a tongue-in-cheek sort of way, the south was able to use the north's low interest credit card. Southern states saw interest rates fall to levels nearly equal to those enjoyed by the traditionally low-interest economies such as Germany (see figure 4-7). Taking advantage of these newly opened capital markets, both the private and public sector increased borrowing. This activity fuelled growth in government and private consumption, thereby inflating and creating bubbles in real estate and property prices that, while increasing GDP growth, masked the weaker economies underlying them and the worsening structural imbalances.

With rapidly growing economies, the eurozone was a success. Southern countries faced no pressure to make the politically difficult decisions required to restrict public spending or restructure their economies in order to maintain or improve their internal competitiveness. As a consequence, productivity relative to northern European trade partners continued to fall, and costs rose in these nations relative to those of their northern neighbours. Northern economies faced the opposite conditions. While accession to the euro had had little impact on their credit conditions, with trade barriers and exchange costs eliminated, and historically higher wages, internal competitiveness within the eurozone demanded these countries focus on productivity gains. Thus, the north was forced to concentrate on competitiveness with the adoption of the euro, while the south, with its expansion of credit, did not face the same conditions.

The first problem of competitiveness was generally ignored as it was assumed that the eurozone itself would facilitate convergence. In theory, greater trade integration would spur convergence, as countries that were less competitive would run a trade deficit, requiring a financial flow into the country as investment. This increase in capital would lead to greater growth in the long run and ultimately convergence among economies. However, such convergence did not occur in the eurozone.

Instead, the trade integration resulted in "twin deficits". Countries that do not enjoy similar productivities or capacities for the production of goods and services will eventually begin to fall into greater and greater debt and deficit as trade flows continue to favour countries with lower production costs, making them more competitive in comparison. Since a country's income cannot be greater than its total expenditure without incurring debt, a trade deficit implies that a country must spend more than it earns, thus trade deficits must be financed by increasing debt burdens. The result is "twin deficits" – a situation where a trade deficit exists and is expanding, causing increases in government deficits due to rising public expenditures, thereby requiring additional borrowing since the economy is already spending more than it generates in income.[100] In sum, deficits mounted on the trade and budget side in southern countries due to competitiveness issues and expanding public sectors.

Under normal circumstances, when a country finds itself uncompetitive with others in a trade environment, floating exchange rates would adjust to rebalance trade. United under a single currency, however, such adjustment between member countries cannot occur. Alternatively, in a complete fiscal and monetary union such as in the United States, the federal system can dictate fiscal and transfer policies to alleviate problems across disparate regions in the country. Again, the eurozone has no significant or similar transfer facilities. While the EU created a monetary union, it failed to complete what some architects might have originally envisioned in a fully integrated Europe – a single federal system that would coordinate EU economic and social outcomes. As a result, trade imbalances caused by relative productivity shifts can neither be addressed through currency devaluation, due to the adoption of a common currency, nor internally through transfers.

As figure 4-5 demonstrates, labour productivity was always much lower in the south compared to northern periphery countries, particularly in Germany, Austria, The Netherlands, and Finland. Further, while labour productivity as a measure of national productivity grew across the union following the euro's adoption, productivity increased more in northern countries. Combined with the fact that before 2008, wages grew faster in the south relative to the north, the north's cost advantage with respect to labour grew over time, leaving southern countries with an increasing cost disadvantage.

Simultaneously, trade deficits widened in southern countries, while in northern countries, greater trade surpluses emerged (figure 4-6). Across the twelve original countries in the eurozone (EU-12), the collective trade balances with the rest of the world did not change significantly. Thus, the data suggest changes in internal trade flows caused the change in regional deficits and surpluses. In other words, once the south had euros to spend, more Spaniards and Portuguese started buying Philips products from The Netherlands and Bosch

---

100 This concept becomes clearer when expressed mathematically: The Y=C+I+G+X-IM where X-IM is the trade surplus (X>IM) or deficit (IM>X) referred to as NX. This can be rearranged using T for total taxes or government revenue as
Y-T-C +T-G = I +NX
Where I = investment
Y –T- C as total private savings S
T-G as the budget deficit or surplus
NX = X-IM
This can be rewritten as
S + T-G = I + NX
If T-G < 0 (budget deficit) then often NX<0 since Investment is positive (one cannot take away the factories, only add them!) and as the budget deficit rises, the trade deficit increases.

appliances from Germany. The resulting reductions in trade deficits in the south as import consumption fell were mirrored by reductions in northern trade surpluses, while the overall EU-12 balance was relatively unaffected.[101]

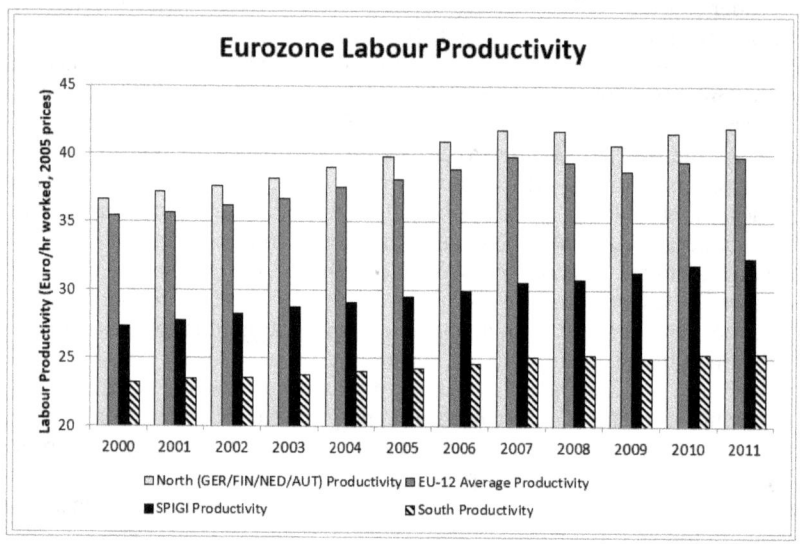

Figure 4-5: From the initiation of the eurozone, there have been large differences between labour productivities in northern and southern periphery states. While productivity growth occurred throughout the decade in all regions, the gap between southern countries and the rest of the eurozone has only widened over the period. This has resulted in cost advantages affecting trade patterns in the eurozone, particularly between northern and southern countries as the north's cost advantages increased. The SPIGI result shows the difference between labour productivities in Ireland and other troubled countries. Ireland's labour productivity is the highest in the eurozone and has continued to grow throughout the crisis, in contrast to other troubled states. Data Source: OECD.

Although often grouped with southern countries, Ireland is structurally quite different. As shown in figure 4-5, Irish levels of productivity were greater than the rest of the southern countries' as indicated by the difference between average southern country productivity levels and that of the south combined with Ireland (SPIGI productivity levels). In fact, Irish productivity has only been exceeded by Luxembourg's since the euro was created, and exceeds that of all

---

101 These results are more rigourously verified in papers such as Nils Holinski, Clemens JM Kool, and Joan Muysken, "Persistent macroeconomic imbalances in the euro area: Causes and consequences." *Federal Reserve Bank of St. Louis Review* 94.January/February 2012 (2012), https://research.stlouisfed.org/publications/review/12/01/1-20Holinski.pdf (accessed 3 August 2015).

northern periphery countries. Furthermore, when one averages Irish annual productivity levels with the south's, the ratio of north to SPIGI country average productivity falls over time, indicating that growth in labour productivity in Ireland was greater than in the southern periphery, or northern states. Higher inflation rates, prior to 2008, were offset by these productivity gains.

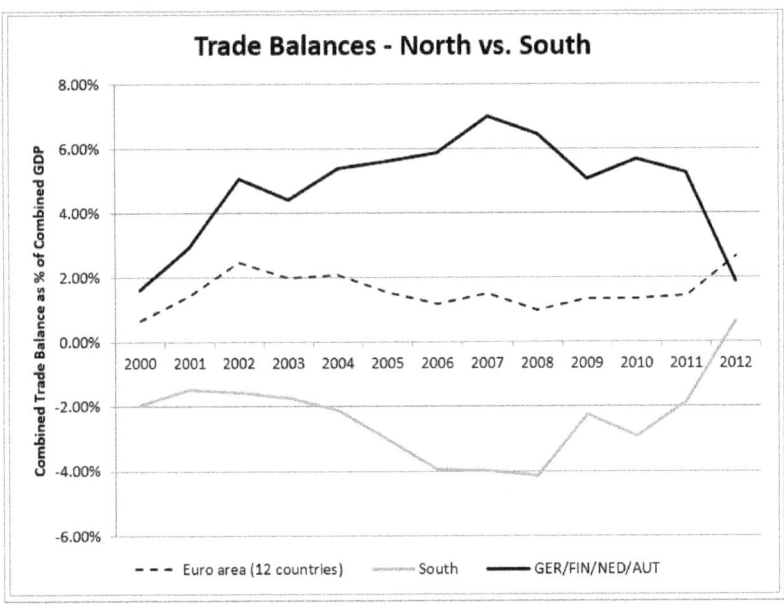

Figure 4-6: Trade balances (exports less imports as a percentage of GDP) were persistently negative for southern countries (Portugal, Italy, Greece, Spain) during the 2000s and deficits increased as credit conditions became easier after 2004. Similarly, northern states experienced growing trade surpluses throughout the period leading up to the crisis. Growth in surpluses appears to mirror deficits in southern states both in the periods leading up to 2008 and afterward during the eurozone crisis. Aggregate trade balance across the twelve original euro countries remained stable and slightly positive throughout the period, suggesting that the change in trade balances appears to have been the result of internal trade flows occurring after the adoption of the euro. Data Source: Eurostat.

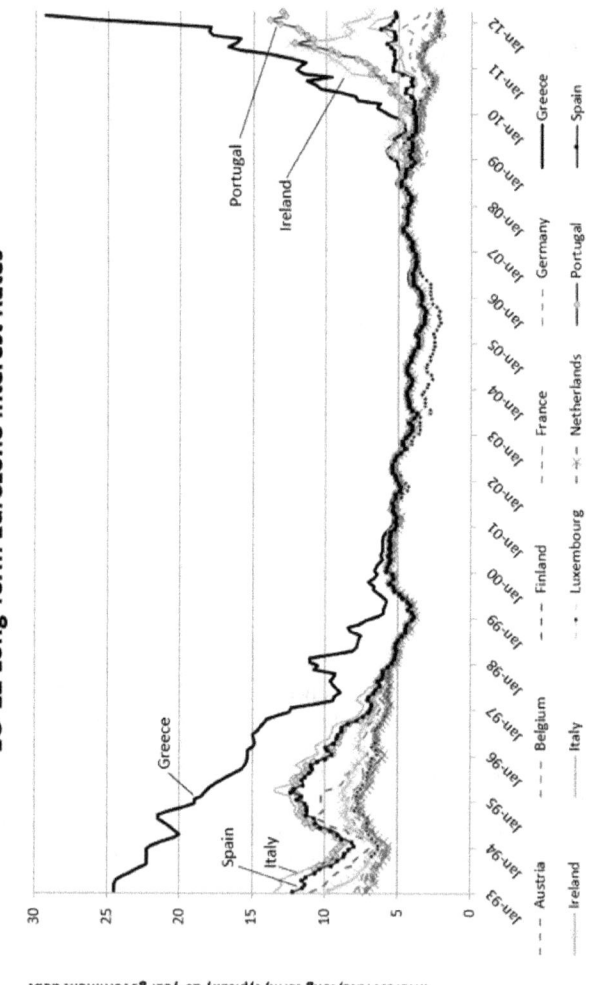

Figure 4-7: Prior to the formation of a common currency, interest rates for sovereign debt of the original twelve countries circulating the euro were quite divergent. With the creation of the euro, interest rates for these countries converged to nearly equal rates. Divergence only occurred again during the financial crisis of 2008 and after Greek debt revelations in 2009. This figure does not include the improvement in interest rates seen in the fall of 2012 and 2013, which is discussed in the following chapter. Data Source: Eurostat.

Relative productivities diverged, with differences in costs between north and south rising throughout the decade. In general, Germany and, to a lesser extent, other northern European states, were the primary beneficiaries. Sustained purchasing under these conditions for southern economies remained possible only through expanded credit markets and, in part, these were financed by the mounting trade surpluses accruing to northern countries in the form of foreign investment.[102] Northern economies improved and grew due to the internal trade advantages productivity growth provided. To make matters better, with a single currency, exchange rates could not appreciate to make the northern goods more expensive, as would normally happen in the world market. Southern economies, although weakened by eroding trade competitiveness caused by the same forces, did not experience slowing growth as shown in figure 4-1, due to favourable cyclical conditions caused by real estate and consumption bubbles. Their economies remained buoyed by the credit flowing in from northern trading partners and the international "savings glut" that, in part, drove property bubbles in North America and the rest of the world during the mid-2000s. Differences in property prices relative to the rest of the eurozone and northern countries, in particular, are apparent from the inception of the euro until 2007 (see figure 4-8).

---

102 In simple economics, the sum of total expenditure across household consumption of domestic goods (C), investment (I), government expenditures of all types (G) and on the trade balance (exports (X) sold to other countries less imports purchased from other countries (M) or (X-M)) must equal national income (Y). As Y=C+I+G+X-M is an identity that states' total expenditure cannot be greater than total income, it must always be true. Redefining Y-C-G as national savings, (S), that is total savings by households and government, this relationship can be expressed as S = I + (X-M). When a trade deficit occurs, (X-M) < 0, expenditures on imports exceed exports sold abroad. Rearranging the previous equation, a trade deficit will imply that investment (I) exceeds new savings available to finance it (S) by the same amount (S – I = (X-M)). In this case, a trade deficit will require that borrowing to finance domestic investment must occur from other countries in an amount equal to the trade deficit as domestic savings will not be able to finance this level of investment expenditure. This borrowing is referred to as Net Foreign Investment or NFI = -(X-M) and refers to the positive flow of credit from other nations to satisfy the shortfall of domestic savings and investment in the presence of a trade deficit. Note also as G, government spending rises, total savings S falls since S = Y-C-G, thus more must be borrowed from abroad to finance a given level of investment if public expenditures increase. This "twin deficits" hypothesis describes the fact that, typically, countries with expanding government expenditure deficits will also incur larger trade deficits. This was apparent in Europe, particularly in southern countries as shown in figure 4-6.

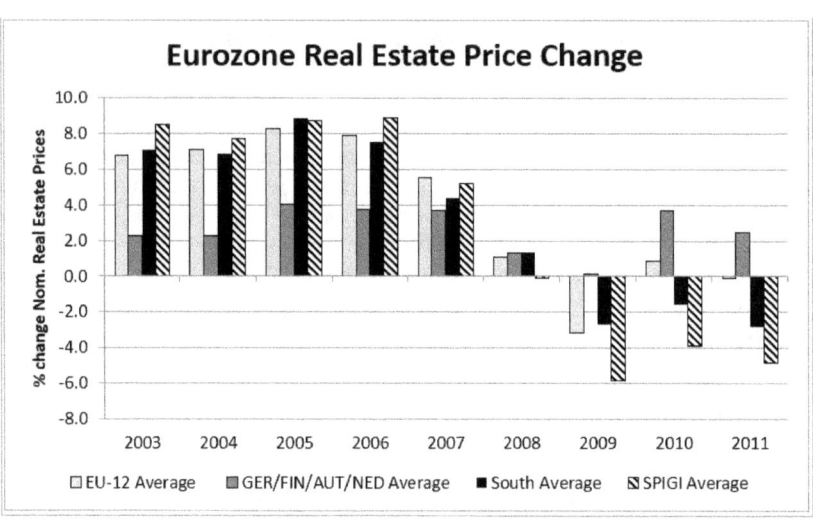

Figure 4-8: From 2003-2007, real estate price appreciation throughout the eurozone and in SPIGI countries were two to three times higher than in northern trade surplus countries such as Germany, Finland, Austria and The Netherlands. These trends reflected Europe-wide conditions. Source data: OECD, Eurostat and GlobalPropertyGuide.com.

In hindsight, growth rates in the south did appear to suggest economic convergence, but these figures were illusory. What was not clearly understood and partially hidden by the apparent growth in the southern economies was the importance of leverage and debt on the economic statistics observed. Persistent trade deficits between the relatively less wealthy southern countries and their wealthier northern partners could have been viewed as an unhealthy divergent force: weaker countries' trade sectors were falling victim to the more competitive north. In fact, the opposite view emerged.

Convergence and trade deficits were not regarded as mutually exclusive. The resulting net foreign investment flows from surplus countries to their southern neighbours, caused by persistent trade deficits, could and would result in increased productivity-enhancing investment. The accumulating debt faced by southern countries in the presence of trade deficits need not have detracted from debt sustainability if returns to such investments were higher than the cost of debt service. In other words, in southern "catch-up" countries, new investment could be expected to yield greater returns in those countries than in countries with higher productivity.

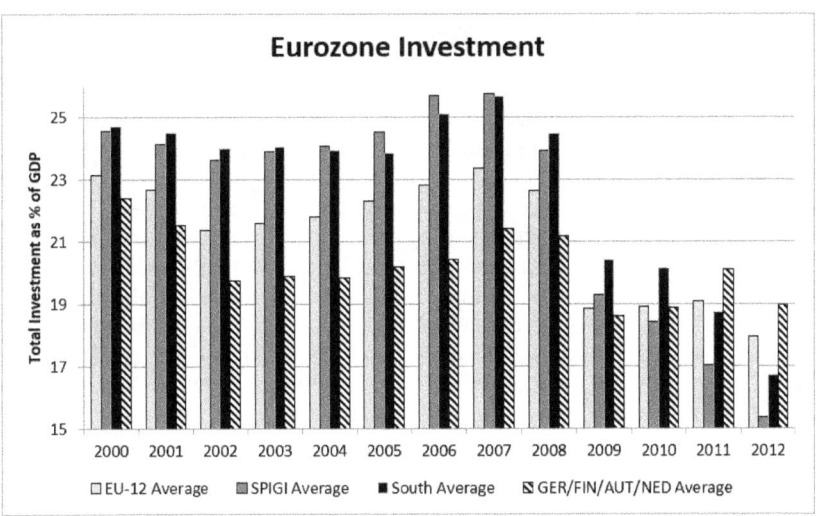

Figure 4-9: Trade imbalances in the period prior to 2008 should have financed net foreign investment flows in southern and SPIGI countries. It appears this did occur as investment slowed in Germany, Finland, Austria and the Netherlands relative to southern states during this period. Given the productivity data, which showed productivity improved for northern states relative to southern ones during the same time, the data is consistent with investment flows financing non-productivity increasing activities such as real estate construction, which would be reinforced by the price data shown in figure 4-8. Source Data: IMF, World Economic Outlook Database.

The evidence, however, does not support this optimistic conclusion. While investment increased in southern and SPIGI countries relative to northern ones (see figure 4-9), the data suggest productivity improvements were not sufficient for such convergence to occur. High investment growth in southern countries, propelled in part by their credit, appears not to have been allocated to productivity-enhancing activities, but instead to debt-financed real estate bubbles, where investment occurred in the form of new construction. The SPIGI economies have not yet recovered from the burst bubbles.

Trade imbalances not only financed real estate investment, they also fuelled both government and private debt. Reductions in gross national saving, as shown in figure 4-10, indicate how both private and public saving declined in southern and SPIGI countries, especially during the real estate boom that occurred between 2004 and 2008. Saving has been consistently lower in southern and SPIGI countries relative to the rest of the union. This debt pattern and the presence of larger public sectors are shown by the higher debt/GDP ratios in these countries (figure 4-11). Stronger growth in the middle part of the decade allowed southern countries to expand the public sector without great impact on the debt/GDP ratio.

Once the financial crisis of 2008 occurred, property bubbles collapsed and rapid and severe recessions followed, as private and public debt levels in the SPIGI countries became unsustainable. Private and public debt levels are shown as they evolved from 2001 to 2011 for the original twelve countries of the eurozone and Cyprus in figure 4-12. From 2001 to 2007, real estate and consumption booms were financed by additional private debt accumulation. By 2011, serious recessions and banking crises caused public debt to balloon as debt/GDP ratios grew much more quickly than in the rest of the eurozone.

Simultaneously, the overhang of accumulated private debt has created significant uncertainty in the eurozone. Countries that saw private debt levels climb, most often due to real estate booms, were now far more susceptible to banking crises, as the quality of loans underlying those private debts rapidly diminished due the sudden crash in real estate prices after 2007. Moreover, the abrupt reduction in debt accumulation that had fuelled the economic booms in much of Europe, especially SPIGI countries, created a contraction in economic activity, further destabilizing banking systems while increasing public expenditures and debt.

As the IMF noted in their OECD Economic Outlook in May 2011, the problem in the eurozone then became one in which public finance burdens were willingly increased because of faulty assumptions regarding the positive economic circumstances enjoyed in the mid-2000s:

> Fiscal consolidation... looked successful, but – as has been a recurrent theme in the OECD's economic history – failure to attain sound underlying public finances was masked by very favourable cyclical developments. Fiscal rules (e.g. the European Stability and Growth Pact) failed to provide incentives to encourage the build-up of a sufficient reserve in good times. The implications of rising private-sector imbalances for the sustainability of public finances were ignored and forecasts of underlying public budgets were too optimistic. A possible correction in financial asset and real estate prices was not factored in and implicit fiscal liabilities were not taken into account.[103]

---

103 OECD *Economic Outlook*, Volume 2011, Issue 1, 320.

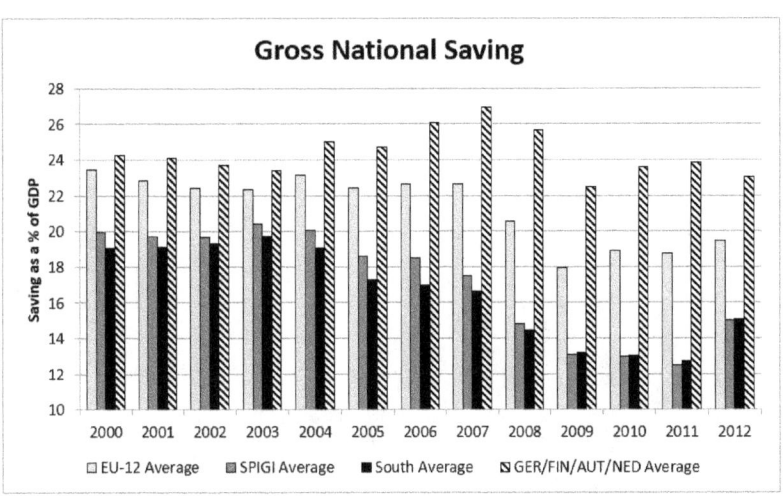

Figure 4-10: Credit inflows between 2000 and 2007 in southern and SPIGI countries also reduced gross domestic savings as both households and governments took on additional debt, especially from 2003 to 2007. Such figures are consistent with increased home prices in the SPIGI and southern economies, and rising trade deficits. The impact of the recessions following the financial crisis in 2008 and the eurozone crisis from 2009 onward is apparent across all countries shown, especially southern and SPIGI nations. Source data: OECD Economic Outlook Database.

What had been a virtuous European circle became the eurozone crisis. Instead of convergence, structural imbalances in trade led to a troubled debt-alliance that left northern countries financing southern neighbours' consumption of northern goods, while helping to fuel property bubbles and expanding public sectors. As productivity improved in the northern countries relative to the south, southern economies became relatively less able to generate income and more reliant on larger debt. Clearly, this fragile partnership would be in danger if credit conditions ever worsened, but, in the mid-2000s, concerns about such risks were considerably downplayed – just another immense miscalculation worldwide that led to the financial crisis of 2008. Growth in southern economies swiftly stopped, and northern creditors found they were holding a bag of potentially toxic liabilities with catastrophic consequences for the eurozone if the debtors decided not to pay them.

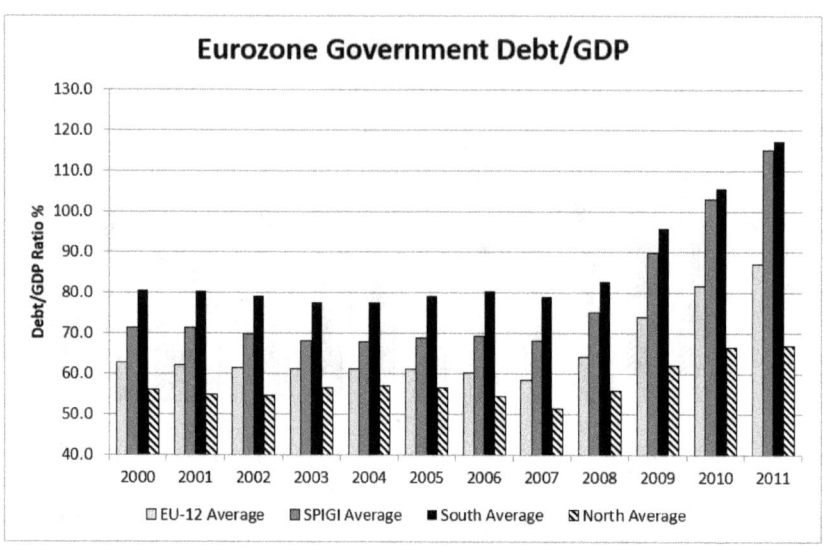

Figure 4-11: Government debt relative to GDP remained higher in southern and SPIGI countries compared to their northern neighbours. Given that growth was also higher in these countries relative to the eurozone, such figures indicate that public sector debt grew more quickly as well. Debt/GDP growth greatly accelerated across Europe, especially for southern and SPIGI countries after the financial crisis of 2007 and then the eurozone crisis in late 2009 and 2010. Toward the end of the period, only northern country debt/GDP ratios had stabilized, reflecting their stronger economic growth. Source: Eurostat.

Private and Public Debt-GDP

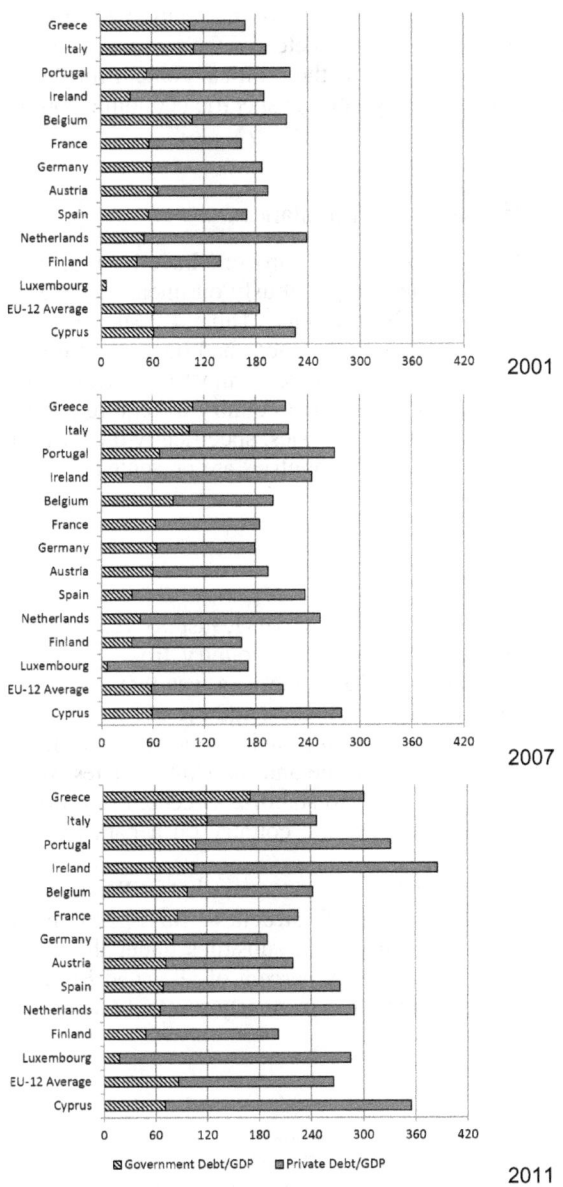

Figure 4-12: Government and private debt relative to GDP in 2001, 2007 and 2011.

The next section of this chapter explores the relative economic and political situations of each of the debtor eurozone countries. Each SPIGI country case study examines the specific conditions that caused the internal recessions. The studies provide a thumbnail sketch of the member state's original motivations to join the EU as well as the political context for their actions. Next, the studies delve more deeply into the specific economic composition of each country.

Country Specific Structural Imbalances

The most troubled countries in the eurozone have been affected by some or all of the structural imbalances previously outlined, however, circumstances of the crises in each have been unique. Table 4-2 summarizes the degree to which symptoms of eurozone imbalances had been present before 2008. The SPIGI countries have been the source of most concern during the eurozone crisis, and Cyprus represents the first country to require a bailout as a direct result of crisis events in other countries, specifically the write-down of Greek debt held privately in 2012. The countries are presented in the order in which the crisis progressed.

Greece

Greece joined the European Union in 1981, just six years after putting an end to a military junta that controlled the country from 1967 to 1975. Joining NATO only a year earlier in 1980, the idea was that NATO would stabilize the country through security guarantees, and the EU would foster it economically and democratically. By virtue of its geographic position that controls the Mediterranean, Western Europe and the United States were strongly supportive of membership in order to stabilize Greece. From the Greek perspective, joining the EU would put the country on a path to development and modernization.[104]

Although still one of the poorest countries in Western Europe, Greece has gained significantly from EC structural funds and investment. Greek farmers have benefited greatly from subsidies under the Common Agricultural Policy. Nonetheless, seventy percent of allocated EU funds go unused. In other words, the government is so poorly run that Greece can only imple-

---

104 Greek Ministry of Foreign Affairs, "Greece's course in the EU," http://www.mfa.gr/en/foreign-policy/greece-in-the-eu/greeces-course-in-the-eu.html. (accessed 3 August 2015).

ment projects that employ a small portion of the funds, creating an absorption rate of only thirty percent.[105]

Greece is also viewed as a 'poor' European, often eschewing the EU culture of consensus and compromise for its own gain. Instead, Greece has used its veto often – a social faux pas. Right after Greece acceded, the Pan Hellenic Movement (PASOK), the social democratic party, which was opposed to EC membership, took power in the Parliament. Greece remained in the EC, but as a spoiler. Typically, the EU countries would agree on something, Greece would veto, and then negotiate a way to be bought off, for example, through agricultural concessions, more structural funds, or protectionist measures. In 2015, Greek prime minister Alexis Tsipras played the same game by putting the EU's bailout proposal to a popular referendum, in effect creating a popular 'veto' in hopes of being able to negotiate a better deal. As a political move, it rattled the other EU member states as Greece once again played the spoiler rejecting the Brussels culture of consensus building.

With regards to the EU's goals for harmonized fiscal policies, Greece has lagged behind the others in terms of each country's targets for inflation, debt, and fiscal balance. The eurozone crisis began with Greek revisions to national debt figures in October 2009 after the election of a new centre-left government, led by George Papandreou. In an audit of public finances, it was revealed that previous Greek governments had, for years, hidden massive debts from the rest of the European Union. Greece's estimated government deficit for 2009 had more than tripled, revised from a previous 3.7 percent of GDP to 12.5 percent shortly after the new government took office. By April 2010, new EU figures suggested the deficit was even larger – nearer to fourteen percent.

The implications of this admission forced investors worldwide to reconsider their faith in the safety of sovereign debt. The EU's own statistical agency, Eurostat, had first suggested Greece was guilty of misreporting financial statistics in 2004. Since 2005, the EU had expressed reservations no fewer than five times regarding the biannual reporting of Greek debt and deficit figures. On November 10, 2009, the European Economic and Financial Affairs Council (ECOFIN) issued a statement calling for an investigation of the ongoing reporting problems in Greece.[106] In its follow-up report issued in August 2010, the European Commission identified two primary causes of

---

105 Nikolaos Zahariadis, "Greece: A Most Enthusiastic, Reluctant European," in *The European Union and the Member States* (eds.) Eleanor E. Zeff and Ellen B Pirro, second edition, (Boulder, CO: Lynne Rienner, 2006), 195.
106 Council of the European Union, Council conclusions on EU Statistics, 2972nd Economic and Financial Affairs Brussels, 10 November 2009, http://www.consilium.europa.eu/uedocs/cms_data/docs/pressdata/en/ecofin/111007.pdf (accessed 3 August 2015).

the repeated pattern of upward revisions: poor accounting procedures and poor governance influencing fiscal reporting. While stated more diplomatically, Greece was charged with allowing official agencies to "cook the books" when politically expedient. The eventual estimate of the Greek deficit would be 15.6 percent of GDP, over four times the level originally reported.

Table 4-2: Maastricht Criteria Levels by Country Group and Selected Countries

	Debt/GDP			Deficit/GDP			Inflation		
	Average Annual Debt to GDP ratio (%)			Average Annual Deficit (-) or Surplus (+) to GDP ratio (%)			Average Yearly Rate of Consumer Price Change		
	2001-2007	2008-2012	2012	2001-2007	2008-2012	2012	2001-2007	2008-2012	2012
Greece	102.5%	143.6%	156.9%	-5.7%	-11.1%	-10.0%	3.4%	2.9%	1.00%
Ireland	29.2%	85.1%	117.6%	1.0%	-14.6%	-7.6%	3.3%	0.4%	1.0%
Portugal	62.5%	96.3%	123.6%	-4.3%	-7.0%	-6.4%	3.1%	1.9%	2.8%
Spain	46.1%	61.8%	84.2%	0.6%	-9.1%	-10.6%	3.2%	2.3%	2.4%
Italy	105.1%	117.9%	127.0%	-3.2%	-3.9%	-3.0%	2.3%	2.4%	3.3%
Cyprus	65.7%	65.1%	85.8%	-2.5%	-4.6%	-6.3%	2.4%	2.8%	3.1%
SPIGI	69.1%	100.9%	121.9%	-2.3%	-9.1%	-7.5%	3.1%	2.0%	2.1%
South	79.1%	104.9%	122.9%	-3.1%	-7.7%	-7.5%	3.0%	2.4%	2.4%
North	55.0%	64.2%	69.9%	-0.4%	-2.2%	-2.1%	1.9%	2.2%	2.9%
EU-12	60.8%	79.7%	91.6%	-1.2%	-5.3%	-4.60%	2.5%	2.2%	2.5%

A swollen public service sector and an ineffective and inefficient tax collection system were the primary causes of the large deficits. Public servants, once hired, had jobs that were constitutionally protected and guaranteed for life. Although originally intended to isolate the public service from political pressures, instead, they became bribes for political support. From 1970 to 2009, public sector employment increased fivefold, creating a powerful political constituency of over 700,000 people consisting of public service workers and their families. Public sector employment growth during this same period was four percent compared to an average growth rate of less than one percent in the private sector.

Table 4-3: Economic Indicators by Group and Selected Eurozone Countries

	Real GDP Growth		Home Prices		Labour Productivity		Trade Balance	
	Average Yearly % Change		Average Yearly % Change		Euros per hour worked at 2005 prices		Average yearly Current Account to GDP ratio (%)	
	2001-2007	2008-2012	2003-2007	2008-2011	2001-2007	2008-2012	2001-2007	2008-2012
Greece	4.2%	-4.4%	5.3%	-3.0%	19.5	20.9	-12.0%	-9.7%
Ireland	5.1%	-1.2%	11.3%	-12.6%	49.1	57.0	13.4%	18.0%
Portugal	1.1%	-1.1%	1.5%	1.5%	16.9	18.1	-8.5%	-6.0%
Spain	3.4%	-0.8%	13.7%	-4.3%	27.8	29.6	-5.0%	-1.9%
Italy	1.3%	-1.4%	6.1%	0.1%	32.2	32.3	0.4%	-0.1%
Cyprus	3.6%	0.2%	8.7%*	-3.5%	19.8	21.2	-2.2%	-5.5%
SPIGI	3.0%	-1.8%	7.6%	-3.7%	29.1	31.6	-2.2%	-0.1%
South	2.5%	-1.9%	6.6%	1.4%	24.1	25.2	-6.1%	-4.6%
North	2.2%	0.2%	3.2%	1.9%	44.3	46.4	5.7%	4.8%
EU-12	2.7%	-0.6%	7.1%	-0.3%	37.5	39.3	3.4%	4.1%

Public sector wages had climbed to a level almost fifty percent greater than in private sector earnings, and accounted for twenty-seven percent of total government expenditures. OECD estimates indicated overstaffing levels in the Greek public sector at over fifty percent. In the decade from 2000 to 2009, wage and social program expenditures in Greece rose by 6.5 per cent annually while revenues increased by only five percent annually. The result was an ever widening government expenditure deficit.[107] From 2004 to 2009, according to documents submitted to the EU by the Greek Ministry of Finance, "output increased in nominal terms by 40 percent, central government primary expenditures increased by 87 percent against an increase of only 31 percent in tax revenues."[108] Over the period of Greek membership in the euro from 2001 to 2007, the average government deficit was 5.7 percent of GDP and the Greek debt-GDP ratio was 102.5 percent (see table 4-2). With respect

---

107 Data on Greek public sector employment from J. Sfakianakis, "The Cost of Protecting Greece's Public Sector," *The New York Times*, 10 October 2012.
108 Greece, Ministry of Finance, "Update of the Hellenic Stability and Growth Programme," submitted to the European Commission, January 2010, 14.

to revenues, tax evasion remained a long-standing problem and one that little was done to correct.

The large, inefficient, and expanding public sector, growing at four times the rate of the private sector, undermined productivity, growth, and trade competitiveness. Additionally, from 2005 to 2007, Greek home prices grew at an average rate of 8.5 percent. The real estate and consumption bubbles in Greece reduced private savings, while increasing private and public debt loads. Debt was sustained by very large and persistent trade deficits, which averaged twelve percent.

Before the financial crisis, Greek economic growth had been among the strongest of the eurozone countries, averaging 4.2 percent annually. However, after 2008, the world financial crisis disrupted the shipping and tourism industries severely impacting local economies. The ensuing recession reduced Greek economic output by 0.2 percent in 2008 and a further 3.5 percent in 2009, straining Greek public finances further as social program costs escalated. The government's own revelations regarding Greek financial mismanagement resulted in an almost immediate series of credit rating downgrades on Greek sovereign debt. Greek ten-year bond yields rose from under 4.5 percent to over eight percent in the period from October 2009 to May 2010, a level almost triple the yield paid on German bonds. In April 2010, Greek two-year bond yields rose to over fifteen percent and five-year bonds exceeded ten percent. Finding international financing of its debt service and operations unsustainable, the Greek government was forced to request a bailout from the EU and IMF on 23 April. On 2 May 2010, the EU and IMF agreed to finance loans totalling €110 billion, granted for three years at an interest rate of 5.5 percent.

Of all the SPIGI countries, Greece alone has suffered from all the economic ills possible: a decline in productivity relative to the northern countries; an increased trade deficit; a housing bubble; declining national savings; an increasing debt to GDP ratio, and a government that is both corrupt and ineffective. As result, Greece has had, by far, the most difficult hill to climb towards economic recovery.

Ireland

Like Greece, Ireland saw membership as a vehicle for development and modernization as well as a way to reduce its economic dependence on the United Kingdom. Whereas, in essence, Ireland was England's first colony, membership in the EU gave it equal status with Britain, allowing the Irish find their own place in continental politics and in the world. Membership in the EU also meant access to CAP and structural or regional development funds to invest in infrastructure and the like, as well as a larger market for Irish goods. By 1975, Ireland had already received 500 million pounds from the European

Community. Not wanting to rock the boat, Ireland has been very supportive of the Commission in almost all of its pursuits. In 1979, Ireland joined the EMS, which allowed the Irish to break the punt's link with the pound sterling for the first time – another symbolic break with Britain.

Historically, one of the poorest countries in Western Europe, by 2007, Ireland became second only to Luxembourg as the richest in the eurozone on a GDP per capita basis. This turnaround earned Ireland the nickname the "Celtic Tiger", putting it in the same league as the so-called Asian Tigers: South Korea; Singapore; Hong Kong; and Taiwan. Its recipe for success included adopting one of the lowest corporate tax rates in Europe and investment in education. The government directed thirty-five percent of EU structural funds to developing human capital, more than any other recipient country, encouraging the growth of a new high tech industry. Subsidies also encouraged high-tech firms to locate in Ireland. By the 2000s, Irish high-tech manufacturing had led to significant trade surpluses with the rest of the world and Europe. Favourable location and relatively lower wages were also often cited as factors in Ireland's economic success.

Annual growth rates of real GDP from 1984 to 2000 averaged 6.3 percent; from 1996 to 2000, they averaged an astounding 10.3 percent. During the period of the euro from 2001 to 2007, real GDP growth continued at a still very high 5.1 percent average pace, despite a period of relative easing during the early 2000s due to the "dot.com" bubble bursting and the information technology slowdown in the United States. High rates of economic growth allowed Ireland to run persistent budget surpluses, reducing its government debt to GDP ratio from over ninety percent to less than forty percent in the decade of the 1990s alone. Debt to GDP ratios continued to fall through 2007 and averaged 29.1 percent from 2001 to 2007 (table 4-2). Again, this performance was among the best in the currency union, and, by 2007, Ireland's debt-GDP ratio was bettered only by Luxembourg.

Unlike other troubled countries in the eurozone, as shown in table 4-3, the most serious source of imbalance in Ireland's economy was a real estate bubble that began to inflate in the early 2000s. Rates of home price increases exceeded fourteen percent in 2003 and 2006 and averaged 11.3 percent between 2003 and 2007, propelled by economic growth, foreign investment, and easy credit. Cheap credit was driven by bond yields on Irish sovereign debt that were often lower than that paid on equivalent German bonds, traditionally the benchmark rate to which other countries' debts have been compared. Growth in high-tech manufacturing, corporate relocation to Ireland, and high levels of foreign investment also encouraged house price increases.

The US real estate bubble in 2007 burst at the same time as Ireland's, and soon, the Irish banking system was in crisis. Banks in Ireland, as in the United States, had financed much of the long-term real estate investment using short-term borrowed credit. As concerns mounted over the ability to repay these loans, Irish banks faced an illiquidity problem. As the Irish economy fell into its first recession since 2003, in an attempt to stabilize the banking system and open credit markets, the Irish government issued an unlimited guarantee backing six of its national banks. The Irish government also implemented deeply unpopular social spending cutbacks in an attempt to reverse a budget deficit that exceeded seven percent of national output, the first deficit since the 1980s. In response to these actions, November 2010 saw one of the largest protests in the country's history.[109]

By the end of the year, the government took out a seventy-five percent ownership stake in order to bailout the Anglo-Irish Bank, the one worst hit by the property collapse. This single bank would eventually lose over €34 billion, worth almost half of its investments and a loss equivalent to almost twenty percent of Irish GDP in 2008. From 2007 to 2009, unemployment climbed from 4.7 percent to twelve percent as the recession worsened. In September 2009, Ireland created the National Asset Management Agency, a "bad bank" in which to transfer the Irish banks' non-performing assets. For a second year, the Irish government also offered an unlimited bank guarantee to back these institutions in another attempt to open credit markets to Irish financial institutions. Credit market conditions, however, only worsened after Greece announced the first of its deficit revisions in November 2009. Irish ten-year sovereign bond yields, which had averaged only a half percent premium over German bonds in 2008, climbed to a level sixty percent greater than the yield on comparable German notes. By the end of 2009, the Irish budget deficit was 13.9 percent of GDP, and the Irish economy had contracted by over three percent. By mid 2010, Irish 10-year bond yields were double those of Germany's; the Irish government had to guarantee Irish bank obligations for a third year. With these bank liabilities, now worth over thirty percent of Irish GDP, the Irish government would no longer finance its expenditure and expanding liability using sovereign credit. It requested a bailout from the IMF and EU, and, on 28 November 2010, was granted an €85 billion rescue package.

Although Ireland was the second country to succumb to the financial crisis, unlike Greece, it had no productivity decline, no trade deficit, and no savings decline. Its debt-to-GDP ratio was healthy as was its government. However, it did suffer from a housing bubble that burst and made the economy go bust.

---

109 John F. Burns, "Demonstrators in Ireland Protest Austerity Plan," *The New York Times*, 27 November 2010.

Portugal

Despite its dictatorship under António de Oliveira Salazar, Portugal was both a founding member of NATO in 1949 and of the European Free Trade Association (EFTA) in 1960 – the EU alternative for those unable or unwilling to join, but still interested in trade. Although Portugal could not have been admitted to the European Community at the time, Salazar would not have wanted to become a member: he was a very keen nationalist preferring intergovernmental organizations. This strong nationalist bent runs through Portugal today.

After Salazar's death in 1970 and the Carnation Revolution that ended the dictatorship in 1974, Western European aid rushed in to protect the nascent democracy. Portugal applied for membership in the European Community in 1977, just one year after they had drafted their constitution. Negotiations began, and Portugal entered the EC along with Spain in 1986. As in Greece and Spain, a key goal of membership was democratization.

Although Portugal does not receive CAP funding, it has received a tremendous influx of development aid from the EU. Nevertheless, Portuguese enthusiasm for the European project has been mixed. As one of the "poor four", being part of the EU has exposed the backwardness of Portuguese agriculture and industry. During the 1994 European Parliament elections, the Social Democrats' (the ruling party) slogan was "European yes, Portugal forever!" The communists, some Greens, and a small right wing party called the Social Democratic Centre Popular Party won nine percent of the vote on an anti-EU platform describing "a Europe bent on turning Portugal into nothing better than a backwater where richer Europeans spend their holidays." Even the socialist president asked, "are we to be the waiters of Europe?"[110] Still, the Portuguese public generally supports European integration and undertook all the requirements necessary to become one of the founding members of the eurozone, albeit one of the weakest.

Even after the introduction of the euro, Portuguese growth faltered. Burdened by a large and inefficient public sector, low productivity throughout the economy, and higher inflation than in the eurozone as a whole, trade deficits averaged over eight percent of GDP. Growth of real GDP averaged 1.1 percent from 2001 to 2007, the lowest among the original eurozone countries. Government deficits averaged over four percent, resulting in government gross debt to GDP ratios climbing in excess of sixty percent. Both deficit and debt ratios persistently exceeded the Maastricht guidelines required of eurozone countries. Despite threatened sanctions, Portugal was not penalized under the EU's Stability and Growth Pact (SGP) rules. Bond yields

---

110 *The Economist*, "Iberia: Navels in Spain and Portugal," 4 June 1994, 52-53.

also remained low; interest rates on Portuguese ten-year bonds averaged only 0.17 percent more than German bonds from 2001 to 2007.

As the worldwide economy worsened, the Portuguese economy also slowed, falling into recession at the end of 2008. Deficits rose to over ten percent of GDP by 2009, with government debt to GDP rising to over seventy percent in 2008 and eighty percent in 2009. In late 2008, Portugal was forced to nationalize one of its largest banks after a banking scandal and severe losses. A second bank also fell victim to management scandal, and, in early 2010, was liquidated by the Portuguese central bank. At the end of 2009, following the Greek deficit revelations, ten-year bond yields on Portuguese debt began to reflect investor concerns regarding that country's debt sustainability. By the end of 2010, Portuguese ten-year debt approached yield levels of seven percent, a level 4.5 percent higher and over two and half times the rate on comparable German debt. With Portuguese debt yields at record highs and unemployment over eleven percent, in April 2011 Portugal approached the IMF and EU for assistance and was granted a €78 billion bailout package.

Although one of the worst battered by the eurozone crisis, anti-European populist parties have not gained much ground. Portuguese economist João Ferreira do Amaral's book, *Why We Should Leave the Euro,* topped the best seller list in 2013, but, in opinion polls, seventy-two percent of Portuguese still wanted to remain in the euro.[111] In 2014, Portugal managed a clean exit from bailout – a success story.

Portugal fell into the crisis due to its weak economy, but not owing to any malfeasance. Portugal suffered from a host of the economic ills: productivity decline; increasing trade deficit; declining national savings; increasing debt-to-GDP ratio, but no housing bubble. Politically, the government is neither corrupt nor ineffective. However, as was the case with Ireland, the government was not able to steer the economy away from the rocks.

Spain

Spain's background and reasons for joining the European Community were similar to Portugal's. As early as the sixties, Spain had free trade agreements with the EC; nevertheless, there was no chance of Spain joining as long as the country was under fascist dictatorship. After Francisco Franco died in 1975, Spain applied for membership in 1977. Like Portugal, the EC gave Spain abundant aid and accepted its application in hopes of stabilizing the region. In 1982, Spain joined NATO; in 1986, Spain joined the EC.

---

111 Patricia Kowsmann and Marcus Walker, "Idea of Euro Exit Finds Currency in Portugal," *Wall Street Journal*, 27 May 2013.

The Spanish have benefited from EU membership by receiving millions in structural funds and CAP supports. In terms of politics, the Spanish have been strong integrationists. They have little trouble with a federal Europe, a common foreign and security policy, or a common currency. Spain does well in Brussels because they usually side with France. Having such a powerful ally combined with its size means that it has greater influence than Portugal and other members of the 'poor four'.

Growth in Spain from 2001 to 2007, spurred by public construction and home building booms, averaged 3.5 percent, well above the rates of most of the original twelve eurozone countries. The high growth rates caused by this activity masked the costs of large and inefficient public works projects throughout the country. Despite these expenditures, government budgets remained in surplus, and the debt-GDP ratio fell to levels well below those in most other countries, achieving a level of 36.3 percent in 2007. Behind these figures, however, a large and persistent trade deficit continued. As in Portugal, economic reforms were deferred, but unlike in Portugal, painful reforms seemed far less justified as high growth continued. Despite this growth, productivity improvements failed to keep pace with northern competitors, and with wage and inflation rates reflected in housing prices, overall Spanish trade competitiveness was persistently challenged, and large trade deficits continued.

In late 2007, the Spanish property bubble burst, as it did in Ireland and the United States. The Spanish banking sector had supported the financing of large public construction projects and real estate in large part through its *cajas*, smaller regional savings banks whose boards and lending decisions were often influenced by local and regional politicians. The bursting of the housing market bubble left many of these institutions in desperate financial circumstances. Still, with economic conditions slowly improving in 2010, authorities chose to support the *cajas* sector by merging several of the most impacted institutions into a single new entity renamed Bankia. Ten-year bond rates on Spanish debt briefly increased to levels one percent higher than German debt in early 2009, then returning to rates only half a percent higher by summer.

Rates began rising again in May 2010 after the Irish bailout. The Spanish economy re-entered recession as property prices fell and default rates continued to escalate, causing losses to mount in the Spanish banking system. In the autumn of 2011, the ECB intervened in markets for Spanish debt, buying limited numbers of Spanish bonds on the secondary market in an effort to reduce interest rates, now more than three percent above German rates. While Spain was "too big to fail," it was also too big to bailout as resources and support for such efforts dwindled after aid was offered to Greece, Ireland, and Portugal. By mid-2012, however, continuing Spanish banking losses required the country to request aid from the EU to recapitalize its banking system; in June 2012, European leaders announced approval for loan guarantees up to €100 billion. Unlike previous bailout efforts, these funds would be made available as needed, and would be made directly to the banking system rather than through the national government. In theory, this tactic would stem the pressure on Spanish sovereign debt rates by avoiding Spain's accumulation of additional debt and the perception of greater default risk. While conditions in bond markets improved in 2012-13 after the ECB guaranteed the necessary funds to ensure the euro would survive, unemployment and economic growth in the region has remained sluggish.

In March 2014, protesters came from all over Spain to participate in a "march of dignity" against government austerity measures. The rally turned violent as demonstrators clashed with police. Unemployment rates had increased to twenty-six percent with youth unemployment reaching fifty-six percent.

Of all the SPIGI countries, Spain was closest to Greece in its economic and political troubles. Spain experienced a productivity decline, an increased trade deficit, a housing bubble, and a decline in national savings. Unlike Greece, it did not suffer from an increasing debt-to-GDP ratio. However, politically, it too had an ineffective and corrupt government.

Italy

As a founding member of the European Coal and Steel Community and one of the largest members of the Union, Italy has always been pro-integration, pro-enlargement, and seen itself as a conciliator during European summits. It benefits a great deal from the EU economically with its regional funds, mostly aimed towards the south, as well as CAP funding. Nevertheless, Italy has had less influence on European politics than might be expected, due to government instability, scandals, and corruption. In addition, Italy suffers from an almost split personality with its extremely wealthy, autonomy-minded north and its less developed south with poorer infrastructure and weak governance.

Although Italy was severely in debt when negotiating entry into the currency union, Prime Minister Romano Prodi was able to persuade Germany to let it join as a way to increase the market for Bavarian dairy products. Prodi recalled how, in 1996, "he pitched 'a big milk pipeline from Bavaria,' pointing to a three-year, 40 percent plunge in the Italian lira that was hurting dairy sales. 'To have Italy outside the euro, a huge quantity of exports from Germany would have been endangered.'"[112] Therefore, Italy became a founding member of the eurozone, but not without costs. Using the opportunity to attack opposition leader and former European Commission president Romano Prodi before Italy's 2005 elections, Prime Minister Silvio Berlusconi called the euro a "disaster" and a "rip-off" that "screwed everybody".[113]

Like Portugal, Italy experienced slow growth throughout the decade of the 2000s, averaging annual rates of growth from 2001 to 2007 of only 1.3 percent. The third largest economy in the eurozone after Germany and France, Italy was allowed to enter the currency union with a debt to GDP ratio in excess of 110 percent in 1999, much greater than originally envisioned by its architects. Deficit levels were also at or above Maastricht treaty limits throughout the period from 2001 to 2007. However, unlike Portugal, Italian deficits were structural in the sense that they reflected slow economic growth and were driven by debt-service. Despite these challenges, by 2007, debt restructuring, permitted by the lower sovereign debt rates available after the euro was introduced, allowed Italy's debt-to-GDP level to be reduced to 103 percent from over 113 percent in 1999. These same low interest rates also created an escalation in housing prices, as they had in several other countries. Nevertheless, these price challenges did not cause inflation to rise relative to levels in the rest of the eurozone as they had in Greece, Ireland, Portugal and Spain. Italy's trade deficit remained slightly positive throughout most of the first decade of the euro, and, even since 2008, has been nearly balanced, although its relative productivity compared to northern eurozone states has declined.

Concerns with respect to Italy's economy have centred on its comparatively large debt level and the cost to service it. While weak economic performance did not improve greatly after adopting the euro, consistent with its Maastricht obligations, Italy did manage to reduce its debt load. Unfortunately, by 2009, these debt levels had again begun to escalate as the worldwide recession of 2008 also caused deficits in Italy to increase, making Italy very sensitive to sovereign debt rates. Since the failure of Lehman Brothers Bank in the United States in the autumn of 2008, yields have averaged over one percent higher than German ten-year bonds, a level more than twenty-five percent higher from what Germany pays creditors. Since 2010, this spread has increased to two percent or more, and, at times, approached levels that could make debt servicing unsustainable. Like Spain, the size of Italy's economy renders it impossible for Europe to bail out; the resources necessary are simply unavailable politically.

---

112 James G. Neuger, "Euro Breakup Talk Increases as Germany Loses Proxy (Update1)," *Bloomberg*, 14 May 2010, http://www.bloomberg.com/apps/news?pid=newsarchive&sid=agwHp5N5FXA8 (accessed 3 August 2015).
113 Filipe Rufino, "Berlusconi attacks euro," *EUObserver*, 29 July 2005.

With unemployment rates of 12.6 percent and youth unemployment at forty-three percent, populist anti-EU parties have gained ground during the crisis. Although Italy has had very strong popular support for integration, averaging seventy percent from 1973-2002, from that point onward, support plummeted to forty-one percent in 2011. Silvio Berlusconi, leader of the main conservative coalition, campaigned on Italy leaving the euro. In 2009, Beppe Grillo, a comedian and Italian television star, founded an anti-establishment political party called MoVimento, or the Five Star Movement. *Time* magazine called him a "European hero" for his jokes "draped around barbed social commentary" and "over-the-top humor to probe the serious social issues that leaders don't want to touch"[114]. In 2013, he upset the status quo by coming in third, ahead of the centrist and outgoing prime minister Mario Monti's party, Civic Choice. Grillo referred to the prime minister as "Rigor Montis" mocking his seriousness.[115] In his blog (see box above), Grillo concludes, "Today to impose a dictatorship, force is no longer necessary. The so called 'reforms…' are enough."[116]

Italy has only some of the problems that the other SPIGI countries have had. It has had a productivity decline as well as a housing bubble, but no issues with a decline in national savings, a trade deficit, or an increasing debt-to-GDP ratio. However, along with Spain and Greece, its government is both ineffectual and corrupt.

Cyprus

A small island economy dominated by Greek heritage, Cyprus joined the European Union in the 2004 enlargement. Its longstanding dispute with Turkey delayed its entry into the Union; it is the only EU member with a permanent United Nations peacekeeping force on its territory. Cyprus joined the common currency in 2008, but only accounted for 0.2 percent of total eurozone output that year. The next smallest economies (Portugal, Ireland and Finland) are each almost ten times larger. Prior to its membership in the euro, Cyprus enjoyed high growth, but also high inflation in the early 2000s. Inflation rates were, in part, driven by another real estate bubble where prices rose at over eight percent per year. Since joining the currency union, Cyprus has also become an offshore banking centre, particularly for Russian depositors eager for access to Europe. The two countries have traditionally had warm relations: the USSR

---

114 Jeff Israely, "Seriously Funny," *Time*, 2 October 2005.
115 "Profile: Beppe Grillo," *BBC News*, 26 February 2013, http://www.bbc.com/news/world-europe-21576869 (accessed 3 August 2015).
116 Beppe Grillo's blog, July 2014, "From Matteotti to Di Matteo #lanuovadittatura—the New Dictatorship," http://www.beppegrillo.it/en/2014/07/from_matteotti_to_di_matteo_la.html. (accessed 3 August 2015).

was one of the first states to recognize Cyprus's independence from the UK in 1960. By 2012, the banking sector in Cyprus accumulated deposits in excess of eight times the island nation's GDP. In addition to banking, Cyprus is also strongly dependent on tourism, making its overall economy very susceptible to symptoms of the European financial crisis.

In July 2011, an explosion at a Cypriot naval station resulted in the destruction of a power station that produced approximately half of Cyprus's electricity. This resulted in several weeks of rolling blackouts, forcing the country to import power at considerable expense. The cost to repair the station was estimated to be over €20 billion, or over ten percent of its GDP. The cost of the electricity imports and blackouts to economic output were large and partially contributed to the recession that occurred in the last half of 2011 and 2012, which, in turn, contributed to a bank crisis, requiring a bailout in 2013. Other contributing factors were the severe economic downturns in other southern European countries, especially Greece, and the second negotiated Greek bailout, which deeply affected the value of Greek bonds held by Cypriot banks. As a result, credit has dried up as have businesses.

Image 4-1: A street of empty shops in Nicosia, Cyprus, August 2015, photo by Janet Constantinides.

Cyprus is an odd case in the eurozone crisis. Although the government is sound according to Transparency International and the World Bank, it has lax banking regulations and turns a blind-eye to possible money laundering from overseas, especially from Russia. As a result, Cyprus is the only country that has had its bank depositors contribute to the bailout. That aside, it also suffered from productivity decline, an increasing trade deficit, and a housing bubble, but had no issue with national savings or its debt-to-GDP ratio.

Conclusions

In summary, the creation of the eurozone has turned out to have serious flaws resulting from the fact that it is a monetary union without a strong fiscal union. Long-term stability of the union would require strong institutional restraints necessary to achieve the sound fiscal footing. The Maastricht treaty requirements were expected to create these conditions: once the eurozone was achieved, many believed fiscal integration would follow. Fiscal pacts, however, are politically messy. While convincing countries to abdicate control of national currencies was difficult, the idea of ceding national fiscal sovereignty to a supranational organization was even more so. With so many countries and varying national ideologies, historical fears, and even national prejudices still existing in the EU, attempts to achieve such a fiscal union were stymied. With growth seeming to occur anyway, the pressure to make such politically difficult decisions faded, but the flaws in the design of the eurozone remained. Worse yet, politics also undermined adherence to Maastricht requirements. Therefore, the institutional brakes intended to ensure debt sustainability were undercut.

Table 4-4: Structural Imbalances among Troubled Countries, 2001-2007.

Country	Productivity decline relative to northern countries	Increasing trade deficit	Housing bubble	Declining National Savings	Increasing Debt/GDP	Corruption	Poor Governance
Greece	✓	✓	✓	✓	✓	✓	✓
Ireland			✓				
Portugal	✓	✓		✓	✓		
Spain	✓	✓	✓	✓		✓	✓
Italy	✓		✓			✓	✓
Cyprus	✓	✓	✓				

Despite these problems, proponents of the currency union reasoned the adoption of the euro would create the political breathing space to allow the realisation of the necessary structural reforms. Strong economic growth among many eurozone countries after the adoption of the euro also seemed to suggest that, at least among poorer countries, an economic convergence was occurring. Unfortunately, the economic growth transpiring during this period was not driven by productivity, improving investment, or market reforms, but by expanding public sectors, consumption and property bubbles. What appeared to be growth that would lead to convergence across economies was really just temporary growth induced by greater credit access – access that was in part propelled by trade imbalances between the north and the south within the eurozone. Table 4-4 below summarizes these imbalances.

Economic convergence in the eurozone required not only strong growth, but underlying productivity and competitiveness improvements to avoid structural imbalances. Achieving such improvements would require difficult internal decisions in many member countries to dismantle uncompetitive institutions that undermined their productivity, including reductions in bloated public sectors, breaking guild control of large sectors of the economy resistant to reform, and removal of public subsidies and barriers to entry in some sectors. These were politically contentious issues, and as labour unrest and riots in Greece, Italy, Portugal and Spain over austerity measures introduced throughout the crisis have shown, it is extremely difficult to reform economies where people have historically relied on such institutions.

Without such reforms, however, convergence cannot occur. The lack of movement towards such reforms, particularly in less-competitive southern countries, created significant economic imbalances. These imbalances, with respect to trade and credit flows, weakened economies and contributed to the emergence of the European financial crisis that has since caused serious unemployment and hardship, not only in southern and SPIGI countries, but in much of Europe as well. In the long-term, if the European common currency union is to be preserved, the flaws of the eurozone must be addressed in order to avoid the development of similar imbalances in the future. Doing so will require addressing the causes of the fiscal and trade imbalances present in the eurozone, and importantly, the institutional structures necessary to stabilize the currency union. Although, as Mario Draghi put it, the European currency union bumblebee was able to fly despite its apparent violation of economic theory, to continue, the bumblebee will now have to learn to fly according to the rules.

Chapter V:
Misperception of European Risk, Market Reactions and Policy Response – A Timeline of the Eurozone Crisis

Introduction

The following chapter presents a timeline of the eurozone crisis. Before the world financial crisis of 2008 and the European financial crisis that followed, optimism dominated the world in many ways. Optimism made it easier to ignore messy details of all sorts, including, in the US, the quality of the mortgages in mortgage-backed securities, and, in the EU, the structure of the European monetary union, its underlying trade and credit flows, as well as its banking and debt composition. As ECB President Mario Draghi noted in July 2012, like a bumblebee, the currency union flew even though it should not have been able to. Since the financial crises, markets have become sceptical and questioning: how and why it flies now matter. Markets must be convinced the union can survive- but can it?

In the United States, one lesson drawn from the financial crisis was that a crisis in a single sector of the economy could unleash consequences that affected the entire financial system, particularly when conditions of high leverage and debt existed. Previously, early warnings concerning real estate markets, in the US and elsewhere, were shrugged off by analysts and policymakers alike. Even in a worst-case scenario, they could not imagine their collapse would seriously affect the whole economy. The fall of Bear Stearns and, then, Lehman Brothers, followed by a cascade of financial failures and near-failures across the US economy and the world, exposed the web of debt that was built on top of the real estate sector. So intertwined is the world economy that it did indeed destabilize the entire international financial system. Given that a single economic sector in one economy could create such turmoil, what could happen if an entire country defaulted on its debts?

"Leverage", or the accumulation of debt, was the key. Debts were utilized to create assets, in this case, mortgages, and those assets were subsequently used to collateralize further borrowing. As long as confidence remained that all the underlying debts were good, the process of leveraging continued and drove increased economic activity as lending begat the ability to borrow more. When confidence faded, lending vanished, and total debt had to be reduced to match the new supply. More often than not, the unwinding of previously accumulated debt occurred through default, resulting in painful economic contractions throughout most of the developed world.[117] Financial market depth and breadth, interlocking webs of debt, and their potential effects on the larger economy would no longer be ignored.

These lessons were not lost on markets when, in late 2009, the new Greek government revealed the true state of its public finances. In Europe, the debt of Greece and other eurozone countries had similarly been leveraged into something much larger. The mistake was that sovereign debt in the eurozone had been considered nearly risk free. During the mid-2000s, a tighter convergence among eurozone country bond rates occurred, suggesting that all member countries posed similarly low risks of default, even those member countries that had previously been considered the least dependable. Reinforcing this assumption, international credit agencies also assigned eurozone members' sovereign bonds investor-grade ratings.[118] Such an interest rate convergence was consistent with a market belief that either eurozone rules would cause previously problematic countries to reform, or that commitment to the currency union would ensure that the fiscal strength of stronger northern economies, such as Germany's, would always support the previously less dependable, peripheral ones if a crisis threatened their solvency.

In hindsight, such market beliefs were clearly questionable: the rules regarding debt and deficit in member states had often been ignored, and the

---

117 The process of bubbles and deleveraging became widely understood in the 1930s. Irving Fisher (1933) coined the term debt-deflation for the effect that such unwinding would have on price levels and the economy. In the 1980s and 1990s, the idea was revisited by more recent scholars, such as Hyman Minsky (1986) and Ben Bernanke (1995), who have considered the process in the context of modern economies and financial markets. While well understood, mainstream analysts and policymakers throughout the 2000s still often ignored the potential dynamics of such a financial crisis, although a few notable exceptions existed before the US housing bubble burst in 2007. Some of the better known examples of analysts and academic researchers who did sound warnings were: Robert Shiller, who recognized both the high tech bubble in the early 2000s and the housing bubble later in the decade; Nouriel Roubini, a professor from New York University who very accurately outlined in a speech to the IMF in September 2006 the financial chain of events that would occur due to the housing bubble bursting a little over a year later; and Raghuram Rajan, a professor at the University of Chicago. Rajan presented a paper entitled "Has Financial Development made the World Riskier?" (Rajan, 2005, fhttps://www.kansascityfed.org/publicat/sympos/2005/pdf/rajan2005.pdf (accessed 3 August 2015)) at the Federal Reserve's annual Jackson Hole conference in 2005 that was politely but apparently skeptically received. In the paper, he outlined the risks of increased financial leverage. Famous analysts included Nassim Nicholas Taleb, whose book *Black Swan* detailed his earlier warnings that markets were unprepared for unexpected shocks. Several other analysts and commentaries warned of unsustainable current account deficits and consumer spending.

118 See for example *The New York Times,* "Ratings Firms misread Signs of Greek Woes," November 30, 2011 for an overview of the role of credit rating agencies. http://www.nytimes. com/2011/11/30/business/ratings-firms-misread-signs-of-greek-woes.html?_r=1&pagewanted=all (accessed 3 August 2015).

rules of the eurozone limited liability among member states for each others' debt. The Greek revelations caused markets to realize and reconsider the unrealistic assumptions that had been made and, as in the US, the change in outlook was immediately felt in credit markets. Lending to Greece evaporated; the eurozone crisis had begun.

During the period from November 2009 through December 2011, market uncertainties worsened as policy reactions proved inadequate, often ill timed, and ineffective. Far from improving, economic conditions deteriorated across the eurozone. Bailout actions meant to save the euro became deeply unpopular in both donor and recipient member states. Perceived treaty limitations constrained ECB actions, and domestic politics constrained EU strategy. The continued decline in market confidence, as exhibited by a relentless rise in EU sovereign bond interest rates, stressed the very fabric of the eurozone, threatening to tear it and the European project apart. In the end, given the price the world demanded to lend to member-state countries, the ECB chose "to do what it takes" and EU leaders adopted unpopular measures in order to save the euro, but only after more than two years of difficult negotiations and political soul-searching.

European Commission @EU_Commission · 24 Nov 2010
#Barroso: "I think it is intellectually and politically dishonest to suggest that the problem is the **euro**" http://bit.ly/hgdjzg

In some ways, the experience of European leaders during the eurozone crisis could be compared to the famous five phases of grief: denial, anger, bargaining, depression, and acceptance.[119] The crisis had come as a shock and threatened to end the currency union that had been the culmination of so many years of European integration efforts. The first reaction was one of denial. Leaders' reactions during the earliest months of the crisis were broadly similar to those seen in late 1980s and early 1990s when Europe implemented fixed exchange rate systems and market pressures emerged to destabilize these rates. As it was two decades earlier, market pressures were predicated on analyses that suggested country-specific fundamentals did not support targeted market outcomes. In the eurozone crisis, interest rates began to climb when markets realized the presence of previously unrealized risk in the sovereign debt markets for particular countries. Once this risk was realized, the price of borrowing adjusted accordingly. Denial affected the willingness of European leaders to accept the causes of the situation in late 2009. Overwhelmingly, European leaders initially blamed the US for the financial crisis, ignoring fundamental problems in their own economies. Where European blame was due, it was assigned to failures of governance in Greece and

---

119 Elisabeth Kübler-Ross, *On Death and Dying* (New York: Scribner's 1969).

not to the larger architecture of the eurozone. EU leaders' outlooks were additionally clouded by overly optimistic projections of imminent and rapid recovery in Europe from both the effects of the US crisis and those later in Greece.

IMF officials were similarly too optimistic regarding economic conditions in Europe and Greece, and underestimated the effects onerous austerity conditions would have across the eurozone.[120] The prevailing viewpoint in 2009 argued the crisis would be short-lived, even in Greece, with growth returning by 2012. Such optimism was reflected in the IMF's use of a Stand-By Arrangement (SBA), in its participation in the first Greek bailout, an arrangement that, by definition, was not to last longer than thirty-six months. By mid-2010, the IMF had already begun to realize the errors in its assessments, and began to reconsider the time that recovery would require. Reflecting that concern, its participation in later bailouts took the form, not of an SBA, but of an Extended Fund Facility, a medium-term program meant to provide assistance to countries over a longer period. Only slowly did the IMF and EU policy-makers begin to appreciate the true threat the crisis posed.

Anger, bargaining and depression – the classic second, third and fourth stages of grief – eventually followed. Anger was manifest across Europe, with eurozone leaders and residents of creditor countries unhappy with Greece initially, and resentful of Ireland and Portugal later on, while citizens of the recipient member states became angrier at the harsh and punitive terms of their aid. Many across the eurozone also seemed to resent the euro for the situation they now found themselves in. The bargaining that followed each crisis promised much; however, in each bailout, the costs seemed undersold while the prospects for success were oversold. Bargaining was ongoing as debtor states struggled to find the resources to save their struggling economies from default, and in creditor states, which were forced to work hard to sell the necessary obligations required to prop up ailing countries in an attempt to resolve the crisis.

The inevitable result was depression, which manifested itself in various ways. Emotionally, the high hopes the currency union had originally created were dashed; economically, a depression would soon exist in each of the aided countries, and even some that had not sought aid. In certain economies, that depression would turn to despair, worsening human welfare and even resulting in a spike in suicides[121] as conditions steadily deteriorated.

The final stage of grief, acceptance, characterizes the point at which eurozone policymakers began to realize effective actions would require deeper

---

120 See IMF (2013), "Greece: Ex Post Evaluation of Exceptional Access under the 2010 Stand-By Arrangement," IMF Country Report No. 13/156, International Monetary Fund.
121 David Stuckler, et al., "Effects of the 2008 recession on health: a first look at European data" *The Lancet*: 378 (9 July 2011): 124-125.

changes than those contemplated in the first two years of the crisis. Reforms would be required, not only of troubled countries, but also of creditor nations. Policies to manage the crisis would require new practices to be implemented if financial and banking stability in the eurozone were to be assured in the short-term. In the longer term, boosting market confidence might even necessitate the formation of a fiscal and banking union. Minimally, it would require greater coordination and oversight regarding the countries' fiscal debt and deficit, and the regulation of the entire union's banking system. By 2012, to preserve the euro, the architecture of the eurozone would require modification in ways that could not even have been contemplated two years earlier.

Timeline of the Crisis

Policy reactions to the eurozone crisis can be separated into two phases. The first represented an evolution of, and an increase in, the original types of policy efforts used to deal with the crisis as it degenerated during its first two years. These policy responses attempted to work within the existing structure of the eurozone and EU Treaty framework. Major policy actions were taken primarily by the eurozone member states and "the Troika", i.e., the EU Commission, aided by the ECB, and the International Monetary Fund (IMF).

The second stage occurred as a complementary set of actions that began to alter the architecture and treaty framework of the currency union, with one set of efforts undertaken by the ECB and the other by the EU Commission in cooperation with eurozone national governments. In this stage of the crisis, the ECB mostly initiated policy actions, while eurozone member states concentrated on treaty reforms meant to alter the long-term structure of the eurozone with respect to fiscal and banking sovereignty. These changes in EU structure and ECB practices would have likely been politically impossible before the crisis. However, after earlier policies that operated within the rules of the EU failed to arrest a worsening situation, a shift of outlook occurred allowing extraordinary measures to be taken.

Necessity is often the mother of invention and so EU reforms have by necessity begun to develop the greater political integration some economic theorists have argued was required since the formation of the currency union. In the following section, a chronological summary of the major events of the crisis between 2009 and 2012 are detailed. While the immediate financial crisis may have ended in the latter half of 2012, conditions in Europe have remained fragile and depressed. More policy responses have been necessary to deal with its aftermath and to avoid another crisis occurring. Some of these efforts are also described.

Image 5-1: The banner on the Berlaymont, the European Commission building in October 2011. Despite the crisis, the Commission's message to the world was pure optimism. Photo by Stephanie Anderson.

October 2009 to July 2011 – A Period of Denial, Anger, Credit Guarantees, and Bailouts

Clearly, EU leaders did not foresee the eurozone crisis coming. In 2009, many European economies appeared to be recovering from the short and sharp downturn that had followed the US financial crisis of 2008. Greek revelations and the market reaction to it caught policymakers off guard and flat-footed in their response. The first policy phase, characterized by limited reactions constrained by the exigencies of the eurosystem, persisted for the first two years of the crisis. These reactions attempted to maintain market confidence through a series of optimistic assessments that Greek (and later Irish and Portuguese) debt problems could be dealt with internally through market reforms. While markets became increasingly driven by what they perceived to be market fundamentals, i.e., country-specific economic conditions, European policymakers emphasized that the situation was under control. As conditions worsened in European sovereign debt markets, leaders tried to "talk the markets down," often listing reasons why they were overreacting. Leaders of the major European economies, particularly Germany and France, and the affected economies of Greece, Ireland and Portugal avoided even mention of the word "default", refusing to admit that new market conditions could become serious problems or that a default was a possibility.

While outwardly attempting to exude confidence, calm, and control, behind closed doors, leaders were apparently taken by surprise and angered by Greek admissions in late 2009. Negotiations to define necessary policy actions were difficult as leaders struggled to understand the implications of the crisis they faced. There was some uncertainty as to whether anything would be done at all to save Greece. For a time, markets were unconvinced any aid would be forthcoming for Greece, leading to a rapid deterioration in Greek bond rates.[122] Contributing to market uncertainty was a lack of action by leaders as market conditions worsened and policy remained undefined through early spring 2010. The new Greek government promised fundamental and wide-ranging reforms to tax collection and government expenditures, yet these promises were deemed neither credible nor sufficient to reverse the course of their sovereign debt crisis. Greek debt was too large. Meanwhile, eurozone leaders struggled to create and justify the political will necessary to support Greece. The EU had no experience in managing a sovereign debt crisis within one of its own member states. Soliciting aid from the IMF, the agency generally tasked with managing aid to countries in such crises, was considered politically embarrassing.[123] Europe was accustomed to providing aid, not requesting it.

The European public, especially in Germany, railed at the idea of their tax euros going to stabilize Greece. This backlash caused German leaders to hesitate in supporting any bailout action. Having struggled with the increased debt levels and slow growth caused by German unification, Germans argued that the principle of independence was paramount. The eurozone was intentionally designed with prohibitions against joint liability. To aid a country, especially one that had "cooked its books" in order to appear in step with Maastricht Treaty rules, would only encourage moral hazard, allowing Greece to avoid the consequences of its own decisions and poor governance.

As credit market conditions for Greece in early 2010 continued to degrade, leaders had to act. Despite popular opposition, they swallowed their pride and requested aid from the IMF as it became clear that: (i) action was necessary – Greece would definitely need external aid if it were to avoid

---

122 For example, see The Economist (2010), "A Greek bailout, and soon?," 28 January 2010 http://www.economist.com/blogs/charlemagne/2010/01/greek_bailout_within_months (accessed 3 August 2015) and IMF (2013), "Greece: Ex Post Evaluation of Exceptional Access under the 2010 Stand-By Arrangement," IMF Country Report No. 13/156, International Monetary Fund.

123 Ibid.

default; (ii) the amount of aid needed was large and would be very politically difficult to raise internally, thus requiring IMF resources; and (iii) the EU needed IMF expertise to develop a coherent policy response.[124]

Despite the distaste leaders expressed for the principle of assistance, there was really no choice. Default by Greece could potentially create a chaotic and unpredictable situation, similar to the one caused by the failure of Lehman Brothers in the United States. Europe's financial institutions were not ready to face another serious shock. They had barely recovered from the fallout following the US financial crisis.

The European/IMF response, the first of the European bailouts, arrived six months after the crisis began. The bailout plan unveiled in May 2010 by the Troika would cost €110 billion, or almost forty-eight percent of Greece's entire GDP from the previous year, and rested on three pillars:

1. Fiscal reduction: Greece would be required to reduce its fiscal deficit by 14.5 percent of GDP by 2014, a huge reduction by international standards. This would be accomplished through a series of expenditure, social benefit and pension reductions, and tax revenue increases.
2. Structural reform: Greece would be required to reduce or eliminate labour market protections, and implement productivity improvements meant to return the economy to growth by 2012.
3. Financial market stability: A dedicated set of funds would support the Greek banking system, thereby avoiding a sector collapse and providing the liquidity necessary to sustain an eventual economic recovery.

To protect Europe from the fallout of the Greek crisis, the ECB began a limited intervention in the secondary markets, buying Greek bonds in an attempt to stabilize interest rates. Intervention also began in Portuguese and Irish markets. In addition, to prevent Greek market instability from spilling over into other eurozone members, in May 2010, the EU created a financial firewall, the European Financial Stability Facility (EFSF). This temporary three-year credit facility, created specifically to address the debt crisis, provided a lending capacity of €500 billion to finance additional bailouts should they be necessary.[125]

Popular opposition to aiding a country that was considered to have fraudulently represented its finances to preserve increasingly profligate spending – spending that provided more generous social and retirement bene-

---

124 Ibid.
125 The EFSF was funded to a level of €440 billion by eurozone countries, and an additional €60 billion was made available by European Financial stability Mechanism (EFSM), a similar facility created and funded by non-euro EU countries.

fits than offered in the countries now expected to provide aid – was understandable. As interest rates fell with the introduction of the euro, debt-driven growth had led to unsustainable increases in the Greek public sector, swelling the size and pay levels of the its civil service. Simultaneously, Greek pension programs had become increasingly underfunded as entitlements became more generous and as publicly provided social benefits expanded.[126] European leaders seemed to resent the politically untenable position they had been put into: protecting the union they had worked hard to create would require aiding the country whose actions now put that union at risk. After Angela Merkel agreed to support the Greek bailout, in May 2010, her party, the Christian Democratic Union (CDU), suffered its worst defeat ever in the state election of Germany's most populous state, North Rhine-Westphalia. Popular resentment was high in Germany and stereotypes of lazy or dishonest Greeks became common in the German press.

Popular Greek anger at the situation the country found itself in was equally venomous, and was directed not only at its own government, but at the EU in general, and especially at Germany. Part of this was a reflexive response to the reactions outside the country, reviving German stereotypes in Greece and opening decades-old wounds. In a radio interview in February 2010, the Greek Deputy Prime Minister, Theodoros Pangalos, stated that Germany had never returned gold stolen from the Bank of Greece by the Nazis. Coming on the heels of a twenty-four hour general strike, he added, "I don't say they have to give back the money necessarily but they have at least to say 'thanks'."[127] Posters depicting Angela Merkel simultaneously as a seductress holding a single rose, and as a Nazi officer with a swastika surrounded by the EU circle of stars with the label "public nuisance", covered Athens. Portrayal of the eurozone crisis as a replay of World War II was ubiquitous in political cartoons and newspapers. In 2012, the newspaper, *Democracy,* led with the headline "Memorandum macht frei" or "(The bailout) Memoradum makes (you) free" in an allusion to the sign over Auschwitz.

Confidence in European sovereign debt had been irreparably impaired despite Greek aid efforts and the creation of the EFSF firewall. Instability in the financial markets soon spread as markets anticipated the need for bailouts in other troubled countries. The first of these was Ireland, where domestic financial conditions there, set off by the bursting of a vast real estate bubble three years earlier in 2007, continued to deteriorate. Given EU rules that

---

126 For a description of events see IMF (2013), "Greece: Ex Post Evaluation of Exceptional Access under the 2010 Stand-By Arrangement," IMF Country Report No. 13/156, June 2013.
127 Andrew Willis, "Germany failed to pay WWII compensation, Greece says," *EUOberver.com*, 25 February 2010, http://euobserver.com/economic/29551 (accessed 3 August 2015).

required member states to manage their banking systems independently, banking guarantees the country had made to prop up its financial system now approached thirty-five percent of GDP. Membership in the currency union meant Ireland would have to acquire the funds needed to save its banks in sovereign debt markets. Although Irish public finances had otherwise remained conservative throughout the past decade and market reforms in that economy had made it among the most competitive in Europe, the cost of borrowing became prohibitive as markets began to recognize the unsustainable position the country was in. As interest rates continued to climb, the Irish government, realizing its situation was irreconcilable, requested an €85 billion bailout in November 2010.

Markets then turned their attention to Portugal. Persistently anaemic growth throughout the previous decade, combined with high sovereign debt levels and an economy that had become less and less competitive as the government failed to enact productivity reforms, resulted in market concerns with ten-year sovereign bond rates rising above ten percent. With a rapidly deteriorating economy and ballooning government deficit, Portugal was correspondingly forced to seek a €78 billion aid package in May 2011. The IMF and EU financed both the Irish and Portuguese bailouts jointly, the latter's aid provided through the new EFSF. Each aid package was based on the same principles Greek aid had been. In return for aid, the country pledged to take on onerous austerity measures. Portugal, like Greece, promised significant structural reforms to make its economy more competitive. In both cases, markets anticipated the need for bailouts months before authorities admitted their necessity. Again, delays occurred for the same reasons as they had in Greece. Contributing countries' electorates rapidly began to suffer from 'bailout' fatigue, as the expansive and expensive credit guarantees were unsuccessful in stemming market pressures. Delays in addressing the problem swiftly and soundly left markets doubting whether the eventual actions taken were enough to stem the tide of the financial contagion now washing over Europe.

Bailouts were intended as a final solution to restore market confidence. Financed by credit guarantees from northern countries, the same countries also demanded stiff austerity conditions in return for aid. Austerity programs, characterized by sharp reductions in government expenditures for pensions, income support, social programs, and public sector workforces, plus state asset sales, played two roles. For bond markets, they were meant to signal reforms and budgetary changes that would ensure future debt stability, allowing credit markets to reopen. In addition, austerity programs addressed the question of moral hazard: if northern economies were to risk their own reserves, the recipient countries would have to engage in permanent reform, especially of any profligate spending practices.

Despite these efforts, however, market pressures continued. Bailout measures, as significant as they were, totalling almost fifty percent of the combined 2009 GDP of the aided countries, did not restore market confidence. Instead, actions seemed "too little and too late". Markets were more impressed by the frictions in implementing these policies – i.e., the denials and delays caused by political scepticism and populist anger in creditor countries that impeded the Troika's efforts – than by the funds themselves.

The progression of interest rate increases, followed by bailouts, followed by concerns arising in a new country is reflected in the pattern of interest rate increases. In each case, a bailout in one country that was intended to arrest the crisis only caused market concerns to focus elsewhere. Eventually, market concerns returned to Greece. Interest rates there continued to rise as markets correctly reasoned the resources pledged in the first bailout were inadequate. Austerity programs that appeared only to create greater recessions in troubled countries led to civil unrest and greater uncertainty. At the same time, they also contributed to a deteriorating economy, causing greater declines in state revenues and worsening debt sustainability. To tame markets, the EU would have to change its approach.

July to December 2011: A Period of Bargaining and Depression as the Economic Crisis Evolves into a Political One

The end of the first phase of the crisis could be defined as occurring when EU leaders began to realize palliative actions were not enough. Austerity measures, social unrest, and political uncertainty had plunged the Greek economy into a far worse recession than the IMF and EU had forecast.[128] Austerity also had similar effects in Ireland and Portugal, especially in the months following their bailouts. These recessions, combined with the uncertainty that now lay like a grey cloud over all of Europe, worsened economic conditions throughout the eurozone. The crisis was not to be short-lived.

As conditions worsened and time went on, leaders realized that treating the symptoms of the crisis was not enough: they would now have to consider creating new EU structures to better deal with the crises and to prevent them in the future. In late 2010, plans were made to implement a permanent eurozone bailout fund through treaty reforms, to replace the EFSF when it expired in mid-2013. The ECB also began to use its ability to support markets through bond purchases in ways that had not been undertaken previously.

---

[128] In a later reappraisal, the IMF reported that it ignored its own internal rules in supporting a bailout to a bankrupt country. Further, it admitted that estimates of the costs to the Greek economy of the austerity measures the first bailout imposed were underestimated. See IMF (2013), "Greece: Ex Post Evaluation of Exceptional Access under the 2010 Stand-By Arrangement," IMF Country Report No. 13/156, International Monetary Fund.

Additionally, the Troika began to consider new means to deal with the crisis, including allowing private creditors, who had been previously protected in bailout efforts in an attempt to maintain bond-market confidence, to realize losses on sovereign bonds.

Greater resources were needed, leading to an understanding that some cost would have to be borne by the private sector regardless of the immediate effects it might create in bond markets. Such measures were both ethically and economically imperative if the crisis were to be long lasting. The Troika now began to consider how they would officially require what would soon be referred to in official documents as "private sector involvement" or PSI in bailout agreements. Unofficially, these efforts have been referred to as debt "haircuts" or bail-ins; those who owned the bonds would now suffer some losses in return for having the rest of the original investment preserved. Although considered previously, it only became official policy when formally announced as part of the second Greek bailout, in July 2011.[129] Supported by the IMF, where the practice was common in IMF-sponsored bailouts elsewhere in the world, the ECB and some EU members of the Troika had resisted the idea during the first phase of the crisis, arguing the threat of private sector losses could further destabilize markets, undermining the purpose of aid efforts. Considering additional resources were needed to stabilize Greece as part of a larger agreement, such concerns were overruled. This important policy decision, however, was only the first in a lengthy negotiation to resolve the second aid package for Greece.

The voters took out their anger on those in charge. In Ireland and Portugal, bailouts were followed by the collapse of the ruling governments, while in Greece the bailout was followed by an immediate drop in support of the newly elected one. Creditor states' electorates suffered from bailout fatigue. Critics, in Germany and elsewhere, argued these efforts violated the terms of the Maastricht Treaty, specifically the prohibitions against countries taking on liability for another country's debt. While such arguments fell upon deaf ears as legislation passed national parliaments and was upheld in German constitutional courts, criticism remained vocal as opponents saw both bailouts and ECB market interventions as contraventions of EU treaties in principle, if not technically.[130] For many, bailouts implied the breaking of a

---

129 So called 'haircuts' on privately held debt had apparently been discussed since at least October of 2010, when comments regarding this option were leaked to the press at an EU summit in Deauville.

130 In Germany, there have been several challenges to the bailouts. Terms of the bailouts have been debated fiercely before being passed by the German Parliament. On 7 September 2011, the German constitutional court ruled against a challenge brought by a coalition of economists, business executives, and lawmakers who had argued that the terms of the bailouts undermined Parliament's ability to determine government spending and budgetary planning.

moral principle, one in which debtors should be exclusively responsible for their own obligations and the consequences of not meeting them. Detractors of bailout efforts argued they soley created moral hazard, protecting both member states who had taken on too much debt, and private investors who financed them from the risk these decisions implied, protecting them from the discipline of the market and encouraging such eventual behaviour again.

Image 5-2: A mural sponsored by the Berlin Artist Program displayed on a building near Oranienburger Strasse from 2011-2012. Photo by Stephanie Anderson.

Given the fact that Greece would require greater support to remain solvent, creditor nations faced a deeper dilemma. Without additional assistance, Greece faced default. Fallout from such an event would pose significant risk to Europe's financial system, especially to France and Germany, the largest creditor nations, whose banks still had the greatest exposure to Greek debt. Electorates and leaders in creditor countries, particularly in Germany, however, had tired of the possibility of continued calls for aid knowing that should it come, they would carry the greatest burden. Voices in Germany and elsewhere began to ask whether such efforts were worthwhile or merely postponing the inevitable – a default. Should a "Grexit", a Greek exit from the euro, just be allowed? The eurozone had to decide whether it was committed to keeping Greece in the currency union. Similarly, Greece had to decide whether it was committed to the conditions staying in the eurozone required. This question would dominate discussions for the next eight months of the crisis from the summer of 2011 through early spring 2012.

The second phase of the crisis marked a period of significantly greater uncertainty as the politics of continued aid worsened. When the initial framework of a new Greek bailout agreement was announced in July of 2011, sovereign debt markets were initially calmed, and bond rates began to fall. As negotiations dragged on into autumn 2011 between the Troika and Greece, it appeared increasingly questionable whether there was the political will to find any solution at all. In Greece, austerity protests worsened. Speculation began to mount as to whether the Greeks themselves would elect to default and leave the euro in order to avoid accepting the greater austerity conditions additional aid would require. Targets mandated in the original aid package regarding tax collection and public workforce cuts in Greece were missed. In creditor nations, leaders were frustrated, suspecting Greek unwillingness and inability to deliver the promised reforms and deficit reductions demanded in the first bailout. Some began to wonder whether instead of Greece leaving the euro, Germany would instead, as the inevitable burden of bailouts appeared to increase.[131] Negotiations became bogged down with recriminations regarding each other's dedication to the European project and the euro.

In the background, bond rates had begun to rise across the southern European states as concerns worsened regarding Spanish and Italian debt, especially given the new policy of bondholder losses that had been invoked. Urged by Europe and the United States, these two countries began pre-emptive austerity programs of their own to reverse rising deficits. In an effort to stabilize the situation in their sovereign bond markets, the ECB also expanded its Securities Markets Program (SMP) begun in May 2010, increasing purchases of Spanish and Italian bonds in August 2011 despite objections from Bundesbank officials in Frankfurt. German protests against these new efforts became so vocal that court challenges were threatened in Germany, and Jürgen Stark, the influential Bundesbank representative on the ECB's Executive Committee, sometimes referred to as its "chief economist", resigned his appointment in symbolic protest.[132] Observers of the crisis began

---

131 Ambrose Evans-Pritchard, the influential international business editor of *The Daily Telegraph* (London) was one of the first to suggest this option. See "Should Germany bail out Club Med or leave the euro altogether?" *Daily Telegraph*, 31 January 2010, http://www.telegraph.co.uk/finance/comment/7119986/Should-Germany-bail-out-Club-Med-or-leave-the-euro-altogether.html (accessed 3 August 2015).

132 There is no such official position as the "chief economist" of the ECB, however Stark's position as the Executive Board member responsible for Monetary Analysis is often referred to in this way. Stark announced his intent to resign in protest in September 2011.

to question whether the willingness to preserve the monetary union was even present among the policy makers tasked with preserving it.

By mid-September, consensus among eurozone members appeared to be breaking down. As conditions worsened in debt markets for troubled countries, the European Commission proposed collectivizing European debt using Eurobonds, bonds that could be swapped for individual nation's debts and backed by the entire eurozone. Eurobond plans called for explicitly backing the debt of troubled nations collectively, by using the resources of the entire eurozone and the strong credit ratings of northern states to restore market confidence by removing the possibility of a default. They also, however, would spread the liability for such debts jointly across the member states. Germany, among other countries, was staunch in its opposition to such proposals, arguing that such actions would not only violate the terms of the Maastricht Treaty, but would further create moral hazard in aided countries, reducing the pressure to enact the difficult economic reforms necessary to increase productivity.[133] Opinion polls indicated a great variance of support for Eurobonds across member state electorates, ranging from a high of sixty-seven percent in Belgium to a low of a mere twenty-six percent in Germany.[134] When France publicly backed German opposition to such plans, the proposals were quietly dropped. Without the resources and official support of Europe's two largest economies, it would be impossible for this proposal to be considered.

The Eurobond controversy demonstrated the strength of one member state's – Germany – influence over EU policy. Merkel championed a diet of fiscal rectitude for other EU countries, a policy that sat well with her ruling CDU/CSU coalition as well as perhaps with her Lutheran upbringing:

Purchases of sovereign debt had actually started in May 2010, but on a very limited scale. The decision in August of 2011 expanded the powers to do so. His resignation followed the resignation of Germany's head of the Bundesbank (the German central bank) Axel Weber over the same measures. In addition to being opposed to the use of monetary policy to reduce pressure on international interest rates for troubled countries, both men had argued previously that such efforts violated the ECB's prohibition of buying country's sovereign debt and also believed the ECB's political independence was being undermined in the face of political pressures due to the debt crisis. The ECB argued that the actions were an attempt to stabilize financial markets, a responsibility within its mandate. Unlike quantitative easing actions in the United States, these purchases did not result in an increase in the money supply as the ECB sterilized these purchases with offsetting bond sales.

133 France also opposed this policy, however, internally it appeared the proposal had much more traction in France than in Germany.

134 Eurobarometer 78, "Europeans, the EU and the Crisis," (Autumn 2012): 40, http://ec.europa.eu/public_opinion/archives/eb/eb78/eb78_cri_en.pdf. (accessed 3 August 2015).

Image 5-3: Grafitti on the Bank of Greece located on 22 Panepistimiou Street in Athens on 10 February 2012. Photo by Nick LaBonde.

If Ms. Merkel refuses to support so-called euro bonds, it is not because it would be like giving free money to the undeserving poor, but because it would not help the redeemed poor take responsibility for their own houses and grow strong for both themselves and their needy neighbors. He who receives, recovers, and profits from society in a time of need has a moral responsibility to pay society back by acting in turn as a strong citizen who can help fill the common chests and sacrifice for his now needy neighbors, who had once helped him. Such is the sacrificial Lutheran society.[135]

Without any other alternatives, German opposition to Eurobonds made it difficult to deal with the immediate bond market issues that besieged European countries in trouble. While outspoken in their opposition to Eurobonds, Germany did eventually agree to a second Greek bailout. Merkel easily won a confidence vote over the decision, although the debate highlighted the political tightrope she was walking within Germany despite her tough stances at European negotiations.

---

[135] Steven Ozement, "German Austerity's Lutheran Core," *The New York Times*, August 11, 2012, http://www.nytimes.com/2012/08/12/opinion/sunday/in-euro-crisis-germany-looks-to-martin-luther.html?_r=0 (accessed 3 August 2015).

Across southern Europe, protests and violent confrontations became more common as austerity policies now gripping these countries affected more and more people. The austerity costs of the previous bailout agreements led to a political backlash in Portugal, and, additionally in Spain and Italy, where austerity efforts had also been undertaken to reduce pressures in their own sovereign debt markets. In Greece, support for Prime Minister George Papandreou's government quickly eroded. Negotiations over the new bailout continued into the autumn despite the apparent agreement the previous July. As fiscal targets were missed, eurozone creditors demanded greater cuts. The Greeks argued that the same austerity measures were responsible for plunging the economy deeper into its current recession, forcing the government to miss its fiscal goals. Critics in Europe countered that easing austerity would only encourage moral hazard. Both sides had logic on their side, however only one had the resources. The golden rule of finance was inevitably invoked – "he who has the gold makes the rules" – but as might be expected, this reality only created additional political resentment.

Despite the fact that a Greek default would almost certainly result in a financial crisis across Europe, countries appeared to hesitate in their efforts to quell the situation. In July 2011, an agreement in principle was announced, but the debate over the details dragged on. Some of the aid promised in the first Greek bailout became a casualty of this inaction. By late summer, speculation was much louder regarding whether an agreement would ever be reached, and some suggested that Greece would be forced to default and leave the euro altogether.

Markets became even more unsettled and rates continued to rise as summer 2011 ended, and the ECB continued its limited intervention into the bond markets, expanding purchases of Spanish and Italian sovereign bonds. Despite these efforts, market conditions for Spanish, Portuguese, Greek, and Italian debt continued to deteriorate, as did the economic conditions across much of Western Europe.

The threat of Italy presented the eurozone with especially grave concerns. Its economy faced severe structural problems, with significant reforms considered necessary to reduce the size of its public sector, open its economy to competition, and liberalize its labour markets to generate greater competitiveness with its European trade partners. Internal politics under successive Berlusconi governments had not resulted in significant economic reforms. The size of the country's debt-to-GDP ratio, while having fallen in the past decade, was still quite large, making Italy extremely vulnerable to increased interest rates that could render the debt unsustainable. Generating 16.8 percent of eurozone output, Italy's economy was almost three times larger than that of Greece, Ireland, and Portugal combined. Using IMF figures from September 2011, Italy's total public debt was over €1.9 trillion ($2.4 trillion in US dollars), larger than the combined annual economic output of twelve of the sixteen other nations in the eurozone, and dwarfing the collective liabilities of Greece, Ireland and Portugal, which totalled €693 billion in the same period. In late summer 2011, the eurozone was stretched politically to support the bailouts already incurred. If Italy were to become unable to support its debts in private markets, EU resources would not be large enough simply to create another bailout. In other words, if Italy fell, the eurozone would, too.

These concerns added to those already troubling markets. As the autumn of 2011 wore on, every day that went by without a Greek deal being reached increased uncertainty and undermined world confidence that Europe would be able to address its problems, or that EU leaders even had control of the situation. Concerns grew deeper that Greece might actually default, as inaction on the part of the Troika to finalize Greece's debt relief suggested a breakup of the eurozone might be imminent. Time appeared to be running out as pending debt payments loomed, and Greece did not have the resources to meet them. Without a deal in place, Europe would not follow through on the previously promised funds that were necessary to avoid a default. Politics, not economics, seemed to be driving the decision making process, and the result was falling bond and stock markets across Europe.

As anxieties grew more shrill, negotiations finally culminated in an eleventh hour deal in late October over the final weekend that Greece had left to come to an agreement. The new bailout arrangement between the Troika and Greece had been difficult to negotiate for both sides. While greeted with relief and approval in most of Europe, the reaction in Greece was not nearly as kind. With a majority of Greeks opposed, the deal was met with outrage in Greece for the additional austerity measures it imposed.[136] In a twist, only four days after the deal was announced and faced with greater opposition than had been expected domestically, Greece's prime minister appeared to back away from the deal, suggesting that acceptance would require a national referendum. European response was immediate and incredulous. Papandreou's reversal seemed only to underline Troika concerns that the Greeks were unwilling partners in the aid efforts being made to avoid a Greek default. The suggestion of a bailout referendum was eventually withdrawn, but the damage was done. The Greek government's indecision was also punished; while it narrowly won a vote of no confidence in the first week of November, negotiations to heal the fractures within the governing party by forming a unity government also failed. As a result, no political party would take power since doing so would require administering the painful bailout

---

136 Polls over the weekend, after the deal was reached, suggested as many as sixty percent of Greeks opposed the deal or thought it would be bad for the country. Reports like this one were common. http://www.reuters.com/article/2011/10/31/us-greece-referendum-idUSTRE 79U5PQ20111031 (accessed 30 November 2014.)

commitments. With the public now blaming establishment politicians in both parties for the troubles the country found itself in, no party wanted to be associated with the controversial bailout.

The result was the imposition of an unelected, technocratic government charged with implementing previously agreed to bailout terms and negotiating a new agreement. It would serve until new elections could be held the following spring. Bailout conditions remained unresolved, and public anger in Greece only worsened as many people felt democracy had been suspended. Politics had also become more uncertain, and, suddenly, it appeared as if democracy might be coming apart in southern Europe as elected governments seemed to be exchanged for unelected ones. Cynics in Greece and elsewhere complained that Berlin and Brussels were now deciding not just economic policy, but governments as well.

These complaints were amplified when almost simultaneously the Italian government fell while the drama of the Greek negotiations and government's failure still dominated the news. Although ostensibly committed to reducing its debt level, the Italian government had failed to implement promised reforms. In what appeared a populist bid for support, prime minister Silvio Berlusconi began to question publicly the austerity calls the Troika were making in exchange for aid elsewhere. Again, the eurozone was taken by surprise as Italy was expected to cooperate in presenting a common EU-Troika front as negotiations continued with Greece. Berlusconi's tactics seemed to backfire, however, when opponents of the Italian government took advantage of the public's disapproval and decreasing support for the sitting government and engineered an unsuccessful budgetary vote. The negative result forced Berlusconi to step down in a matter of days. Events that followed his step down mirrored events in Greece only days before.

As in Athens, once more opposition parties in Italy were unwilling to take the reins of power to implement what were certain to be unpopular policies in the midst of the greater crisis in Europe. Italy's ruling government was also replaced by a technocratic one, with a mandate extending to the next election in 2013. Its leader, former European commissioner Mario Monti, portrayed himself as an agreeable partner in attempting to stabilize the crisis. Like the interim administration in Greece, the new Italian government's charge was to implement the austerity measures and market reforms necessary to maintain the country's perceived debt sustainability, which had been eroded both by a worsening recession and rising bond rates, and now political crisis. Again, those bearing the costs of austerity wondered whether democracy had been suspended and whether their interests were being sacrificed for those elsewhere.

Political dramas continued across southern Europe. The government of Spain fell a week after the Italian government did. Deeply unpopular, the sitting government was defeated in an election landslide over its management of the economy, which was widely blamed for both the recession that had occurred after the Spanish real estate bubble had burst in 2007, and for the austerity measures implemented to appease sovereign bond pressures. By the end of November 2011, three governments had fallen in less than a month. In less than a year, the crisis had taken down all five SPIGI governments, each failing due to the political fallout of austerity actions taken to earn Troika aid and seemingly made necessary by credit market conditions. These political upheavals only reinforced the political discontent spreading across Europe. In each case, from the first bailout in Greece to the bailouts that followed in Ireland and Portugal, after the voluntary actions taken in Italy and Spain through to the second bailout agreement for Greece, and all the efforts in between to calm markets, quite the opposite had happened. Actions taken to address the crisis seemingly only made it worse, and far from reducing uncertainty, confidence in the monetary union's future grew more pessimistic.

December 2011 to March 2013: A Period of Acceptance – Recognizing the Need for Structural Reforms

As the end of the year drew near, the events of 2011 had left the European continent unsure of its future. Markets were more uncertain after a year of efforts to address the financial crisis than at the beginning almost twelve months earlier. Politics had grown more and more acrimonious between "Club Med" southern states and their northern creditors. Not only were EU leaders challenged to find workable agreements among countries, they were also constrained by their own domestic politics, which were becoming increasingly resentful of the bailout efforts. In the north, the tolerance for greater accommodation of their troubled southern neighbours, particularly in Germany, Austria, and Finland, was quickly running out, as was their patience to see meaningful reform. In Mediterranean countries, resentment was growing too, at the increasing pain austerity measures were inflicting on society, as pensions and social programs were cut while recessions worsened. Street protests in Spain, Portugal, and especially Italy had become larger, more vocal, and more violent, making the negotiations to stem the crisis that much more difficult.

As the crisis degenerated, the "blame game" poisoned politics across the continent, serving no useful purpose. Whoever was responsible, the mistakes leading up to the crisis could not be undone. Many began to argue more loudly that to recreate confidence in the markets, deeper structural reforms that both addressed the problems that led to the crisis and signified a greater commitment to the union, were necessary.

The first signal of this change came with the ECB in December 2011. Throughout the crisis, although conservative in its approach, critics claimed its actions violated fundamental principles that were argued to be at the core of the monetary union. The ECB had been modelled on the German Bundesbank, and like the Bundesbank before it, it was expected by many, especially those in Germany, to remain politically independent, and committed to only one goal – stabilizing prices and the currency. Independence in this case implied avoiding any discretionary actions that might ease political conditions or be seen to interfere with market outcomes to favour member states. Actions the previous summer to support Spain and Italy on international bond markets had been seen by some to cross that line. Pundits of European policy, however, had complained loudly, especially in the British and US press that the bank could do much more if it would only release itself from the shackles of its perceived role as a passive central bank. Specifically, these critics wanted the central bank to act more forcefully, like the Federal Reserve had in the United States in 2008.

As financial crises cause banks to become illiquid, banks become unable to borrow due to market fears regarding their solvency, and such fears tend to become self-fulfilling. Banks fail as they cannot obtain financing to cover their debt obligations despite the fact that they may be fundamentally sound. The potential means to arrest such crises had been known since the 1870s when Walter Bagehot wrote *Lombard Street*. That account described how a central bank, acting as a lender of last resort, could arrest financial crises by providing massive quantities of liquidity into financial markets.[137] Such actions, he argued, reverse the destructive expectations process causing the crisis by restoring its liquidity and faith in the financial system, thus allowing it to function once again. Used successfully in numerous financial crises since, including in the United States in 2008, it appeared the financial markets would only be satisfied if the central bank in Europe followed the script that had worked so often before. Previous efforts had been too little, too late; only something far more impressive could staunch bleeding in European financial markets now.

Doubts regarding the euro's future were leading deposits to flee troubled and weaker countries' banks for those in stronger countries such as Germany, or causing deposits to flee the union altogether. The euro continued its fall in international currency markets as confidence dwindled that it would survive. Credit markets within Europe had dried up, and this lack of lending was turning a financial crisis into a full-blown recession as businesses were starved of the credit they needed to operate or expand. Rising unemployment and worsening demand only made conditions worse as investors became increasingly unwilling to take business risks in Europe. Finally, these same effects were worsening sovereign bond markets across much of the continent, and especially for those countries that faced worsening banking conditions as

---

137 Walter Bagehot, *Lombard Street*, (New York: Scribner, Armstong & Co, 1873).

investors began to consider which country might be next to suffer a banking crisis like those seen in Ireland and Portugal.

In 2011, the 'too big to fail' and 'too big to bail' countries, Spain and Italy, had begun having difficulty in their bond markets. ECB bond-buying efforts in the late summer of 2011 had only slowed this for a time, but, as the year ended, conditions again began to deteriorate as interest rates on Italian and Spanish sovereign debt climbed ever higher. Banks in troubled SPIGI economies, in particular, were known to have significant amounts of debt due early in the New Year, and credit markets had almost dried up as financial institutions anticipated the credit scarcity this would cause. Under current conditions, it did not appear that financing this amount of debt would be possible, and market analysts had already begun the process of predicting which banks were likely to fail when the inevitable credit crunch came in early 2012.

Market watchers feared these failures could tip new countries into crisis, particularly Italy and Spain. It seemed clear that the resources and willingness to address such bailouts, should they occur, had been exhausted over the previous year. In fact, given the scale of these economies, there could likely never have been the resources to address failures of the magnitude these countries would represent.

The second phase of the crisis, one in which Europe began to address the crisis in new and more creative ways, began on 21 December 2011. On this day, and to the surprise of the markets, the ECB began leveraging its options as a central bank in ways that were not used during the first two years of the crisis, and on a much more massive scale. To address the financial concerns now roiling markets, particularly the concerns regarding the large amounts of debt that would have to be financed in the New Year, the ECB unexpectedly announced a bold new lending program, one meant to eliminate such concerns on the market, not just for a short time, but for good. Opening its massive purse, the ECB allowed banks across the euro-area access to three-year low-interest loans, referred to officially as the ECB's Long Term Refinancing Operation (LTRO). These loans allowed banks to refinance the debt obligations coming due, neatly avoiding what appeared to be an impending financial crisis. They also allowed financial institutions the ability to earn income by using lower interest loans to purchase higher yielding sovereign debt in their own countries, which reduced pressures in sovereign debt markets as well. The scale of the loans was unprecedented: in the course of twenty-four hours, almost half a trillion euros in credit was extended to beleaguered European banks.

The injection of liquidity the ECB's actions represented immediately caused market concerns to ease and eurozone sovereign bond rates to decline. While the crisis was by no means thought to be over, 2011 ended on an optimistic note that few would have thought possible less than two weeks before.

To emphasize its willingness to stabilize the crisis, a second round of loans was offered in February 2012, and together, the two actions poured more than €1 trillion into eurozone banks. This unprecedented ECB effort to restore liquidity to eurozone financial institutions seemed to be the type of effort the markets had been looking for. Whereas only weeks before, many market watchers had written off the euro and anticipated its failure as only a matter of time, like the new shoots of spring beginning to emerge from winter's darkness across Europe, there seemed to be new hope that the crisis could yet find a solution. The LTRO succeeded, allowing credit markets to loosen and sovereign bond rates to decline, giving the eurozone some much needed breathing space to develop longer-term policies.

The change in the ECB's role seemed to coincide with its new leader Mario Draghi taking the reins of the bank. An Italian, educated in economics in the United States, he had taken over the previous November for Jean-Claude Trichet, who had presided over the bank since 2003. Trichet had long defended the bank's conservative approach to the crisis, and, earlier in the summer of 2011, had even presided over the ECB raising interest rates twice, which actually reduced liquidity in the eurozone, to combat what he saw as an inflation threat in countries such as Germany.[138] These actions had many market observers suggesting that the ECB had not taken the threat the crisis posed to Europe's credit markets seriously enough. They argued the ECB was doing exactly the opposite of what was needed given the crisis. Draghi's elevation to the post of ECB president had increased hopes that he would oversee a bank charting a different course. The LTRO efforts marked this sea change. The reduction of ECB interest rates Draghi had presided over in the weeks since his appointment had also stoked such hopes, but the massive injection the LTRO actions represented were a turning point. Coupled with the fact that they were an example of using extraordinary and non-traditional means to combat the market turmoil, these actions were interpreted by many observers as signaling the ECB was now willing to use its considerable financial power to take a much more active role in arresting the crisis.

---

138 In fact, Trichet had argued that eurozone governments needed to rein in deficits. His move to raise interest rates was seen as ending what he argued might be perceived as too generous support of eurozone economies. The decision to raise interest rates suggested that the bank would remain vigorously independent of concerns regarding economic conditions and the potential effects of the financial crisis, and would instead follow its price stability mandate. This increase in interest rates is now widely regarded as having been premature, and two days after Draghi assumed office, the ECB promptly reduced rates by a quarter percent on 3 November 2011, and then again on 8 December 2011. These changes fully reversed the interest rate increases made under Trichet in April and July 2011. Between July 2012 and September 2014 the ECB continued to lower interest rates to what was considered the absolute minimum possible – a level of 0.05 percent (nearly zero).

The ECB actions and the effects these had on credit markets also allowed EU leaders some breathing room to reconsider their policy strategy. Whereas during the first phase of the crisis from 2009 to the end of 2011, EU policy had focused on stemming immediate issues – reacting to sovereign debt problems in markets with bailouts and bail-ins, and developing a firewall to shield additional countries should the contagion in sovereign debt markets spread – in the second phase of the crisis, the EU would now focus on addressing the long-term problems that had contributed to it in the first place. The strategy utilized such efforts as a one-two punch in combination with the ECB efforts to attempt to convince markets they could control the crisis.

To show their new commitment to ensuring that such a crisis could not happen again, and to reinforce their commitment to fiscal discipline, the eurozone countries devised a new "fiscal compact", in which all members agreed to enact national legislation requiring limits on national debt and deficits. Specifically, the compact required eurozone countries to implement constitutional-level laws requiring their structural deficits not exceed one-half of one percent of a country's GDP and to agree to mandated debt reductions if the debt-to-GDP ratios exceeded the Maastricht maximum of sixty percent.[139] Exceptions would only be allowed under special circumstances and would require the approval of the European Commission. The agreement came into force in January 2013.

The ECB's LTRO actions had also allowed the EU to take additional actions to strengthen the union against adverse conditions in the future. During this period of calm, the Troika concluded a comprehensive new Greek aid plan in February 2012. Worth €130 billion, the package included significant new austerity actions, and required additional structural reforms and privatization of Greek government assets. The agreement also included strong conditionality, specifying the Greek actions to be implemented before funding payments could be released. Funds would be disbursed to a kind of international escrow account to ensure they were used as specified. Previously announced private sector "haircuts" imposed losses to private bondholders of 53.5 percent in a debt-buyback financed by the EFSF. Overall, the agreement decreased Greek debt by an estimated €110 billion, and allowed the plan to lower the Greek debt-to-GDP ratio from a forecasted level of 198 percent to

---

139 The structural deficit refers to the deficit occurring after accounting for expenditures demanded by the business cycle – the deficit that would occur if the economy was at full employment. For example, increases in unemployment and social benefits costs in a recession would be netted out of a structural deficit computation. The compact basically reinforced the Maastricht limits of three percent deficits and a sixty percent debt-GDP goal, creating stronger rules to ensure countries could not ignore these limits. All countries had to pass national legislation to agree to these rules and the Compact came into effect when twelve states had ratified the rule, which occurred after Finland did so in January 2013.

160 percent in 2012, and predicted a decline to 120.5 percent by 2020.[140] In March 2012, the eurozone also finalized the implementation of its permanent bailout fund, a lending capacity worth €500 billion called the European Stability Mechanism (ESM), to replace the EFSF that was due to expire in June 2013.[141]

As 2012 marched on, however, the period of calm that characterized the spring began to fade, precipitated by a series of rapid political and financial shocks. In what followed, the necessity of a more activist ECB was confirmed. The comparative tranquillity of markets in the first months of the new year would soon be shattered by a perfect storm of new political challenges that would eventually make the instability of late 2011 seem less dramatic in comparison. It is unclear whether these challenges could have been overcome without the willingness of the ECB to become much more actively engaged than many thought it was ever intended to be.

Two political shocks dominated events in the crisis only a few weeks following the successful negotiation of the final Greek aid package. While the governments had changed in all of the SPIGI countries by the end of 2011, the first major change in creditor countries occurred May 2012. French elections resulted in the defeat of the French president Nicolas Sarkozy. Sarkozy and Germany's chancellor Angela Merkel, leaders of the eurozone's two largest economies, nicknamed in the press 'Merkozy', had previously combined their political and economic power to guide eurozone policy since the crisis in Greece first began. Merkel went so far as to endorse Sarkozy's re-election even before he had announced it himself – a move that was out of the ordinary in a union where national sovereignty and independence was a fundamental principle. Sarkozy had seemed a bit embarrassed by Merkel's diplomatic gesture, remarking, "I did not know she voted in France."[142] In any case, the people did not oblige. The replacement of Sarkozy with the newly elected socialist president François Hollande, whose party was not allied with chancellor Merkel's policies, broke this political association, leaving Germany alone as the dominant voice of eurozone creditor countries and sharply reducing German potential political influence. Witticisms abounded as to whether Merkel would like her policy with a "sauce Hol-

---

140 See Eurogroup Statement, February 21, 2012. National central banks and states in the in the EU, including the ECB holding Greek bonds were exempt from the write-down. Profits made on these debts were to be allocated to the bailout.
141 Actual funds allocated to the ESM, including funds previously allocated to the EFSF, as well as funds allocated in previous bailout actions, were expected to total €700 billion, with €200 billion kept as a capital reserve.
142 William Boston and William Horobin, "Merkel to Back Sarkozy in Re-Election," *The Wall Street Journal*, 30 January 2012 .http://online.wsj.com/news/articles/SB10001424052970204740904577190293163105890 (accessed 3 August 2015).

lande-aise" – a reference to the anticipated compromises she might now have to accept.

Sarkozy's electoral defeat occurred on the same day as elections in Greece. Widely viewed as a de facto referendum on the second Greek bailout and Greece's willingness to remain in the eurozone, the results of the election were inconclusive; no party was able to create a ruling coalition. Voters, clearly frustrated by the deep austerity measures imposed on their economy, punished the usual mainstream parties by instead supporting many more populist and anti-bailout candidates than had been expected. Results of the election underscored concerns that the Greeks might not have the capacity or willingness to abide by the most recent bailout agreement or the willingness to commit to measures that avoided default. In reaction to the election, market sentiments shifted as optimism again evaporated. Markets began to prepare for a potential "Grexit". A period of uncertainty followed while a second election was held culminating in a vote six weeks later.

The resulting narrow victory by parties supporting the bailout allowed a thin majority coalition government to be formed. While the results of the second election were widely interpreted as confirming Greek willingness to remain in the eurozone, the lack of a result in the first election and the tenuous nature of the resulting ruling coalition after the second did not reassure markets. Lingering uncertainty remained. The election ambiguity also proved financially costly, delaying the implementation of the Greek bailout reforms required in the second agreement reached three months earlier, causing markets to worry further whether Greece could accept the terms required to remain in the currency union.

As if these shocks were not enough, in quick succession, a third test of the eurozone occurred in June 2012, even before the Greek elections were resolved. While attention was centred on the Greek elections, it also became clear that Spain would require a significant recapitalization of several of its largest banks. Despite ongoing efforts, the country was unable to finance sustainably the required resources needed to stabilize its banking system. The result was a new request for aid in the eurozone. Apprehensions regarding the continuing threat of a default in Greece, and now a financial crisis in Spain, had a contagious effect on Italian sovereign debt markets, and bond rates for Italy soon began to climb. Within a period of two months, the eurozone had moved from a period of relative calm to conditions in which three simultaneous threats had now emerged: an unresolved election in Greece; a banking crisis in Spain; and now a potentially looming sovereign debt crisis in Italy. In addition, the election loss of Nicholas Sarkozy in France left overall EU leadership in doubt.

Conditions were different at this stage from what they had been in years past. Unlike previous aid negotiations, Spain, as the fourth largest economy in the eurozone, found it commanded significant bargaining power over the terms of any bailout due to its economic size. Unlike Greece, Ireland, and Portugal, its size meant that it had to be dealt with swiftly as the threat it posed to Europe's financial system was an order of magnitude larger than the others. The narrative was also somewhat different. Although Spain had borrowed heavily during its housing boom, it had also pre-emptively implemented significant austerity measures and was committed to important structural reforms as it attempted to address the challenges the crisis had posed. Its debt relative to GDP was rising quickly, but was not yet at the levels seen in previously troubled countries.

The problem became how to deal with the banking crisis without creating another sovereign debt crisis. Given the simultaneous uncertainty created by political conditions in Greece and the threat of contagion a Spanish financial crisis failure could create in Europe, especially in Italy, the eurozone changed its previous bailout strategy and designed an aid package in which the burden on Spanish sovereign debt would be minimized. The agreement reached a week before the second Greek election created a guarantee to finance up to €100 billion in aid specifically to support a Spanish bank bailout. Unlike previous bailouts, Spain was able to negotiate a deal that did not include similarly onerous austerity conditions to those imposed on Greece, Ireland, and Portugal.[143]

Still, the agreement to offer Spain credit guarantees and the resolution of Greek elections did not quell market concerns, and sovereign bond rates remained high. Exacerbating the situation, on 25 June 2012, Cyprus also requested bailout aid. Since its entry into the eurozone in 2008, the Cypriot banking industry had boomed as an offshore banking centre catering to eastern European and non-EU states, amassing total deposits seven times larger than its GDP. Clearly if such a banking sector fell into trouble, the national government would not have the finances to tackle the problem alone. The banking sector had also accumulated significant amounts of Greek debt. Its banks had bet heavily that, like previous bailouts, private debt-holders would not be held accountable for losses in the most recent negotiation concluded in February 2012. They were wrong. The recent Greek bailout agreement, which included significant private sector write-downs, had imposed harsh losses on private banks holding Greek debt and severely destabilized

---

143 The Spanish government argued determinedly that the credit guarantee of €100 billion should be paid directly to banks, thereby avoiding an increase in sovereign debt. Other eurozone countries resisted this plan arguing that under the current rules of the eurozone the debt had to be assumed by the national government, which could then assign it to a national bank recapitalization program. The final agreement specified the debt would be assigned to Spain's total sovereign debt load. Conditionality, with respect to the loan, however, was otherwise limited.

Cyprus's banking system, prompting the request.[144] The amount of aid needed was scant relative to previous packages, but given conditions – the uncertainty still surrounding Greece, Spain's banking problems, Italy's worsening debt rates, and now Cyprus's request for aid – fears began to mount of an imminent set of sovereign debt crises occurring across countries like dominos that could serve a death knell to the currency union. The euro's exchange rate against major currencies fell to levels not seen since the start of the crisis, and a virtual bank run began across eurozone economies, particularly in southern states, as deposit holders attempted to transfer their wealth out of the eurozone or into safe-haven economies, especially in Germany, for example, by investing in Berlin real estate.

The seemingly relentless sequence of challenges that buffeted the eurozone over the late spring and early summer of 2012 was like a relentless flood-tide that threatened to wash away any defences that Europe had been able to mount against the crisis so far. Facing mounting volatility in currency and bond markets, Europe's leaders seemed frozen. Merkel's sudden political weakness after the loss of her closest ally meant that EU policy could soon be thwarted by internal dissension. What if Germany and the more conservative northern countries could not convince southern countries, now seemingly allied with France, to follow the previous austerity script? Would this force Germany to leave the euro? Could it undermine Merkel's support at home? Political paralysis threatened to undermine Europe's ability to act just when it might be facing its darkest hour. Uncertainty continued to worsen, and markets seemed to brace for the eventuality of a eurozone break up.

It was at this darkest hour that the ECB once more surprised markets by acting in a way everyone knew it could, but few had assumed it would. Conditions and confidence in the eurozone now, however, had deteriorated to the point where the ECB's official mandate seemed almost a contradiction. Charged with maintaining price stability and maintaining the stability of the currency, it now faced a choice. Price stability typically meant limited activism, however, without action, the euro as a currency could fail. Given conditions, the ECB was forced to act, and, at the end of July 2012, it unleashed what the media dubbed the "big bazooka".[145]

---

144 While the Cypriot government, as part of the eurozone, had approved the recent Greek bailout agreement, a credit downgrade in autumn 2011 and recent events had caused its sovereign rates also to climb to unsustainable levels, and the costs necessary to stabilize its banking system made bailout aid necessary.

145 See for example, BBC News, "Euro crisis: Has the ECB created a big bazooka?, http://www.bbc.com/news/business-19096992 (accessed 3 August 2015)or *SpiegelOnline*, "Buying Bonds against the Crisis: How the ECB Plans to Use Its Bazooka" 6 August 2012, http://www.spiegel.de/international/europe/how-the-ecb-plans-to-use-its-big-bazooka-a-848417.html (accessed 3 August 2015).

Abiding by its mandate to maintain the stability of the euro, during what seemed like an otherwise routine speech in London, ECB president Mario Draghi promised very clearly that the ECB would do "whatever it takes" using its unlimited euro-resources to stabilize the situation.[146] This statement, while only a comment in an otherwise seemingly innocuous speech describing the currency union's recent experiences, was immediately understood to imply the ECB now stood willing to enter sovereign debt markets in an unlimited way.[147] Calling on its potential to be a lender of last resort, the central bank had finally indicated it was willing to do what many had argued for since shortly after the eurozone crisis had begun. The ECB was now implicitly threatening to use its unlimited power to purchase eurozone sovereign debt as necessary to stabilize markets. Actions would no longer be limited, as they had been in previous programs to protect sovereign interest rates.[148]

The initial announcement had an immediate impact on markets, which began to stabilize after sovereign bond rates had reached record levels for Spain and Italy. Following this statement, a month later, the ECB unveiled its Outright Monetary Transactions (OMT) programme, formalizing the conditions under which the ECB would intervene in sovereign bond markets. The programme clearly indicated that in cases where a country had applied for assistance, and agreed to the conditions under which the assistance was made, the ECB would be willing to purchase an unlimited quantity of government bonds on the secondary market to reduce interest rate pressures. The roles of the ECB and the Troika were now clear. The Troika would define the conditions under which bailouts could ensure sustainable debt levels. The ECB would then stand ready to ensure interest rates were maintained to safeguard that sustainability. In principle, a bailout agreement should now resolve any future questions regarding a country's debt sustainability.

Eliminating such concerns also implied the euro's stability was far sounder. As long as a country abided by the terms of its aid agreement, the risk of default was removed. Moral hazard also seemed under control; a country would receive aid only if it abided by these conditions. After this announcement, sovereign bond rates of troubled countries began to decline rapidly, and soon approached levels not seen since the beginning of the crisis.

---

146 Mario Draghi, speech to the Global Investment Conference, London, 26 July 2012.
147 During Spanish bailout discussions the potential to enter secondary bond markets had been widely discussed by legal and economic experts and officials.
148 The previous Securities Markets Programme, or SMP, had been limited in the sense that all transactions were "sterilized", purchases of one country's sovereign debt were balanced by equivalent value sales of another's, thereby leaving the money supply in the eurozone unaffected, thereby minimizing any inflationary effect this otherwise might have. In this way actions to stabilize currency conditions were tempered by the need to maintain price stability by minimizing any perceived inflationary such actions might cause.

Buttressing the ECB's efforts in the summer of 2012, the European Commission and ECB also followed up on previous policy initiatives and released initial plans for a banking union that September.[149] Under these reforms, The ECB would also now be the sole regulator of major banks in the eurozone, and, as such, would have the power to support them directly should recapitalization ever be necessary. This reform would, in principle, permanently allow the link between financial crises and sovereign debt crises to be broken, adding an element of stability to the eurozone that had been missing since its formation. This reform came into effect in autumn of 2014. The reforms also defined a single set of rules to resolve bank failures should they occur, allowing such efforts to be completed much more quickly to minimize the disruption and uncertainty they could cause to financial markets. Final rules were adopted in December of 2014. Other new rules to define common capital requirements and other regulatory standards that all financial institutions in the EU must comply with, were passed in 2013 and 2014. These were meant to prevent such failures and to eliminate the patchwork of unique and different national bank regulations that had previously existed and that had contributed to the crisis. In principle, the banking union initially proposed would also release individual countries from the responsibility to guarantee their own banks deposits up to €100,000 to help break the so-called "doom loop". Such rules proved controversial though and eventually remained the responsibility of national banks, but the new banking union rules directed that a single pan-European deposit guarantee mechanism be considered by 2019.[150]

As an indication of the reform effort's success and the calming effects of the ECB actions taken in July and August, Spain's bank bailout required "only" €39.5 billion in aid to recapitalize its banking system.[151] This was in stark contrast to the €100 billion that had been initially approved. The additional funds were not needed – a testament to the turnaround that had occurred in the

---

149 See "Communication from the Commission: A Roadmap towards a Banking Union" (September 2012) http://ec.europa.eu/finance/general-policy/banking-union/index_en.htm (accessed 30 August 2015).

150 For a discussion of the rules enacted, see "Banking Union: restoring financial stability in the Eurozone" European Commission memo, 15 April 2014, http://ec.europa.eu/finance/general-policy/docs/banking-union/banking-union-memo_en.pdf (Accessed August 30, 2015), and Understanding the Banking Union," February 27, 2015 European Commission Banking and Finance newsletter, http://ec.europa.eu/information_society/newsroom/cf/fisma/item-detail.cfm?item_id=20758&newsletter_id=166&lang=en (Accessed August 30, 2015). Support for trouble banks now comes primarily from the ECB in times of crisis, or they are resolved (closed) according to the common mechanism agreed upon, however, a common European pool of funds to guarantee deposits up to €100,000 across Europe could not be agreed upon. The agreement specified this matter would be revisited before 2019 to determine if such a common pool was warranted.

151 An additional €1.9 was made available in February 2013.

crisis. The acute phase of the eurozone crisis was over, but the road to economic recovery would still be a long one and stood several years away.

From Financial Crisis to Political Crisis

The ECB's final intervention in summer of 2012 and the ensuing efforts to create the missing banking union and make permanent the ESM firewall combined to end the financial crisis that had plagued the eurozone for nearly four years. Questions regarding whether the euro would fail as a common currency quickly faded. At this point, the political crisis began: could governments convince voters that the economic decisions made were in their best interests?

2012 ended, much like it had begun, with a new confidence that the euro-area had weathered the storm. Euro-country bond rates began to realize further reductions as confidence returned to the borrowing markets. As the financial crisis subsided, it became clearer the challenges the eurozone faced were now long-term: how to deal with the deep economic recessions caused by the crisis, especially in the SPIGI countries. As of 2015, unemployment rates exceeded twenty-three percent in Spain and Greece and thirteen percent in Italy, Portugal, and Cyprus. Potentially more troubling, youth unemployment rates in these countries have risen to more than fifty percent. Even the healthiest creditor nations have seen very sluggish growth, too little to reduce unemployment to "normal" levels. In fact, since 2012, much of Europe has been forced to accept a "new normal", with persistent and elevated unemployment levels and limited economic expansion.

Political uncertainty also continued. In February 2013, new Italian elections resulted in no clear electoral winner. Populist protest parties with no clear agenda secured a significant portion of the vote. A weak Italian coalition eventually formed in late April with its policy agenda seemingly defined as a dedication to maintaining membership in the euro, but under terms that benefited the Italian people, in other words, with growth rather than austerity. Political conditions in that country have, nevertheless, remained volatile. Enrico Letta was sworn in as Italy's new prime minister, succeeding Mario Monti after the April 2013 elections, but was soon replaced by Matteo Renzi in February 2014. Populist resentment of austerity actions and opposition to labour market reforms have continued to make change in Italy difficult, and economic conditions have remained very weak.

Cyprus, which had requested aid in late June 2012, continued to negotiate the terms of its bailout until late November 2012 when the Troika's terms were made public. These specified severe austerity measures, reductions in public jobs and salaries, pension and benefit cuts, and tax increases. The value of the bailout package would be €17.5 billion, with €10 billion financed by Troika funding and the remainder through Cyprus's restructuring and austerity programs. Final agreement on the bailout, however, did not take place until March 2013 to accommodate a Cypriot federal election in which a change of government took place. What followed was an unfortunate set of errors during a two-week period in which the new government was supposed to finalize the program.

The initial plan to finance Cyprus's share of the bailout had included a tax on all existing bank deposits in addition to a series of other austerity actions and reforms. Some refer to such actions as a "bail-in" as citizens' deposits become part of the resources used during the bailout. A political backlash, however, resulted as this plan was unveiled and the general population rose up against these costs being imposed on small businesses, regular citizens, and the least wealthy in the economy. This reaction caused the government to backtrack from its bailout agreement, and, for a time, it threatened to default rather than accept the Troika's terms. The political deadlock resulted in a national financial crisis where all banks closed for a week and financial transactions were severely limited. Economic chaos followed on the island as most commerce ground to a halt. Avoiding a default, the plan that eventually emerged imposed a tax only on deposits over €100,000, limiting public contribution to the bailout to the more affluent, and to those wealthy foreign depositors who had previously benefited from the tax advantages of keeping their funds in Cypriot banks. The damage, however, was done. The Troika and the Cypriot government accepted the package, but the weeklong stalemate caused by clumsy negotiations underlined the political disparity among countries in the currency union. Large nations still called the shots; small ones would have to abide by them. The final result was a serious economic recession in Cyprus, one likely made much worse by the ham-fisted course of bailout negotiations. Lessons learned also informed the banking union negotiations underway at the time.

In Germany, the September 2013 election returned chancellor Angela Merkel and her ruling party, the Christian Democratic Union/Christian Social Union, to power with its strongest showing since 1990. Nevertheless, her success did not rub off on her former coalition partners, the Free Democrats, whose electoral collapse left them without representation in the Bundestag. Short five seats, Merkel had no choice but to form a grand coalition with the former opposition, the Social Democratic Party (SDP). Since then, the strong showing of Merkel's CDU/CSU party has allowed her to limit her coalition partner's power, resulting in little change with respect to the German crisis policies with their emphasis on austerity and reform. Germany's economy remained sluggish, but, by mid-2014, growth began to approach healthy levels. Still, in part due to international tensions and consequent trade sanctions with Russia that occurred after that country's invasion of the Crimea in early 2014, the economy has not grown at rates seen in other major economies such as the United States or the United Kingdom.

Since his election in 2012, François Hollande, France's socialist president, has seen his approval ratings fall to thirteen percent, becoming the least popular president in France's history.[152] This fall in support coincides with a worsening of the economy characterized by little growth and increasing unemployment. Again, the government has had difficulty reigning in its deficit and finds itself in conflict with the EU over its potential to exceed official union deficit limits agreed to under the Fiscal Compact. As a result, relations with Brussels – and more importantly with Berlin – are strained, resulting in even less consensus regarding economic policy across the European Union.

Conditions in some of the bailout countries and their neighbours in this period actually improved at a faster rate than in some creditor nations. Ireland recorded strong growth in 2013 and 2014, achieving general unemployment rates better than they were in 2009. Portugal's return to growth has been slower, but it, too, has seen an improvement in unemployment, although the youth rate still remains significantly elevated. Both countries have since reentered sovereign debt markets and exited their bailout agreements, with Ireland completing its agreement in December 2013, and Portugal in May 2014. Growth is also stronger in Spain compared to the rest of the euro-area, but high unemployment rates persist, hovering near twenty-three percent.

Although crisis conditions subsided in sovereign bond and exchange markets since the summer of 2012, economic conditions have remained weak across much of the eurozone, aside from those countries noted above. Germany and other northern economies have struggled with weak growth, and a lack of demand across the continent threatened the continent with deflation. Across the EU, frustration with slow growth and especially with the slow improvement of unemployment rates has worsened. Elections in 2014 resulted in a large number of populist and anti-EU parties being elected to the EU Parliament.

Despite the ongoing economic malaise in many countries, debate has continued to rage among capitals regarding continuing austerity actions, the necessity and speed of labour market reforms and deficit reductions. Similarly, the EU has found it very difficult to implement new policies meant to more speedily repair current economic conditions and restore growth in the union, a problem that may now be the union's greatest challenge.

These challenges have been most significant in Greece, where economic conditions improved very slowly after 2012. In mid-2014, five years after the outbreak of the crisis, the recession officially ended as the Greek economy recorded positive growth. Greece was able to return to credit markets in mid-

---

152 *Le Monde*, "François Hollande devient le président le plus impopulaire de la Ve République" 4 September 2014, http://www.lemonde.fr/les-decodeurs/article/2014/09/04/francois-hollande-devient-officiellement-le-president-le-plus-impopulaire_4482376_4355770.html (accessed 3 August 2015).

2014, issuing new debt at competitive interest rates. Nevertheless, unemployment levels remained high. Tied by the austerity straitjacket of the 2012-bailout conditions, most people in Greece saw little improvement in their economic livelihoods. As a result, populist parties promising to ease austerity conditions and demand better bailout terms gained clout.

A Greek Popular Revolt: The 2015 Referendum

The Greek coalition government elected in 2012 was able to rule only until January 2015 when it was defeated by a coalition of left-wing anti-bailout parties. Prior to the election, the Samaras government was persistently chastised by its Troika creditors to speed up reforms. Simultaneously, in its domestic politics, it had to contend with rising electoral discontent over the slow pace of economic improvement. Overall, Greece has epitomized the potential conflict Rodrik outlined between electoral accountability, state sovereignty, and deep integration at a supranational level. Reforms demanded by EU creditors left the sitting government no choice but to accede, but doing so undermined its political support as imposed austerity actions including labour market, pension and institutional reform proved very unpopular. It also proved destabilizing to the coalition. In June 2013, one of the coalition partners withdrew, leaving the remaining coalition with a slim three-seat majority, and with even less political sway to push through additional reforms.

In April 2014, the country re-entered the bond markets for the first time in four years, selling €3 billion euros worth of five-year bonds, offered at a yield of 4.95 percent. This return to borrowing was made possible both because of the decline in interest rates Greece had enjoyed as markets become more complacent regarding eurozone woes, and because of the relatively high yield they provided in an otherwise very low yield international environment. Investors were willing to take the risk this relatively higher yield provided. The success of the bond sale was in part caused by the fact that the Greek government had experienced revenue problems that made looming debt payments problematic, even despite the February 2012 bailout. Terms of that bailout had been severe, and despite the size of the aid package, the size of Greece's debt still left little room for error. The election and economic uncertainty that followed the agreement in second bailout agreement in 2012, when two elections were needed to establish a victor, had reduced revenues, and the lack of reform and slower than anticipated growth since the last bailout had suggested a third bailout of approximately €50 billion might still be needed between 2015 and 2020. Avoiding such a politically unpalatable outcome had increased pressure from Troika creditors on the Greek government to speed up reforms and left the Greek government looking for additional revenue options. In February 2014, negotiations began between the Troika and Greece regarding the possibility of approximately €15 billion in additional debt relief, but again, to elicit such aid, creditors demanded Greece accelerate the pace of unpopular reforms in return. In Rodrik's trilemma, the government found itself in a vice between an unhappy electorate and an impatient EU. Bond markets offered what seemed to be a possible solution.

Despite the success of the bond sale, the Samaras government remained unpopular and was branded a lackey of foreign interests by the opposition. To bolster its domestic political position, the Samaras government suggested it might attempt to leave its bailout program early by relying instead on additional bond financing to meet debt commitments. The appeal of such a solution to the domestic audience was clear. If the government could leave the bailout program, the harsh conditionality and austerity the Troika had demanded would no longer be relevant, allowing the government to claim that the Greek peoples' sacrifices and government efforts had been worthwhile and successful. Furthermore, it would undermine the ability of the opposition to continue accusing the government of putting the Troika's interests ahead of the electorate's.

Nevertheless, such a move was risky. Since Greece's position was still precarious, bond markets might see the withdrawal from the bailout program as increasing the chances of default by removing the crutch of external financial support the program provided. It also increased the possibility of moral hazard. Under such circumstances, Greece would have little incentive to continue with its unpopular domestic reforms. Unsurprisingly, Troika reaction to the idea of Greece leaving its bailout program ranged from sceptical to outright irritation. Some EU states saw this suggested course of action as both potentially undermining the commitment to Greek reform they desired as well as to the stability of the euro. In addition, they argued such a withdrawal would only result in another debt crisis down the road. By September, market concerns seemed to side with the Troika's, and were reflected in Greek sovereign debt interest rates, which after enjoying a steady two-year decline, suddenly began to increase once more.

Faced with plunging support domestically, and difficulties maintaining its coalition, the Greek government in late 2014 made a bold move. It called an early presidential election, a procedural move, akin to a vote of confidence, to establish support from its coalition, as such an election occurs in the legislature. Under these circumstances, if the ruling party's candidate does not gain majority support, a general election must be called. The Samaras government played a high risk game of 'chicken', betting that its reluctant coalition partners would not dare subject the country to a general election for fear of losing to the anti-bailout Syriza party, which was well ahead in the polls, and whose win might threaten economic calamity if they attempted to abandon the bailout terms. The gamble, however, did not work. In late December 2014, the Samara's candidate for President did not gain majority support, forcing a general election in late January 2015.

The outcome of that election was a win for Syriza and a coalition of left wing, mainly anti-bailout parties. Alexis Tsipras, who had risen to prominence in the 2012 elections on an anti-austerity platform, formed a new government on the promise that he would force the Troika to offer a new deal, a renegotiation of the current bailout and one in which the people were put ahead of EU finances. Difficult and sometimes heated bargaining between the new Greek government and the Troika commenced, and the Greek crisis that had seemed to be very slowly healing suddenly began to haemorrhage as efforts to find a fresh solution with the new government dragged on.

The election of the Syriza government marked a political turning point in the eurozone crisis focusing on the question of austerity. Syriza maintained that austerity should be reduced and debt forgiveness extended, while difficult market reforms in Greece should also be slowed or stopped. The EU saw this position as a threat on several levels. Financially, such policies would hurt the taxpayers of Europe as collectively they held the majority of Greek debt after the bailout of 2012. Politically, such a position would be portrayed in creditor states as allowing a government that was blamed with causing the crisis in 2009 to avoid paying its bills. It would also mark an about face in the policy position of creditor nations throughout the crisis, which have trumpeted the need for financial and structural reform (austerity) as the solution.

Ultimately, these questions represented a face-off between the European Union and one of its member states. As in Rodrik's trilemma, which would lose out: the deeply integrated economies; domestic preferences; or the sovereign state? In other words, something had to give. Would the euro fail or would the Greek people's preferences be ignored or would the EU become a federation where the Greek people's preferences would be assimilated with Europe's as a whole, meaning sovereign states would be replaced by federated ones? After 2012, domestic preferences lost, but the fiscal and banking reforms adopted may indicate that the EU is on the path to becoming more akin to a federation. The new Greek situation in 2015 offered another opportunity to potentially reframe the structure of the EU within Rodrik's trilemma.

On 20 February 2015 the Troika and the new Greek government announced an agreement that would extend the previous bailout another four months, allowing the new government time to meet looming debt obligations. Afterward, the Greek government was to begin discussions on a new third bailout, as its need became rapidly apparent.

Tax revenues remained uncollected under the new Greek government as it became uncertain whether previously imposed increases in taxes would remain permanent. The sudden new political uncertainty had also tipped the frail Greek economy back into contraction. Avoiding another bailout would always have been difficult given the ground previously lost in the summer of 2012, and the events of early 2015 forced the country to fall off the fiscal tightrope. A new bailout would now be necessary, but under what terms? The new Greek government had been elected on a promise to roll-back the hated austerity conditions of the previous bailout many Greeks blamed for their current misfortunes. The Troika, and especially EU governments, saw the reversal of such conditions a recipe not only for future disaster, but also as a domestic threat to their own governments given existing anti-bailout sentiment in their countries.

Initially, the February agreement appeared to solve the most recent debt crunch; the Syriza government seemed like it would be able to make future debt payments as negotiations went on, however, the deal came with conditions attached. Greece was to identify new reforms and plans regarding how they would be achieved. However, the new Greek government and the Troika did not see eye-to-eye on what reforms were needed. This process began a series of new negotiations in which Greek officials produced successive plans that were then rejected by Troika officials, particularly EU ministers, who found them repeatedly lacking in substance. So unhappy was Brussels with Syriza that one EU official quipped, "They are living in cloud-cuckoo land." Yanis Varoufakis, Greece's finance minister, said he welcomed the animosity directed at him across the eurozone.[153] As long as such plans were not produced, a needed €7.2 billion to cover Greek debt obligations in the coming months through summer 2015 would not be released. A second impasse began as talks dragged on while deadlines loomed ever closer.

Yanis Varoufakis @yanisvaroufakis · Apr 26
FDR, 1936: "They are unanimous in their hate for me; and I welcome their hatred." A quotation close to my heart (& reality) these days
4.1K   3.6K

In May 2015, Greece officially entered recession again after recording two consecutive quarters of negative growth (the last quarter of 2014 and the first of 2015). Greece's fiscal position continued to worsen as tax revenues further declined, due both to the lack of growth and uncertainty over what taxes were even owed in the previous year, given the possibility the new government might repeal previous tax increases. With negotiations dragging, the Troika withheld the next tranche of bailout aid promised in February 2015. Greek bond rates began to soar, and by April 2015 exceeded ten percent. Any return to the bond markets was now financially impossible.

---

153 Charlemagne, "The sorry saga of Syriza" *The Economist*, 9 May 2015, 51.

In April, Greek Prime Minister Alexis Tsipras travelled to Moscow to discuss the situation with Russian President Vladimir Putin, to the dismay of many in the EU. In the end, Greece did not break ranks with the EU over Russian sanctions, and Tsipras left with only Putin's moral support.[154] Although unsuccessful, the effort further infuriated some European officials who questioned whether Greece was really serious about coming to an agreement that would release the final tranche of bailout aid from the 2012 agreement and necessary to meet looming debt payments. It was now clear a new bailout deal would be needed, however, it was unclear whether Greece might instead choose to default on existing loans before such an agreement could be reached. Worse, some EU officials even worried whether Greece was seriously trying to avoid such a result.

In May 2015, the Greek government made its debt payments despite the cash-crunch. With domestic revenues collapsing, the Greek government managed to pull enough funds together to meet its obligations, but these efforts included passing a measure that infuriated the mayors of the many cities and towns who, along with other state entities, were told they had to hand over any spare cash to the state to aid its repayment efforts. Remarkably, while tempers flared in Brussels and Athens, financial markets in the rest of the EU were generally unfazed with this new round of uncertainty regarding Greece's future in the monetary union. Fears in 2015 that a "Grexit" would precipitate a euro failure were far more muted in this round of Greece-EU negotiations, and bond rates of other SPIGI countries remained relatively stable, unlike events in 2011 and 2012.

Many observers saw the risk of the crisis as mainly one that threatened Greece and the political leaders involved in negotiations. The rest of the currency union behaved as if it were an optimal one, one in which the benefits of staying were clearly greater than losing the currency. Accordingly, markets were unwilling to bet against the euro and the currency. Some pundits even argued a Greek exit might, in fact, bolster the euro as it would demonstrate the newfound strength of the currency union's financial rules. Daniel Gros, the director of the Center for European Policy Studies, remarked after the February negotiation that it symbolized "...a basic clash between national democratic accountability and European rules and obligations... The European Union can't work if every new government can't keep the commitments of previous governments."[155]

---

154 Denis Pinchuk and Renee Maltezou, "Greek PM gets support, not money from Putin" *Reuters*, 8 April 2015, http://www.reuters.com/article/2015/04/08/us-russia-greece-idUSKBN0MZ0KJ20150408 (accessed 3 August 2015).
155 Liz Alderman and James Kanter, "Eurozone Officials Reach Accord with Greece to Extend Bailout", New York Times 20 February 2015, http://www.nytimes.com/2015/02/21/business/international/greece-debt-eurozone-finance-ministers.html?_r=0 (accessed 3 August 2015).

This time the crisis seemed political, not financial, at least for the rest of the EU. When asked whether the EU finance officials and negotiators had ignored the Greek electorate's preferences, Jeroen Dijsselbloem, the head of the group of eurozone finance ministers, remarked, "In the Eurogroup we have to work with 19 ministers who have 19 mandates," adding "[and] we have to reach a joint decision." Decisions "will always be about money and about conditions," he added.[156] In other words, the debate was not about what to do to solve a financial dilemma, but rather about the principles and organization of the supranational institutions of the EU and eurozone. The threat the new Greek crisis posed was as much about how the EU would continue to be organized in the future; whether national democratic accountability would be superseded by the member states' responsibilities under the Maastricht rules and similar treaty obligations; or whether Europe would face the fact that its current structure left little room to directly recognize, reflect, and be held accountable for the preferences of its citizens. If the union were to become more reflective of the people's preferences, it would have to become more of a federation.

By June, positions had hardened between Greece and the rest of Europe. Even France, which had initially seemed sympathetic to the new Greek government's questioning of the European status quo and emphasis on austerity, became tired of the lack of progress in negotiations. Further, it had become apparent that Greece was not willing to bargain in the way Europe was used to. Instead of avoiding overt conflict with other parties and striving for a consensus, Greek politicians brought disputes into the public arena. The media increasingly reported on the personal feelings expressed by Greek participants, and, in particular, by their German antagonists. As the month dragged on, the Greek government failed to provide any new proposals over which to negotiate and seemed instead to become more vocal regarding their demands that the Troika reduce the austerity of previous bailouts. Europe and Troika members became more frustrated with Greece's apparent lack of willingness to come to a compromise. Any trust left between sides seemed to melt away and negotiations seemed to move backward as Troika members, more uncertain than ever about Greece's commitment to meet any bailout conditions should an agreement be reached, began to offer not less but often more austerity in their bargaining positions. Eventually, as the deadlock continued, Greece ran out of resources and was forced to miss a €1.6 billion payment in June 2015 on an outstanding IMF debt.

---

156 Ibid.

Image 5-4: Greeks waiting in long lines at ATMs to find ones that still had cash to dispense, Athens, summer 2015. Photo by Peter Stavropoulos.

This event was not technically a default, but world markets reacted as if it had been.[157] Greek sovereign 10-year bond rates climbed to over fifteen percent. Unlike events in 2011 and 2012, other SPIGI countries' rates were hardly affected. This time, markets seemed to take as given the integrity of the euro as a currency; the only question was whether Greece would leave the eurozone. Withdrawals from Greek banks, which had been accelerating since spring 2015 turned into a torrential outflow of cash as savers in Greece looked to protect their deposits. The ECB continued to lend to Greek banks to maintain their liquidity and to avoid failure; however, with the missed bond payment and the threat of default, it was unsure for how long. In a final attempt to come to an agreement, in late June just before the looming IMF payment was due, Greece and its Troika creditors engaged in a final set of round-the-clock negotiations.

The Troika, despite the misgivings of some member countries, made one final offer in late June. The proposed deal allowed some concessions from previous bargaining positions, but after so many months of zero progress the terms were harsh, and required increased Greek austerity in many areas. In a surprise move on 26 June the Greek negotiating team abandoned talks, and, after banks had closed that Friday, prime minister Tsipras, announced he

---

157 By IMF rules, such a missed payment is not classified by the IMF as a default. Instead, Greece was ruled to be "in arrears". However, by missing the payment, Greece became the first developed economy ever to do so. It was also the Fund's largest missed payment.

would call a national referendum for July 5th, allowing Greek citizens to decide whether to accept the final deal offered.

This decision simultaneously roiled financial markets in Europe and Greece, and enraged many negotiators involved in the bailout talks. Withdrawal requests from Greek banks morphed from a steady stream to a flood as citizens attempted to move money out of their accounts to safeguard their savings if Greece abandoned the euro and returned to drachmas or another currency, which now seemed much more likely. The ECB did not increase bank support to offset this liquidity crunch and, on 29 June, faced with potential runs when banks opened for business on that Monday morning, Greek banks remained closed, and customers were limited to teller-machine withdrawals to a maximum of €60 per day. International transfers were halted. The Athens's stock exchange closed. As had happened in Cyprus, capital controls had been imposed on the country to avoid the failure of the country's banks. These institutions would remain closed until after the referendum was completed.

The referendum asked Greeks:

Should the plan of agreement be accepted, which was submitted by the European Commission, the European Central Bank, and the International Monetary Fund in the Eurogroup of 25.06.2015 and comprises of two parts, which constitute their unified proposal?
The first document is entitled "Reforms For The Completion Of The Current Program and Beyond" and the second "Preliminary Debt Sustainability Analysis".
NOT ACCEPTED/NO
ACCEPTED/YES[158]

The following week saw frenzied campaigning in Greece by both pro- and anti-bailout forces. Tsipras went on television to ask the people to vote "no" so as to bolster Greece's negotiating position. He explained that the referendum was not a vote on leaving the euro or the EU, but, as he put it on the cover of his Twitter page, a vote "for a Greece of dignity, for a Europe of Democracy".[159] Those inclined to vote yes disagreed fearing a no-vote would result in Greece leaving the euro, and financial calamity. Those against accepting the referendum question noted the question merely asked people if they supported accepting the terms the Troika had offered. A no-vote, they argued, would only allow further negotiations. As can be seen from the question, neither side could claim with certainty their view was correct. Many found the referendum language

---

[158] Referendum (translated) question presented to Greeks in July 2015 http://fortune.com/2015/06/29/greece-bailout-referendum-ballot/ (accessed 30 August 2015).
[159] https://twitter.com/tsipras_eu?ref_src=twsrc^tfw (accessed 30 August 2015).

unclear and confusing.¹⁶⁰ Moreover, the Council of Europe said the vote fell short of its standards, not allowing the public the minimum of two weeks to deliberate.¹⁶¹ The Council of State, Greece's highest court, was also brought into the fray, ruling that the vote was legal.¹⁶²

Alexis Tsipras @tsipras_eu · Jul 1
Sunday's #referendum is not about whether or not #Greece remains in the Eurozone. #dimopsifisma
559   320

On Sunday, 5 July, the Greek people rejected the question resoundingly, with over sixty percent of ballots cast rejecting the conditions. While Greek markets and banks remained closed, as soon as world financial markets opened, Greek bond-yields soared, with the two-year bond rate reaching forty-eight percent. SPIGI bond yields, and even German and French yields, all briefly jumped. European and Greek negotiators were forced to meet to defuse the looming crisis, and to determine whether Greece would leave the euro. On 13 July, the Greek government eventually accepted a set of conditions that would open new bailout talks and release short-term credit to pay current debt obligations and those debts now in arrears. The terms were worse than those offered prior to the referendum.

In the following days, as a line of credit was made to Greece to allow the country to pay its debt obligations, including those now overdue, the Greek parliament also met to pass the conditions of the new loan guarantee package, thereby allowing bailout negotiations to begin. This capitulation to Troika demands created a mutiny within the ruling government's coalition. Nevertheless, on 14 August a bailout agreement was struck, worth €86 billion. In the end, the additional uncertainty, uncollected revenues and the economic contraction that had occurred since the January elections had cost Greece and the Troika an estimated 36 billion more than what had been estimated the previous December.

Following the acceptance of the third Greek bailout program, the Greek government passed the necessary measures to see the program go into effect. These votes were not without cost, requiring the support of opposition parties

---

160 "The Greek referendum question makes (almost) no sense", *BBC News*, 29 June 2015 http://www.bbc.com/news/world-europe-33311422 (accessed 30 August 2015).
161 "Greek referendum falls short of standards – Council of Europe" *Reuters* 1 July 2015 http://www.reuters.com/article/2015/07/01/eurozone-greece-rights-idUSL8N0ZH3IO2015070 (accessed 30 August 2015).
162 Nick Fletcher and Julia Kollewe, "Greek debt crisis: referendum to go ahead as court rejects appeal" *The Guardian* 3 July 2015 http://www.theguardian.com/business/live/2015/jul/03/greek-debt-crisis-council-of-state-to-rule-on-referendum-live (accessed 30 August 2015).

to offset the defections within the ruling coalition's own ranks. In response, prime minister Tsipras announced his resignation on 20 August and a new national election was called.

On 20 September, Syriza party won a clear victory, falling only six seats short of an outright majority. Tsipras quickly moved to form a coalition with the much smaller Independent Greeks (ANEL), meaning he would not have to partner with either of the two parties that had ruled Greece for the past forty years, the centre-right New Democracy and the centre-left PASOK. The election was a victory for Tsipras, and the hard-earned bailout agreement negotiated the previous month, which he promised to implement. Although he failed to change Greece's relationship with its creditors, voters rewarded his gumption.[163] Reaction from Brussels was swift to congratulate Tsipras, but also quick to remind him that much needed to be done with no time to lose.

In Athens, the mood remained sombre, and unlike the January election when Tsipras first came to power, this time there were no illusions regarding a new approach to crisis policies. Weary of the prolonged self-examination, political and economic uncertainty, and the exhausting austerity they had experienced over the past several years, Greek voter apathy and abstentions from the vote reached record highs during this election. As Tsipras and Syriza celebrated a new beginning and a fresh start, most Greeks seemed more concerned with their everyday struggles than politics. In many ways a feeling of defeat fell over much of Greece. Despite the outcome of the parliamentary election, Greek politics remain fractured, and it is unclear whether Greece's problems are over, although the populism that had challenged the Troika's policies has now been replaced by a sense of inevitability.

Nevertheless, Greece's problems are Europe's problems. Whether Greece leaves the eurozone or muddles through, there are implications for the European Union. Yanis Varoufakis, a former finance minister of Greece, argued in a *New York Times* op-ed piece, "If the 'Athens Spring' – when the Greek people courageously rejected the catastrophic austerity conditions of the previous bailouts – has one lesson to teach, it is that Greece will recover only when the European Union makes the transition from 'We the states' to 'We the European people.'"[164]

---

163 Suzanne Daley, "Alexis Tsipras Given a Second Chance by Greek Voters" *New York Times*, 20 September 2015, http://www.nytimes.com/2015/09/21/world/europe/greece-election-tsipras.html .(accessed 21 September 2015).
164 Yanis Varoufakis, "How Europe Crushed Greece" *New York Times*, 9 September 2015 http://www.nytimes.com/2015/09/09/opinion/yanis-varoufakis-how-europe-crushed-greece.html (accessed 12 September 2015).

Conclusions

Despite warnings from different quarters including from some academics and even some EU officials, in general, both the public and politicians had great confidence in the euro. Therefore, when the eurozone crisis struck, the European reaction followed the same path as the stages of grief. The first reaction to tremors in the eurozone was to deny the common currency was to blame. Next, anger flared as European nations criticized others for their problems. In the next phase, bargaining ensued and both economic and psychological depression set in. The final phase, acceptance, was reached when the ECB and eurozone countries implemented the structural changes necessary to end the economic crisis.

Six years after the beginning of the crisis, it is, again, centred in Greece alone, exactly where it started in 2009. However, this time, the damage has been contained. The causes of the turmoil in 2015 were indecision and conflict between the government of Greece and the governments and institutions of the Troika. While tumultuous for Greece, in 2015, European markets were only minimally affected. The crisis is now purely political and the dilemma Rodrik's trilemma poses is now stark. Despite the democratic wishes of the Greek people, solutions contrary to that will were imposed on the country by the state and the overall institutions of the greater EU. As Rodrik predicted, under conditions like those the common currency creates of deep integration of national economies, national governments must first react to the rest of the world, or in this case the governance of Europe, over the wishes of its own people.

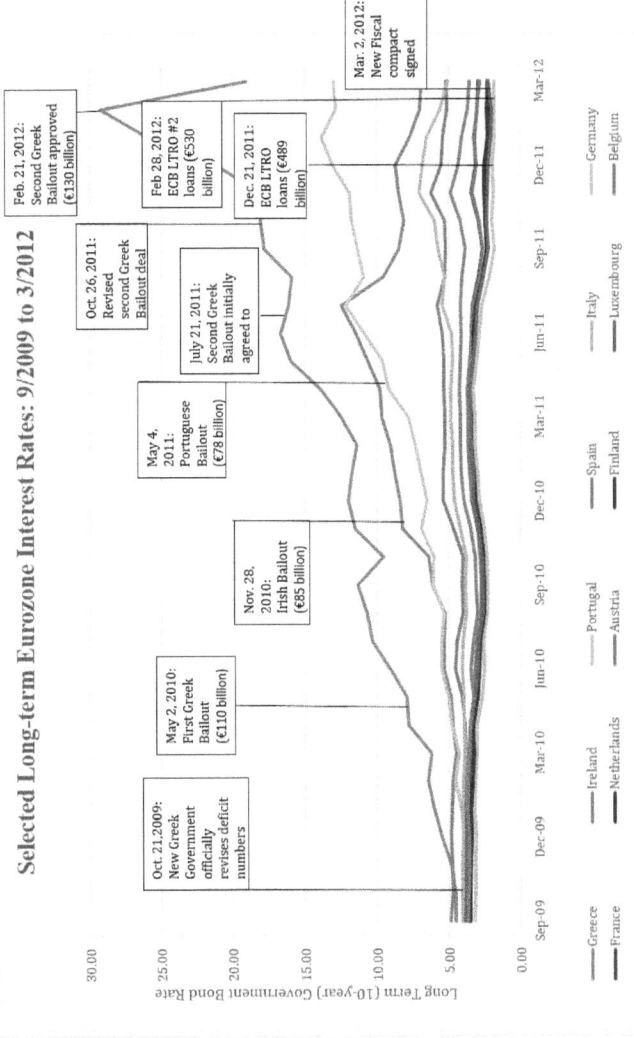

Figure 5-1: European Sovereign Interest Rates Timeline: September 2009 to March 2012. Average monthly government 10-year or equivalent long-term bond rates. Greek interest rates hit a maximum value of almost 30% just as that country's second bailout was finalized. The rate reflects an expected write-down in Greek debt. Spanish, Portuguese and Italian sovereign debt all hit highs in this period just prior to the ECB's LTRO loans were made available. Source Data: Eurostat.

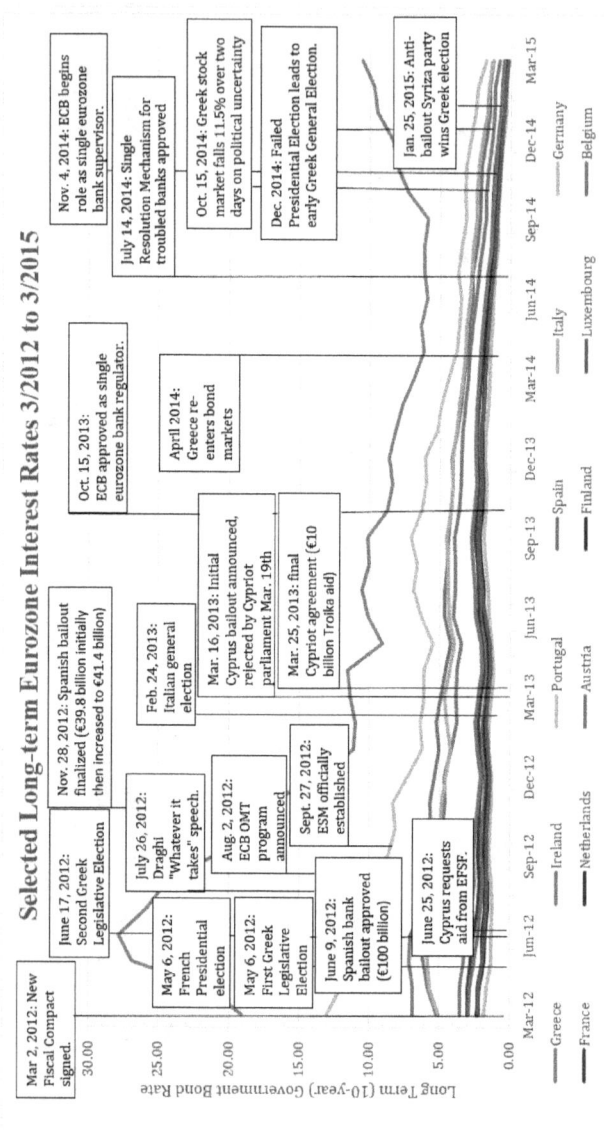

Figure 5-2: European Sovereign Interest Rates Timeline: August 2011 to May 2013. Average monthly government 10-year or equivalent long-term sovereign bond rates. Greek, Spanish and Italian bonds all reached maximum values in summer 2012, just before the ECB's declaration to do "whatever it takes" to support the euro. After the announcement, rates declined through the remainder of 2012. By summer of 2013 the twelve original Euro countries' rates had returned to levels not seen since the start of the crisis. Source Data: Eurostat.

Chapter VI:
Counterfactuals, Costs, and Conclusions

The eurozone crisis was the result of an imperfect currency union. As many theorists predicted, member states were neither similar enough nor integrated enough to withstand financial shocks, like those of 2008 and 2009, without serious consequences. Why was the currency union not optimally designed? Because, originally, the political will did not exist. Member states did not want to give up their sovereignty in the ways necessary to create a more flexible currency union, capable of bending without breaking, in the face of such strains. As established in previous chapters, the member states drew the line at certain measures such as joint liability of debt, a fully implemented banking union, or, more generally, a political and fiscal union that could have allowed the currency zone to better accommodate external shocks. Without these foundations, the eurozone appears to have been akin to a financial house of cards.

Why pursue a currency union without first securing the political support necessary to get it to function properly? Is this not a case of putting the cart before the horse? The answer may lie with Robert Schuman who warned, "Europe will not be made all at once, or according to a single plan. It will be built through concrete achievements which first create a de facto solidarity."[165] The purpose of the euro seems not only to have been to facilitate greater economic integration, but to generate the solidarity necessary to create, as stated in the Treaty of Rome, "an ever closer union". In other words, the economic union was a precursor to political union. As the European Union was still member-state centric, the only way to convince national governments to surrender more sovereignty to Brussels was slowly to build toward greater integration over time, while simultaneously creating public support for such measures. Having a tangible piece of Europe in one's pocket to husband everyday might hasten the process of European integration.

Did the introduction of the euro increase European solidarity? Did the eurozone crisis? The answers seem to be a qualified yes, even after the financial crisis. According to public opinion polls, in absolute terms, the introduction of the euro cultivated a feeling of 'Europeaness' among a percentage the citizenry, and the crisis has led to more citizen support rather than to less. On the other hand, this achievement is tainted by the antipathy the crisis has generated within certain segments of the population. While support for pan-European institutions may have increased over time, it appears not to

---

165 The Schuman Declaration, 9 May 1950, http://europa.eu/about-eu/basic-information/symbols/europe-day/schuman-declaration/index_en.htm (accessed 31 August 2015).

have created enthusiasm, at least politically. Turnout for European Parliamentary elections is generally low and declining. Furthermore, the voter more likely to turn out for elections is the angry one: one more likely to cast his or her ballot as a statement of dissatisfaction. This would explain apparent contradictions between EU polls that suggest greater support for the EU and the euro and recent European Parliament election results, where anti-EU parties won a significant minority of seats. Although opinion polls demonstrate that the idea of the euro did increase solidarity among the citizens as Schuman predicted, the crisis also intensified and broadened the anti-EU voices on either end of the political spectrum. Eventually, if conditions caused by the crisis persist, they could undermine the progress toward greater integration the EU and euro have achieved.

This greater acceptance of the euro may explain why the EU has worked so hard to ensure the euro's survival since 2009. The costs of the crisis have, in part, been determined by the response of Europe to it. Political leaders in Europe made a decision to protect the euro and the economic union it represented. Have these efforts been worth it? What costs have they avoided? The benefits of a currency union have been previously described, but the costs of maintaining the currency throughout the crisis have not been negligible financially or politically.

The following sections describe estimates of the immediate economic costs that might have occurred had the euro failed. Next, the chapter assesses the economic and political costs and benefits of the measures taken to protect the euro, in particular, the choice of greater fiscal austerity. Actions to protect the euro have been of two sorts: palliative actions in response to the immediate crisis; and structural changes that were heretofore unimaginable before the crisis. Finally, the authors discuss lessons learned from the crisis, specifically, that while strides have been made toward a more integrated continent; the Union is still not one of equals. The EU is still member-state centric; each member state is self interested in terms of politics, and these realties make reform difficult. Nevertheless, the eurozone crisis has been a momentous event in the evolution of the European Union.

Where are We Now? Economic and Political Costs

In 2014, conditions in sovereign debt markets were the best they had been since before the European financial crisis began, but the same could not be said for most of the eurozone's economies, many of which have suffered from severe unemployment and economic recession as a consequence. Was the price of the policies used worth it? Is the eurozone better off than had nothing been done or had the euro been allowed to fail?

Economic costs

Answering these questions requires an estimate of outcomes as they would have been had the currency union collapsed. While such estimates are too complex to hope to predict exactly, many calculations were attempted to determine the possible losses such a collapse would have caused. Table 6-1 estimates how each of the first twelve and largest economies of the eurozone would have been impacted by the collapse of the monetary union given conditions in late 2011 and early 2012. The consequences were grim. In SPIGI countries, the average decline in economic output two years after the break up of the eurozone was estimated to be 12.5 percent, and among the other seven nations, the average decline was predicted to total 9.9 percent.

Table 6-1: Potential Economic Impacts of a eurozone Failure (Spring 2012 estimates). Sources: *Der Spiegel*, ING.

Country	Change in Output (change two years after last year of Euro)	Change in Unemployment (change two years after last year of Euro)	Change in Inflation Rate (relative to last year of Euro)
Greece	-15.4%	+23.8%	+18.6%
Ireland	-8.9%	+19.4%	+9.5%
Portugal	-14.9%	+18.0%	+13.1%
Spain	-11.0%	+26.7%	+12.9%
Italy	-12.3%	+12.3%	+10.3%
Germany	-9.2%	+9.3%	-0.9%
Austria	-9.7%	+8.6%	+0.8%
Finland	-8.4%	11.7%	+0.8%
Netherlands	-10.8%	+8.8%	+0.7%
France	-11.6%	+15.9%	+1.2%
Belgium	-10.4%	+11.8%	+1.1%
Luxembourg	-9.3%	+8.4%	+0.8%
SPIGI Average	**-12.5%**	**+20.0%**	**+12.9%**
Non-SPIGI Average	**-9.9%**	**+10.6%**	**+0.6%**
12-Country Average	**-11.0%**	**+14.6%**	**+5.7%**

The stark differences and damages caused by a break-up of the currency union were reflected in other measures as well. Unemployment would have been even more severely impacted, rising by an average of twenty percent in SPIGI nations and 10.6 percent in the remainder. A eurozone break up would have been worse than any previous recession since World War II.

As previously noted, labour market rigidities would make economies less able to adjust internally to an external shock, worsening economic outcomes in those countries where rigidities were the most severe. For example, if, after such a negative economic shock, labour released in one sector could not be quickly absorbed into another, then unemployment outcomes would be worse and persist longer. In SPIGI countries, these rigidities have been measured as higher. In other words, differences in labour rules by country result in more rigid wages, more closed professions, or greater cultural differences that result in a greater reluctance of people to leave their country for a new member state. These rigidities partly explain the more severe employment outcomes predicted in these countries had the euro failed. Differences in these same rigidities have been very important in understanding the regional disparities that have actually occurred during the crisis as countries with more open labour markets have been far less affected than others.

Predictions based on the data in table 6-1 also demonstrated that inflation would vary by country. In SPIGI member states, the re-adoption of national currencies would result in precipitous declines in exchange rates relative to levels during the time of the euro, which would lead to rapid increases in the costs of imports, causing very high inflation. Since unemployment was predicted to rise, had the euro also failed, this would have led to even worse conditions than had unemployment risen alone, as people would have had less money with which to buy more expensive goods. Conversely, in stronger eurozone countries, the price effects were forecast to be much more moderate as these stronger economies would be better able to manage their currencies to stabilize domestic price shocks. Depending on the country, exchange rates in countries less troubled by the crisis, the northern and central creditor countries, would vary little or actually appreciate; quite the opposite to that effect experienced in SPIGI nations, again suggesting that weaker economies would have fared worse regardless of whether the euro survived or failed.

How do the outcomes that actually occurred compare to these predicted outcomes? Results in table 6-1 can be compared to the actual outcomes that occurred during the crisis to get some sense of both the success and cost of the policies implemented. A comparison suggests that policy efforts have allowed some economies to avoid the potentially devastating recessions a monetary union failure could have caused. In particular, those states in northern and central Europe, that have acted as creditor nations during the crisis, have experienced far better outcomes than they might have. Aided states, however, particularly those in the south, have not fared as well. SPIGI economies that were either forced to implement severe austerity measures as a condition of their aid or, like Spain and Italy, that did so defensively, have experienced severe recessions. In some cases, the recessions that occurred were almost as harsh as the predicted outcomes had the euro failed.

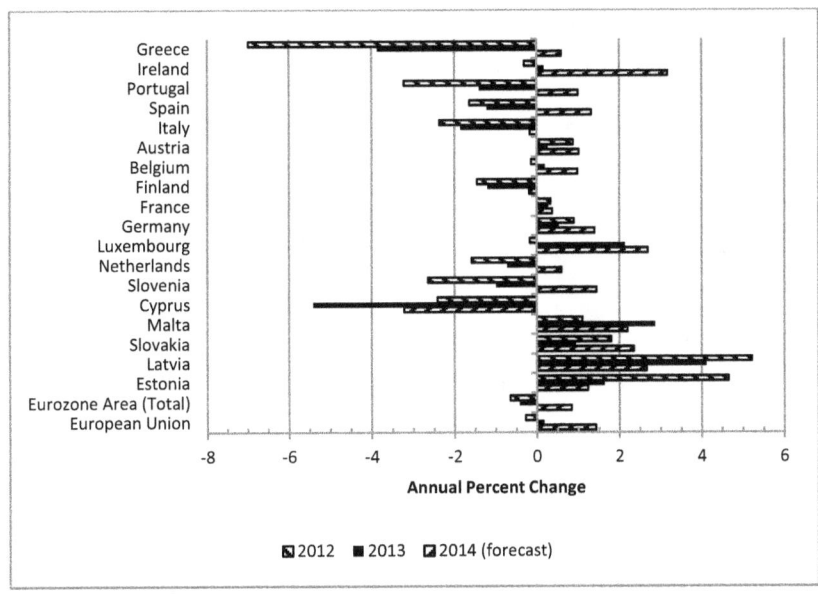

Figure 6-1: Eurozone Country Real GDP Annual Growth Rates: 2012 to 2014. Growth slowed to its lowest levels in many countries in 2012 as the majority of countries using the euro were in recession when the crisis reached its worst point. In 2013, growth rates improved in most countries; however, in eight of the countries using the euro, and in the eurozone as a whole, growth was still negative. By October 2014, growth was forecast to return to all states using the euro except Cyprus, Italy, and Finland. EU countries not using the euro averaged better growth rates than those using the common currency in all three years. Source data: IMF World Economic Outlook October 2014.

The severity of the recessions some countries have faced can be seen in the growth and unemployment outcomes that occurred since 2012, the worst year of the crisis. Figure 6-1 describes the GDP growth outcomes in 2012 and 2013, and forecasted outcomes for 2014. Output across the eurozone in 2012 contracted at an annual rate of 0.7 percent, and the recession continued into 2013 with contraction continuing at a 0.4 percent pace. In the sub-group of the original twelve that, combined, contribute over ninety-eight percent of total eurozone output, the 2012 contraction was worse than in the eurozone as a whole. Among these countries, the growth rate averaged negative 1.3 percent of GDP measured at an annual rate, and fell another 0.6 percent the following year. Across these countries, however, economic outcomes varied significantly.

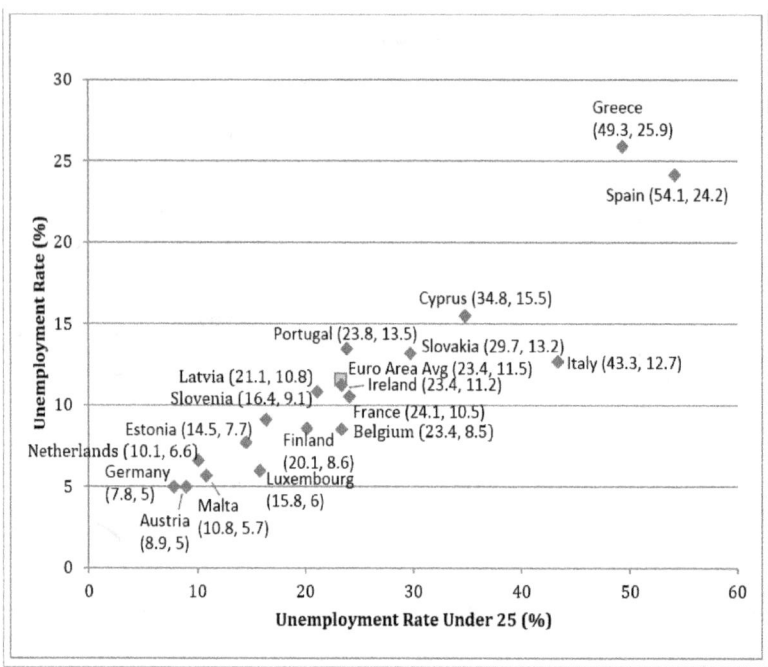

Figure 6-2: Eurozone Unemployment Rates (August 2014). Data labels identify the country and its respective youth (under 25) and overall unemployment rates. In most countries, rates are far above what would be expected at full employment, and, in several countries, they are at depression levels, especially in Greece and Spain. On average, almost one in four youth willing to work in the eurozone are unemployed. In Spain and Greece, it is half, with one in four people in the overall workforce still unemployed almost five years after the crisis began and two years after the ECB intervened, promising to "do what it takes" to avoid the failure of the euro in the summer of 2012. Source data: Eurostat.

The worst outcomes have, not unexpectedly, occurred in southern states. Greek output declined by seven percent in 2012. Another 3.9 percent decline occurred in 2013, resulting in a reduction of over ten percent of the economy's income in only two years, and approximately twenty-five percent since the crisis began in 2009. Only in 2014 was growth projected to return and the recession predicted to end. Other southern Europe countries have also been hard hit by the crisis. Cyprus's economy fell by over 2.4 percent in 2012 and, after their banking crisis and Troika-financed bailout, declined a further

5.4 percent in 2013, with a further contraction of 2.3 percent in 2014.[166] Portugal experienced an economic contraction of 3.3 percent in 2012 and a further 1.4 percent in 2013 before returning to growth. Italy and Spain also saw recessions last across 2012 and 2013. Of the SPIGI countries and Cyprus, only Ireland avoided contraction after 2012, returning to growth by 2013 and experiencing the strongest growth of any of the original twelve countries in 2014. However, Irish growth figures can be deceiving. A labour exodus during the crisis resulted in many of the most talented workers leaving for opportunities elsewhere. Mortgage failures also continued to occur in the housing market, leaving banks weak and construction moribund for several years after the bailout.[167]

At the other end of the spectrum, seven countries of the seventeen using the euro in 2012 experienced positive growth in 2012, albeit weak. Among the largest economies, Germany barely saw any growth in 2012, recording an increase in output of only 0.9 percent, while France recorded growth of 0.3 percent. For comparison, in 2012 Australian growth was 3.6 percent, the United States' growth was 2.3 percent, while in Canada it was 1.7 percent, and in Japan 1.5 percent, highlighting how the crisis worsened outcomes in Europe relative to similar developed economies worldwide.

Unemployment outcomes across the eurozone two years after the summer of 2012, the worst year of the crisis, are shown in figure 6-2.[168] As one might expect given growth figures, unemployment rates were generally very high across the monetary union and followed a worsening trend as the crisis continued. A full five years after those 2009 elections in Greece that precipitated the crisis, unemployment rates were still very high. In August 2014, the unemployment rate across the euro-area was 11.5 percent, 1.5 percent more than in the same month in 2009, which itself was elevated because of the effects of the recession that followed the 2008 financial crisis. Worse was the unemployment rate for those under twenty-five years of age, reaching 23.5 percent in the eurozone overall and in the double-digits in every eurozone country except

---

166 2013 and 2014 figures were reported as preliminary by Eurostat at the time of this writing.
167 By mid-2013, the effects of the real estate crisis in that country were still being felt with 15.8 percent of all mortgages found to be over ninety days in arrears, and 26.9 percent over ninety days overdue for buy-to-let mortgages. Twenty-five percent of small and medium size business loans held by banks were judged to be "impaired", and bank lending had slowed significantly, further slowing business and consumer activity. The credit crunch in Ireland was especially obvious in the statistics for bank loan refusal rates compared to other countries in the EU, where Ireland ranked second highest (IMF 2013b). See IMF country Report 13/163, "Ireland, Tenth Review under the extended arrangement," June 2013. Since that time credit has continued to be difficult despite a general recovery in the Irish economy.
168 By spring of 2015, European unemployment rates still stubbornly remained very close to those recorded the summer previous and shown in figure 6-2. The overall eurozone unemployment rate had fallen from 11.5 percent in August 2014 to 11.3 percent in March 2015, and youth unemployment across the eurozone from 23.8 percent to 22.7 percent over the same period.

Germany and Austria. Conditions were worst in Greece and Spain where the overall unemployment rate in each country hovered at nearly twenty-five percent, and where among those twenty-four years old and younger, it remained at nearly fifty percent or more. Among the other SPIGI states, Portugal and Italy still had unemployment rates in the thirteen percent range, with youth unemployment over twenty percent in Portugal and over forty percent in Italy. Only Ireland had actually achieved unemployment rate improvements relative to 2009 with both its overall and youth unemployment rates below those at the beginning of the crisis. However, such figures are deceiving considering that, in 2009, Ireland was already in a deep slump after its housing market bust, and that it has a history of using emigration to solve unemployment issues at home. Across the rest of the eurozone, only Germany, Estonia, Latvia, Slovakia, and Malta recorded improved unemployment rates since 2009. Again, the previously mentioned developed economies outside of Europe have all seen dramatic improvements in their employment conditions, emphasizing the stagnation that has taken place over the past five years in the EU.

For policy-makers, youth unemployment figures are potentially the most worrisome economic outcome of the crisis. The crisis has clearly had a differential impact on the peoples of Europe, both geographically and also demographically where a disproportionate share of the cost has fallen on young people. The potential implications and political fallout such a "lost generation" might have on the continent in the future are of grave concern. Overall, even if robust growth were to return to Europe, the rates of unemployment now present will take years to clear out of labour markets, with costs in potential output, earnings, and in depressed demand remaining high for years to come. The costs to future productivity will likewise be high as prolonged periods of unemployment undermine future human capital and depreciate people's skillsets. Clearly, such conditions could also sow the seeds of political discontent and social instability in a union already challenged by the events of the past several years.

Another trend is apparent in figure 6-4. Across the eurozone, deficits have been slashed. Compared to 2012, most countries are at or below the Maastricht required deficit limit of three percent of GDP. Those that are not have also reduced their deficits, most very significantly.[169] Despite the slow recovery, the majority of countries in the eurozone have embarked on an EU-mandated fiscal reduction to bring their deficit and debt targets back in line with EU requirements as defined by the Maastricht treaty and the more recent fiscal compact agreed to in 2012.

---

169 The exceptions are Slovenia and Finland. The former endured a banking crisis in 2013, resulting in bank aid, which caused the deficit to rise, while in Finland, the country had already achieved its target and an economic slowdown caused the deficit as a share of GDP to rise. This was allowable since its debt/GDP ratio was below sixty percent.

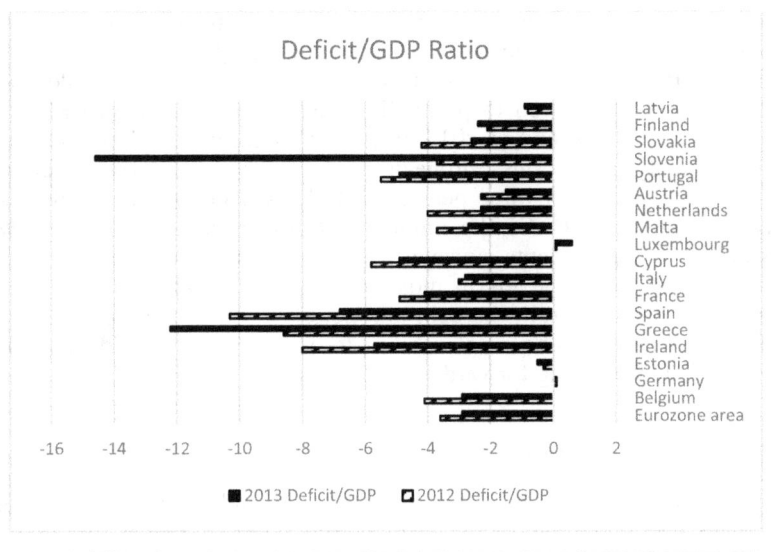

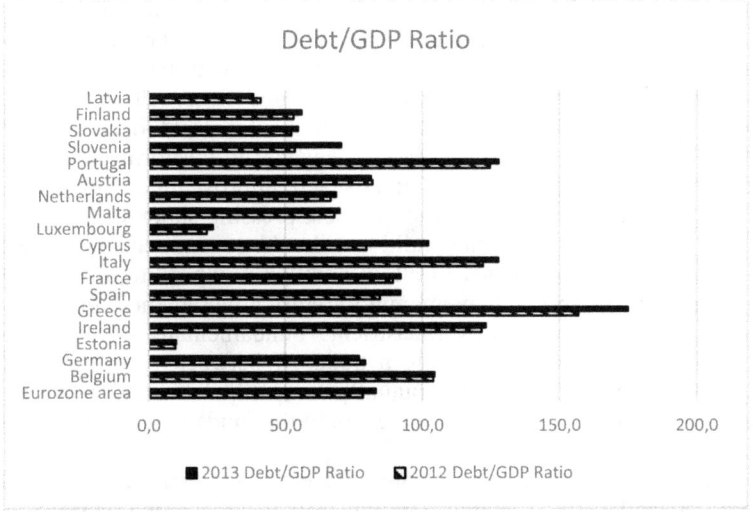

Figures 6-3 and 6-4: Eurozone Country Debt and Deficit to GDP levels (2012): Poor economic conditions in 2012 due to the eurozone crisis took a toll on deficit and debt levels. Only six countries in the currency union met their deficit target defined by the Maastricht Treaty, and only five were able to meet their debt-to-GDP requirement. This outcome suggests the trade-off that faced the currency union: either the eurozone would have to relax its Maastricht requirements or significant additional austerity would be necessary for most countries to reach these goals. Clearly, such a policy could threaten to worsen economic conditions at a time when most members were already in recession.

Slow growth and high unemployment have taken their toll on the fiscal positions of eurozone countries, too. Debt and deficit levels have spiralled as economic contraction has reduced tax revenues and increased social program costs. Compared to pre-crisis levels, the impact of the eurozone crisis is clear. By the end of 2013, only five countries could claim to meet the basic treaty obligations European monetary union requires – maintaining deficit levels under three percent of GDP and gross debt levels under sixty percent of GDP. Of the remaining thirteen states, most were well outside these requirements, and will remain so for some time. Simultaneously, unemployment levels in most countries will remain elevated for a number of years. Overall, the debt and deficit in the eurozone has significant implications for the area's ability to address growth and unemployment challenges moving forward.

Austerity versus Stimulus

The eurozone now faces a dilemma. Creditor and aided member states alike face weak economic conditions. The common currency means that troubled economies cannot simply devalue their currencies to stimulate their economies through greater exports. If treaty obligations were to be strictly followed in the future, significant austerity would be required in the countries where deficit and debt outcomes exceed Maastricht guidelines. Alternatively, even if treaty requirements were relaxed, given the levels of debt and deficit, member states have little fiscal space to engage in any form of stimulative policy to reverse current growth trends and improve unemployment outcomes. These circumstances lead to the most pressing short run policy questions. First, to improve current conditions, should governments be allowed to relax Maastricht requirements to allow additional expenditures intended to rekindle growth, or should they attempt to return government deficit and debt outcomes to those required by Maastricht? Fundamentally, this question is about policy effectiveness: is there a trade-off between "greater austerity" and growth, or are these policies mutually compatible? Second, if there were a desire to stimulate economies, where would the funds for such efforts come from?

This first question has dominated the eurozone crisis political debate since 2010 and reflects a longstanding policy debate in theoretical economics. Traditional macroeconomics would suggest that, in times of recession, governments should not reduce their fiscal position. Among "Keynesian" economists, policy advice would go further and advocate the expansion of government expenditures and deficits when economic conditions are like those in the eurozone, as other countries did in the aftermath of the world financial crisis of 2008.[170] In contrast, opponents argue that governments cannot stimulate economic activity in any real or permanent manner. Therefore, governments should only ensure stable economic finances: debt or deficit should be limited to long term efforts to increase capacity and capital that would otherwise not be provided privately or in optimal quantities. As a result, many creditor countries, particularly those that have proven the most fiscally conservative through the crisis – Germany, Austria, The Netherlands, and Finland – support lowering deficit and debt, or an austerity policy when government deficits exceed the Maastricht threshold of three percent.

Some advocating this argument would go even further, suggesting just the opposite view to Keynesians, that additional austerity would not hurt growth and might actually help it by creating additional confidence in bond markets through a demonstrated dedication to fiscal prudence. Such increases in confidence, they argue, would then lead to expansionary effects in the private sector economy, resulting in growth without increasing debt. Which viewpoint is true is an empirical question.

Since 2010, the eurozone has provided a useful Petri dish for a policy experiment across developed nations, as countries collectively increased austerity in reaction to events in bond markets following Greece's revelations regarding its debt and deficit. Major economies that had previously been focused on economic recovery after the worldwide financial crisis of 2008 now had a new fear – too much debt and becoming "the next Greece" in the eyes of bond markets. The debate to stimulate or cut back occurred among global leaders at the G-20 economic summit meeting in Toronto in June 2010. On one side, US president Barack Obama went to the summit with a plan to convince G-20 countries of the need for stimulus and a worldwide focus on job creation. At this meeting, however, Britain's prime minister David Cameron, Germany's chancellor Angela Merkel, and Canadian prime minister Stephen Harper's arguments for austerity carried the conference. As a result, world economic policy made a sharp U-turn, shifting its focus to debt, not recovery. Governments rapidly began to raise taxes and decrease expenditure.

---

170 The best known of these was likely the American Recovery and Reinvestment Act of 2009 in the United States that allocated over $700 billion in stimulus funds to stem the recession that followed the 2008 financial crisis there.

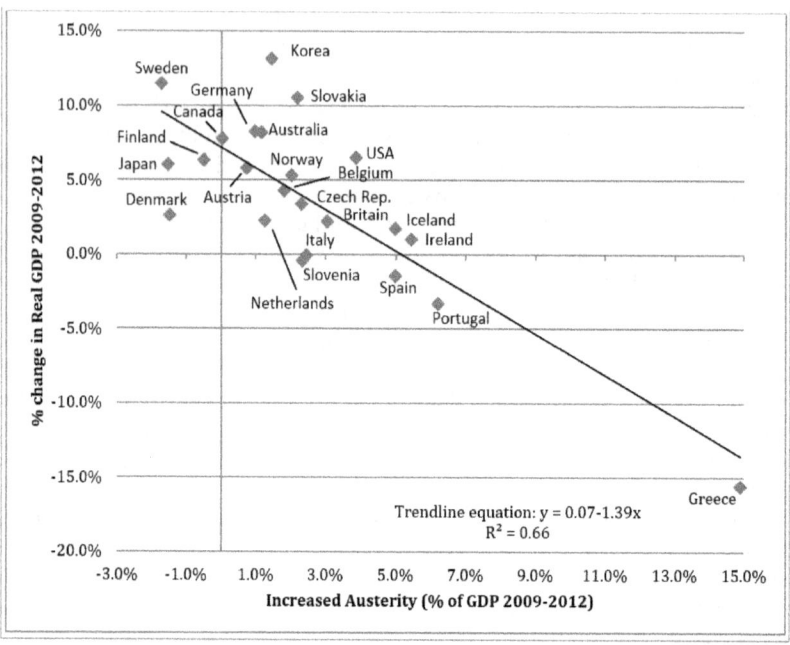

Figure 6-5: Austerity and Growth across Selected Countries: The relationship between increased austerity, (total combined increases in fiscal revenues and expenditure reductions), as a proportion of GDP generally appears to decrease real GDP growth. Using a cross-section of twenty-three developed countries' data from 2009 to 2012, the trend line shows that, on average, a one percent increase in austerity was associated with a 1.39 percent decrease in real GDP growth. Source Data: IMF Fiscal Monitor, October 2012 and World Economic Outlook Database, figure and computation created by the authors.

What has been the effect of these policies? While a simple association is not proof of causality, figure 6-5 uses the IMF's online data from 2009 to 2012 to summarize growth and austerity outcomes; each point shows a single country's austerity and growth outcome over this period. Of the twenty-three countries included in figure 6-5, some were recovering or had recovered from the financial crisis of 2008 and associated recession afterward (such as the United States) while some were still in recession or had slipped back into recession (like many of the countries affected by the eurozone crisis). While recovering countries tended to see tax revenues increase after the recession because of improved economic conditions, the majority of the countries shown here reduced their fiscal position regardless of the state of their economies by some combination of increased taxes or reduced expenditures. On average, across the countries shown, government austerity increased by 2.5

percent of GDP. The collection of countries shown includes thirteen from the eurozone where austerity increased by an average 3.5 percent of GDP. Austerity in the eurozone ranged from a low of -0.5 percent in Finland, when GDP grew by 6.4 percent over the same period (Finland's fiscal position increased as a percent of GDP, the opposite of austerity) to a high of 14.9 percent in Greece. Greece's government increased its tax revenues and decreased expenditure by an amount equivalent to 14.9 percent of the economy's output. At the same time, Greece's economic output contracted by almost sixteen percent over the three year period.

To estimate the implied relationship in Figure 6-5 between austerity and growth, a simple regression analysis was conducted, which is summarized by the trend line shown in the figure. More austerity, (from increased tax revenues, decreased expenditures or both) as measured by the total change in a country's fiscal position as a percentage of its economic output between 2009 and 2012, is shown by moving rightward along the horizontal axis of the chart. A country's economic growth over the same period is shown on the vertical axis as the percentage change in GDP. As shown by the estimated trend line's negative slope, on average, an increase in austerity relative to GDP of one percent (increased taxes and/or reduced expenditures) was associated with 1.39 percent decline in economic growth.[171] The data from this period support a view consistent with Keynesian economists: that economic growth slows when a government contributes less and takes more from the economy. There appears to be little evidence that greater austerity is consistent with increased growth. More sophisticated analyses also reinforce the results shown. The International Monetary Fund (IMF) issued a widely read report in late 2012 that detailed its analysis of the cost of austerity's efforts on world economic growth.[172] It concluded that the effects of increased austerity across the world likely decreased economic growth significantly.

---

171 One must not interpret the relationship presented between austerity and growth as causal. The trend line only summarizes the average correspondence. A more carefully detailed structural study is necessary to determine whether this is causal. A traditional Keynesian framework would argue greater austerity is causal with respect to output contraction, and that the degree of contraction is determined by the fiscal multiplier. A discussion can be found in Blanchard and Leigh regarding the possible size of multipliers at the time of the data presented: Oliver J. Blanchard, and Daniel Leigh, *Growth forecast errors and fiscal multipliers*.,no. w18779, National Bureau of Economic Research, 2013, http://www.sindacalmente.org/sites/www.sindacalmente.org/files/wp1301_studio_fmi.pdf (accessed 22 August 2015).

172 See IMF, World Economic Outlook, October 2012. The analysis did not just rely on the simple relationship shown in figure 6-5, it also relied on an analysis of IMF forecasts and actual outcomes to determine whether the IMF estimates of what is known as the "fiscal multiplier" were consistently underestimated. This is reported in more detail in Oliver Blanchard and Daniel Leigh, "Growth Forecast Errors and Fiscal Multipliers" IMF Work-

These results have important implications for European macroeconomic policy. First, they suggest less austerity would be better than more. To promote growth, especially in the economies most affected by the crisis, austerity demands may have to be reduced, and, stimulus may, in fact, be appropriate. However, how would such a policy change be financed? Few options exist. Delivering aid in the form of EU grants or external stimulus could be one possibility, but where would these funds come from? Creditor countries have already financed several bailouts, and have exhausted the public's political will to extend further financing to the troubled countries, especially to the extent that would be necessary to meaningfully increase employment and growth in those troubled economies of Europe.

Alternatively, troubled countries could finance their own stimulus, but, again, where would the funds come from? The troubled economies that might benefit most from such stimulus are exactly the countries that have been unable to access international credit markets during the crisis. While all the SPIGI countries have since resumed new borrowing on sovereign debt markets, the expansion of credit necessary to stimulate their economies may not be possible, and embarking on such efforts could undermine the newly restored confidence these countries have been able to earn regarding their debt. Creditor countries would likely have to be the source of funds, and again, the political will does not seem to be present. Given these practical constraints, reducing austerity demands is probably the most realistic means to deliver swifter recovery within the troubled economies. Opponents to such plans, however, would argue that such actions could undermine the future stability of the currency and reduce the incentives for economic reforms that are necessary to make troubled economies more competitive.

A focus on troubled economies, however, threatens to lose sight of the potential for economic improvement elsewhere. With respect to stimulating the most troubled economies in Europe, it is possible that stimulus in the least troubled economies could be an effective recovery policy. Specifically, if the strongest economies were to take actions to stimulate their own economies internally, such growth could lead to two positive outcomes where recovery is needed most. First, growth in the strongest economies is likely to increase export demand from weaker economies. It could also create employment for migrants from high unemployment states. Increased incomes in wealthier economies could also stimulate tourism and other economic activity in southern economies in Europe, thereby further aiding their growth. Second, strong growth in creditor economies is also likely to increase inflation in these countries, raising wage levels. Such a change could improve the relative competitiveness of weaker eurozone economies, further stimulating their

---

ing Paper WP/13/1, (January 2013) https://www.imf.org/external/pubs/ft/wp/2013/wp1301.pdf.

export growth. Stimulus in creditor economies would also have another advantage of avoiding the type of political resistance increasing financing to troubled countries would create. Since growth in creditor economies has not been strong, efforts to improve growth in these countries would likely be welcomed. As is clear in figure 6-5 though, the opposite has occurred as economies across the eurozone have consolidated their fiscal budgets.

The problem of finding funds to stimulate troubled economies in the eurozone was well illustrated by the EU's response in 2012 and 2013. In 2012, a "Growth Pact" championed by France was suggested as a means of balancing Germany's efforts to achieve the Fiscal Compact. In June 2012, the EU announced it would allocate €130 billion to programs to be used to help troubled economies in the eurozone recover. Nevertheless, practically no new funds were on offer. Almost half of the announced funds were merely repurposed from existing EU regional development funds. Further, the remaining funds pledged were contingent on private sector contributions that would have to come from external private investment with the ECB providing limited loan guarantees. Of course, given conditions in the eurozone, there was little private appetite to provide such funding.[173]

In 2013, an additional EU sponsored Youth Unemployment Initiative promised €6 billion in aid for the jobless. However, such an effort was far less than was necessary to make a dent in the EU's unemployment problem given the economy's €13 trillion size. Such efforts suggest the difficulty in defining meaningful policy under the eurozone's current economic circumstances and such announcements appear to be made more for political effect than to accomplish meaningful change.

The most politically acceptable policies are likely to be those that focus on improving short-term recovery in creditor nation economies. Such efforts could focus on increasing economic activity in the strongest eurozone economies, Germany's for example, then allowing this increased demand to raise export demand in troubled economies elsewhere. In this way, the stronger economies could pull the weaker ones out of recession through stronger growth. Furthermore, higher growth in stronger countries could result in greater wage growth in these economies, thereby increasing the relative competitiveness of the troubled economies where internal devaluation has caused wage costs to fall. Such plans also have the additional benefit of being more politically acceptable as stimulus funds are used in the countries providing them. Ultimately, political constraints bind more tightly than economic. Indeed, Germany has already indicated that it is unwilling to expand its fiscal budget to finance growth oriented policies and unwilling to relax Maastricht commitments for other countries.

---

173 Similar programs were also been announced in 2014 regarding expansion of infrastructure expenditures, but few new funds were pledged to the efforts.

Political Costs

What would have happened politically had the euro broken up? In the end, Angela Merkel chose to support the euro because, as she put it, "If the euro falls, then Europe falls."[174] The European Union derives much of its legitimacy from economic prosperity; therefore, the feared depression that would have ensued with a breakup of the euro would have discredited the European project. Fritz W. Scharf and Walter Lacqueur both went so far as to argue that the damage had already been done. According to Scharf, the EU's legitimacy has already suffered as it proved itself unable to deliver the prosperity promised in the euro.[175] Lacqueur stated the eurozone crisis put Europe as a whole on the road to decline, rendering it merely a living "museum or a cultural amusement park for the nouveau riche of globalization."[176] So important is the euro to the EU that Wolfgang Münchau asked, "What is the point of the EU beyond the eurozone?" He posited that between the European Economic Area and the proposed Transatlantic Free Trade Area, there were few advantages to a country outside the euro to remain in the EU.

What of it? What would it mean if the European Union ceased to exist, as we know it? Practically speaking, without the European level of governance,[177] member states would have to renationalize policy, which would be less efficient and give them less influence in the world. As Charles Kupchan explained:

> From London to Berlin to Warsaw, Europe is experiencing a renationalization of political life, with countries clawing back the sovereignty they once willingly sacrificed in pursuit of a collective ideal. ... If these trends continue, they could compromise one of the most significant and unlikely accomplishments of the 20th century: an integrated Europe, at peace with itself, seeking to project power as a cohesive whole. The result would be individual nations consigned to geopolitical irrelevance – and a United States bereft of a partner willing or able to shoulder global burdens.[178]

---

174 Peter Spiegel, "If the euro falls, Europe falls", part 3 of the series "How the euro was saved" *Financial Times*, 15 May 2014.
175 Fritz W. Scharpf, *"Political Legitimacy in a Non-Optimal Currency Area,"* KFG Working Paper 52 (Berlin: *Freie Universität Berlin* 2013) http://userpage.fu-berlin.de/kfgeu/kfgwp/wpseries/WorkingPaperKFG_52.pdf *(accessed 3 August 2015).*
176 "'An Anxious Continent': Walter Laqueur on Europe's Decline" *Der Spiegel*, 26 July 2013, www.spiegel.de/international/europe/interview-with-historian-walter-laqueur-on-the-decline-of-europe-a-912837.html (accessed 3 August 2015).
177 For more on multi-level governance, see Liesbet Hooghe and Gary Marks, *Multilevel Governance and European Integration* (Lanham, MD: Rowman & Littlefield, 2001).
178 Charles Kupchan, "As Nationalism Rises, Will the European Union Fail?" *Washington Post*, 29 August 2010.

Integration takes advantage of economies and politics of scale to increase the prosperity and influence of all participants. Economically, integration has increased the wealth of every member state. Politically, integration has stabilized nascent democracies, for example, in Greece, Spain, and Portugal. The EU has strengthened the voice of Europe in international affairs. *En bref*, European integration coincides with the longest period of peace and prosperity Europe has ever known. Ultimately, Merkel was right: the euro is too big to fail because the European project is too big to fail, hence, the importance of the euro.

In general, the Europeans at the grassroots level recognize these accomplishments. In a Eurobarometer poll, a majority of people pointed to free movement of people, goods and services as well as peace among the member states as the top two accomplishments of the EU. The euro came in third above student exchange programs, the EU's political and diplomatic influence in the world, the EU's economic power, social welfare and the Common Agricultural Policy.[179]

Andrew Moravcsik thought reports of Europe's demise were greatly exaggerated:

> The euro crisis itself has even allowed European policy to intensify in existing areas, such as monetary and banking regulation. And even a collapse of the euro would not jeopardize the existence of the EU, despite what such commentators as Walter Laqueur and Wolfgang Münchau have at times suggested. Whatever the outcome of the crisis, the EU will remain without rival the most ambitious and successful example of voluntary international cooperation in world history.[180]

How much damage did the eurozone crisis cause the European Union politically? Certainly, the EU's image was tarnished during the crisis, but, at the same time, support for the euro remained positive. Opinion polls demonstrate that, although backing for the EU and the euro dipped during the eurozone crisis, at the same time, many Europeans recognized that more integration was the solution. Trust in the EU went down significantly, and, yet, it still remained the most trusted governmental entity surpassing trust in both national governments and parliaments. Furthermore, it persisted as the organization of choice to resolve the crisis. According to the polls, SPIGI country residents (excluding Greece) actually felt closer to other Europeans after the crisis. The power of the idea of the euro endured, increasing the foundations of solidarity on which further integration could take root.

---

179 Eurobarometer 81, (spring 2014), 32.
180 Andrew Moravcsik, "Europe After the Crisis: How to Sustain a Common Currency" *Foreign Affairs* (May/June 2012) https://www.foreignaffairs.com/articles/europe/2012-05-01/europe-after-crisis (accessed 3 August 2015).

Did the eurozone crisis spawn a new age of Euro-scepticism under the extreme right? While the extreme right received a strong boost from the crisis, their support may wane as economic conditions improve. The extreme right has always flourished under the 'politics of despair': when people are desperate, desperate solutions seem more plausible. Moreover, people are prone to vote extreme right when they want to punish the mainstream parties. They are also more likely to turn out in an election.[181] Although the right had a stunning victory in the 2014 European Parliament elections, turnout was the lowest ever at 42.5 percent. Most likely, those who made the effort to vote were disproportionately supportive of the right compared to the electorate as a whole. In general, the extreme right does better among the less educated whereas the EU has greater support among the more highly educated. Eurobarometer polls show that the EU continues to have strong support from this larger demographic.[182]

The following opinion polls document public sentiment towards the euro, in general, and towards the EU during the crisis. The advent of the euro in 2002 boosted a small amount of pro-Europe feeling. The crisis itself activated some rally-round-the-flag support among some SPIGI citizens, especially, and in several eurozone countries, in general; however, it accentuated suspicion of the euro in non-eurozone countries and in specific eurozone ones (e.g. Germany and Greece). Broadly speaking, the more directly a member state was affected by the crisis, for better or even for worse, the more likely the crisis was to create pro-Europe support among its inhabitants.

Public Attitudes Towards the Euro

How successful is the euro as a political tool, that is, as a device to enhance public support for the integration project? In general, the answer is quite good. Contrary to Scharf, Thomas Risse argued, "In sum, there is an emerging demos in the European polity and it has been strengthened during the euro crisis."[183] Both the introduction of the euro and – perhaps counter-intuitively – the subsequent crisis created an uptick in European feeling among the people, especially those in the eurozone.

The European Union feted the arrival of the euro on New Year's 2002 as the birth of a new age. Once the fanfare subsided, public support for the euro

---

181 Anger is a great motivator in getting people to the polls. See Nicholas A. Valentino, *et al.*, "Election night's alright [sic] for fighting: The role of emotions in political participation", *The Journal of Politics* 73 (2011): 156-170.
182 For more in-depth analysis, see Marcel Lubbers, *Exclusionist electorates. Extreme rightwing voting in Western Europe*, (Nijmegen: KUN/ICS, 2001).
183 Thomas Risse, "No Demos? Identities and Public Spheres in the Euro Crisis," *JCMS: Journal of Common Market Studies* 52.6 (2014): 1215.

remained strong. In 2002, Eurobarometer asked whether citizens were more likely to feel 'European' after using the common currency for a year. The great majority of the people felt no change. However, on average, eighteen percent did feel more European, and a much more significant thirty-two percent did in Ireland and Italy (see figure 6-6). In terms of creating more European solidarity, the introduction of the euro had negligible negative consequences.

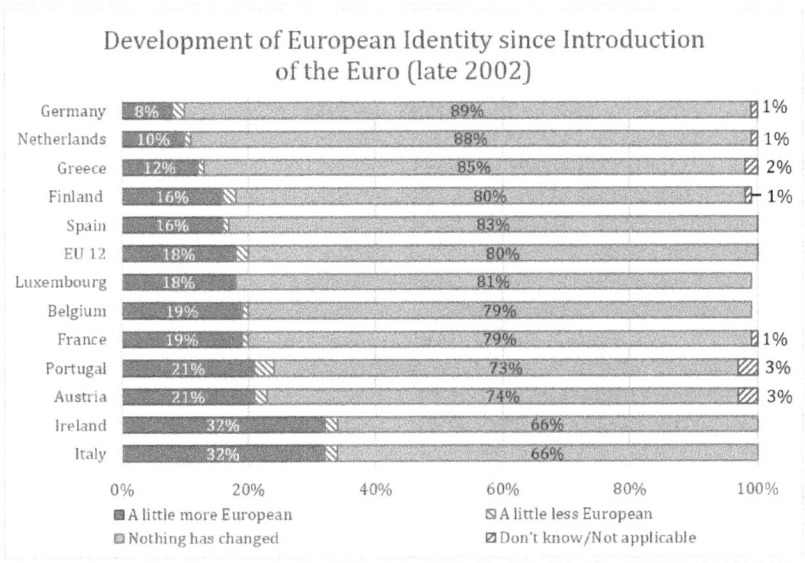

Figure 6-6: Flash Eurobarometer 139 "The euro, one year later" (2002), 71.

Certainly, Europeans were 'happy' about it. Luxembourgers, the Irish and the Belgians were happiest about the euro; Portugal, Italy, Greece and Spain were all in the middle. Sixty-eight percent of Germans were unhappy about losing the Deutsche Mark, a symbol of post-War regrowth and rehabilitation. Overall, fifty percent were happy or very happy. Removing Germany from the average, 62.5 percent of the other eleven eurozone countries were 'happy' about the euro.

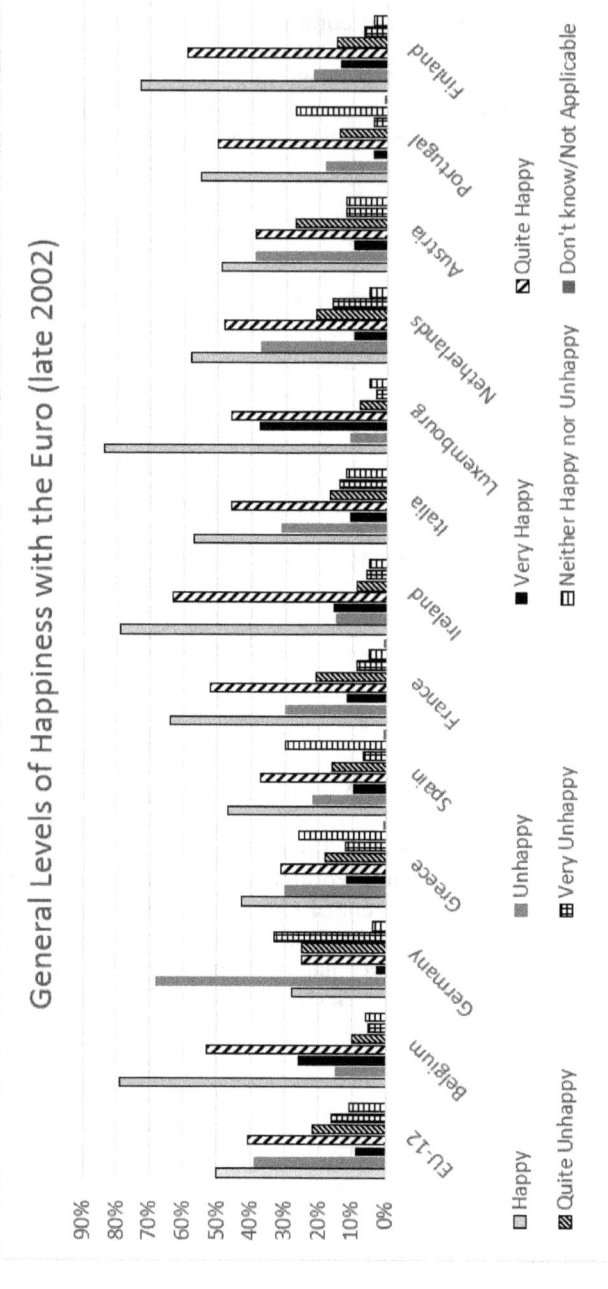

Figure 6-7: Flash Eurobarometer 139, "The Euro, one year later" (2002), p. 74.

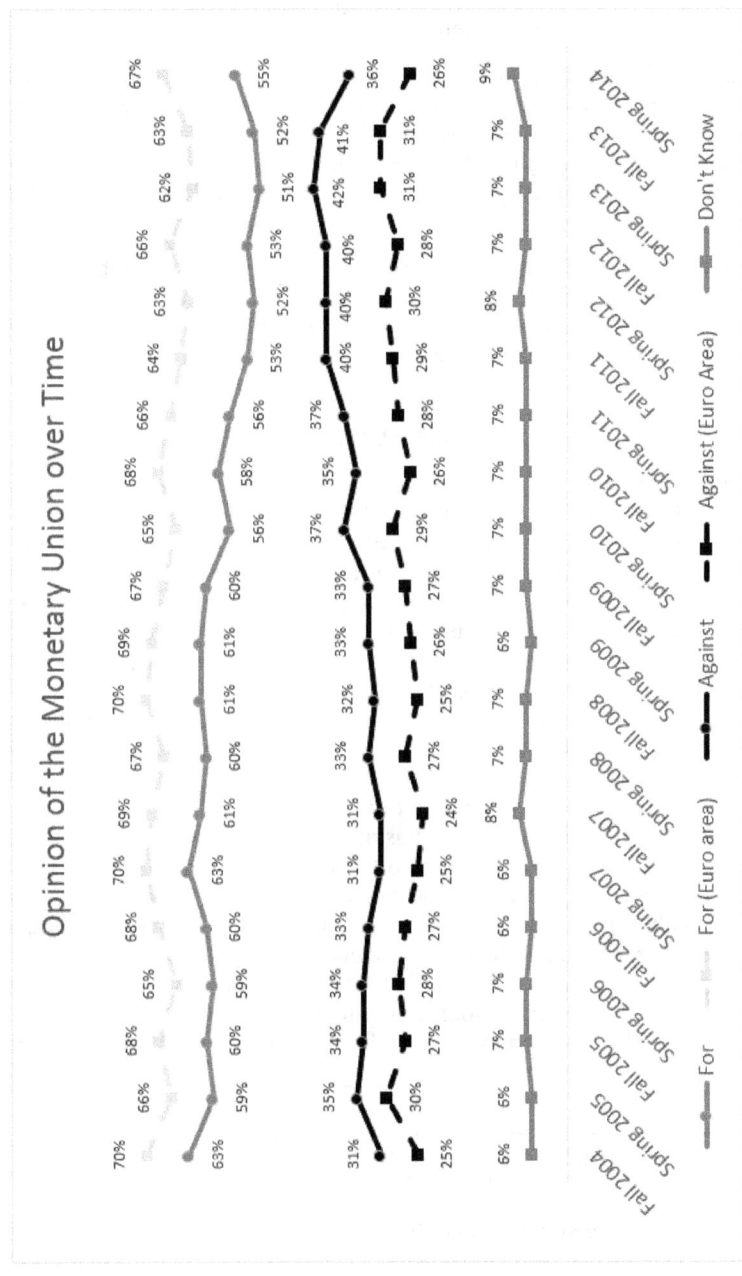

Figure 6-8: Standard Eurobarometer 81 (spring 2014) 19.

Despite the overall levels of 'happiness', the pollsters at Eurobarometer worried about the general downward trend from a year earlier:

> Changes in the level of satisfaction are worrying. This seems to result from a number of elements on which negative opinions were expressed as part of this survey, such as difficulties experienced in using the euro and the feeling of being cheated upon when converting prices. But this could also be explained by the adverse economic background in which the survey took place.[184]

Two lessons can be taken from the above quotation. First, the numbers were still high albeit down from a year earlier. Second, adverse economic conditions affect popular support for the euro. Therefore, one can predict that popular support for the euro vacillates depending on the health of the economy.

Public Attitudes During the Eurozone Crisis

The eurozone crisis has had a mixed effect on the public. Very often, the people will pull together during a crisis, what is known as the "rally-round-the-flag" effect. Despite some anger and disillusionment, people agreed that more integration was the answer. In 2012, more than seventy percent of respondents agreed that the following measures would be effective in tackling the financial and economic crisis: "a stronger coordination of economic policy among all the EU member states"; "a stronger coordination of economic and financial policies" among eurozone countries; and "a more important role for the EU in regulating financial services".[185] A whopping eighty-five percent agreed that "as a consequence of the crisis, EU countries will have to work more closely together." A majority believed the crisis would make the EU stronger in the long run.[186]

The economic and financial crisis has also not cooled enthusiasm for the euro. The following graph charts support for the common currency from 2004 to 2014. Among all EU countries, support for the euro fell to its lowest ebb in 2013 with fifty-one percent, showing that even at its lowest point, a majority of Europeans were in favour of the euro. Among eurozone countries, that is, the people the most affected, 2013 also had the lowest showing of sixty-two percent. The graph demonstrates that support for the euro is extremely resilient. The main opposition to the euro comes from those outside it.[187]

---

184 Flash Eurobarometer 139 "The €uro, one year later" (2002), 75.
185 Standard Eurobarometer 78 (autumn 2012), 28.
186 Ibid., 40.
187 Standard Eurobarometer 81 (spring 2014), 19.

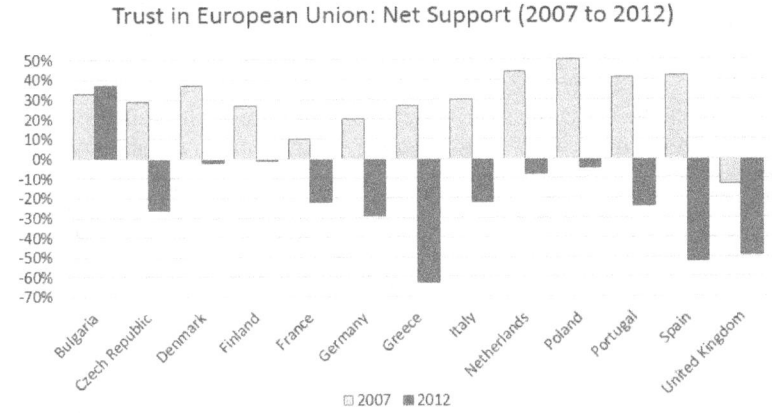

Figure 6-9: Net trust change in support for the European Union from 2007-2012. Jose Ignacio Torreblanca and Mark Leonard, "The continent-wide rise of Euroscepticism" European Council on Foreign Relations Policy Memo, May 2013 http://www.ecfr.eu/page/-/ECFR79_EUROSCEPTICISM_BRIEF_AW.pdf (accessed 3 August 2015).

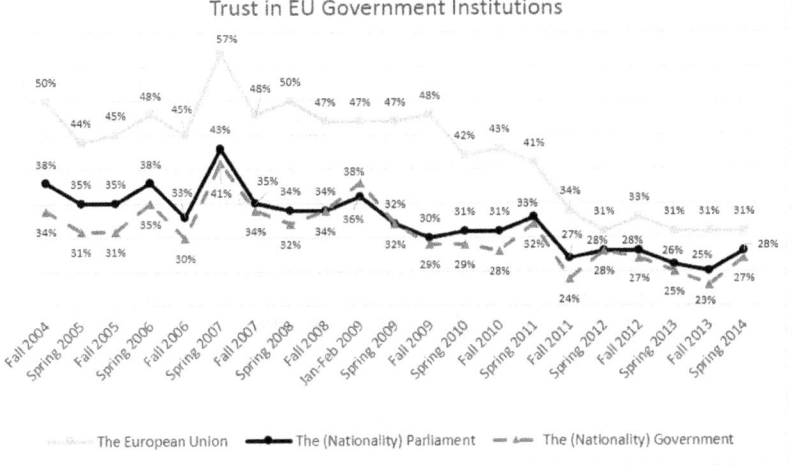

Figure 6-10: Eurobarometer 81 spring 2014, 19.

Trust in the EU fell to record levels in 2013, making headlines,[188] but although true, the numbers were not as negative as one might think. The European Council on Foreign Relations took Eurobarometer figures to determine net trust in the EU. Their chart below shows the severe decline in the people's trust of the EU from 2007 to 2012.[189] That said, the European Union remains more trusted than national governments, national parliaments, the IMF, the G-20, and the United States.[190] The following time series demonstrates that the EU has held its place as the most trusted institution over the past ten years.[191] In other words, despite these steep declines, the EU remains the most trusted governmental organization among those polled. While the people were unhappy with the economic situation, they choose not to change horses. Daniel Debomy argued that while more people might say "no" to the EU, in general support for the euro remained.[192]

In the spring 2014 Eurobarometer, many indicators regarding the EU were on the rise, most likely because the economy was doing better.[193] In terms of identity, the crisis has made forty-one percent of EU citizens overall feel closer to each other.[194] In eurozone countries, 43.2 percent felt closer. Among the SPIGI countries, the figure jumped to 48.6 percent. If one adds in Cyprus, the average increases to 50.5.[195] Therefore, the more one is affected by the crisis, the more likely the citizen is to have a feeling of increased closeness with his and her fellow Europeans. Notably, socio-demographics made no difference in the responses to these questions.[196] Moreover, with the upturn in the economy, the spring 2014 Eurobarometer showed the highest levels of feelings of EU citizenship since 2010. Fully sixty-five percent of respondents said they felt they were EU citizens, a six percent increase from the year before. Most interestingly, the six point increase was reflected in the category "yes, definitely".[197] The German Marshall fund concluded "The

---

188 See for example Ian Traynor, "Crisis for Europe as trust hits record low" 24 April 2013, http://www.theguardian.com/world/2013/apr/24/trust-eu-falls-record-low (accessed 3 August 2015).
189 Jose Ignacio Torreblanca and Mark Leonard, "The continent-wide rise of Euroscepticism" European Council on Foreign Relations Policy Memo, May 2013 http://www.ecfr.eu/page/-/ECFR79_EUROSCEPTICISM_BRIEF_AW.pdf (accessed 3 August 2015).
190 Standard Eurobarometer 78 (autumn 2012), 17.
191 Standard Eurobarometer 81 (spring 2014), 19.
192 Daniel Debomy, "EU No, Euro Yes?: European Public Opinions Facing the Crisis (2007-2012)" Notre Europe: Jacques Delors Institute, Policy Paper 90, 27 March 2013, http://www.notre-europe.eu/media/publicopinioneurozonecrisis-debomy-ne-jdi-mar13.pdf?pdf=ok (accessed 3 August 2015).
193 http://ec.europa.eu/public_opinion/archives/eb/eb81/eb81_publ_en.pdf, 6.
194 Standard Eurobarometer 80 (Autumn 2013) "Europeans, The European Union, and the Crisis" http://ec.europa.eu/public_opinion/archives/eb/eb80/eb80_cri_en.pdf, 40.
195 Ibid. These averages were calculated using the figures on 40.
196 Ibid., 41-43.
197 Standard Eurobarometer 81 (spring 2014), First Results, 28.

Great Recession and the sovereign debt crisis left Europeans somewhat unsure about the euro but still committed to the European Union as an economic entity. Public opinion seems to support the argument that crises tend to lead to more citizen support for integration rather than less."[198]

Nevertheless, decisions in the EU are not made by continental majority. Instead they are made at the country level, so it is important not to confuse a general result across the EU for a meaningful one. After all, it could take only one country to leave the euro and/or a major country like Germany to pull its support for the eurozone to crumble. Pan-European support will not translate in to pro-European action. Therefore, it is unclear whether support for the euro and the EU has improved or not in a meaningful way that could lead to greater reform. Ultimately, it is easier to say "no" than to come up with structural modifications that pass muster with every member state.

The Rise of Euro-Scepticism

While a majority of Europeans continued to support the European project, almost half became much more anti-EU. EC president José Manuel Barroso warned: "Socially and politically, one policy that is only seen as austerity is, of course, not sustainable. ... We haven't done everything right ... The policy has reached its limits because it has to have a minimum of political and social support."[199] Economic contraction and unemployment – especially youth unemployment – led to despair. In Gallup polls from Spring 2011, more people believed their economic situation was deteriorating rather than improving, with numbers reaching seventy-one percent and sixty-one percent in Greece and Portugal respectively.[200]

The rise of extreme right parties and the popularity of their nationalist and protectionist messages during periods of economic crisis may be due to their ability to provide scapegoats. Historically, these have been foreigners as they have blamed immigration policies, but, during the crisis, they have blamed the EU. In The Netherlands, the Party for Freedom, came in third in the 2010 parliamentary elections. Their leader, Geer Wilders, advocated returning to the guilder. In Finland, the True Finn party won nineteen percent of the vote in the 2011 elections. In 2012, in France, National Front candidate Marine Le Pen came in third in the presidential election with almost eighteen

---

198 German Marshall Fund, Transatlantic Trends, Key Findings 2010, 13, http://trends.gmfus.org/files/archived/doc/2010_English_Key.pdf (accessed 3 August 2015).
199 Ian Traynor, EU near austerity limit, says Barroso" *The Guardian,* 22 April 2013, http://www.theguardian.com/world/2013/apr/22/eu-near-austerity-limit-barroso?INTCMP=SRC (accessed 3 August 2015).
200 Bruce Stokes, "What Europeans Think About the Eurocrisis" German Marshall Fund, January 2012, http://www.gmfus.org/file/2552/download (accessed 3 August 2015).

percent of the vote. In Greece, in 2012, the neo-Nazi Golden Dawn, running on an anti-austerity and anti-immigrant platform, had its best showing winning seven percent of the vote and seats in the Hellenic parliament.

Other anti-establishment or simply anti-EU or euro parties have done well during the crisis, too. In the UK, the United Kingdom Independence Party (UKIP) has improved its standing, garnering almost one quarter of the vote in local elections and coming in third with 12.6 percent of the vote in the 2015 general election. UKIP's popularity has even forced the prime minister, David Cameron, to promise a referendum on Britain's membership in the EU should he win re-election. He did, and the referendum is tentatively scheduled for 2017.

In Italy, Beppo Grillo began the Five Star Movement in 2010. On an anti-establishment and anti-euro platform, his party won over twenty-five percent of the vote in the 2013 election. In Germany, the anti-euro, although not anti-EU, party, Alternative for Germany, founded in 2013, won 4.7 percent of the vote in the general election, just shy of the five percent threshold needed to win a seat in the Bundestag. With many academic and intellectual supporters, the party used slogans such as "The euro splits Europe", "The courage to tell the truth: Citizens are what matter to our system, and nothing else," and "So that Europe doesn't fail due to the euro"[201]. One year later, the party won seven out of Germany's ninety-six seats in the European Parliament and secured seats in the state parliaments of Saxony, Brandenburg, and Thuringia.

Together, these anti-EU parties had their best showing to date in the 2014 European Parliament election. They gained ten percent more seats in parliament bringing the number of anti-Europe parties in the EP to thirty percent.[202] This statistic should, however, be taken with a grain of salt. The European Parliament saw its lowest turnout in 2014 of 42.5 percent, the latest in a thirty-year-long downward trend. For better or for worse, most voters were apathetic. In addition, as explained earlier, support for the extreme right usually spikes during periods of economic strife, meaning that this rise will be as short or long-lived as the recession. Finally, the European Parliament has restricted powers; therefore, the rise in anti-EU MEPs will most likely have limited impact on the EU, especially considering that this group is so nationalist that it seldom crosses state lines to cooperate together within the EP setting.

---

201 In German, these slogans were "Der Euro spaltet Europa", "Mut zur Wahrheit. Die Bürger sind systemrelevant. Sonst nichts", and "Damit Europa nicht am Euro Scheitert".
202 *The Economist* "The Euroskeptic Union" 31 May 2014.

The Eurozone Crisis and Anti-Semitism

Special attention must also be drawn to the rise of anti-Semitism in the context of the eurozone crisis. According to a poll from the Anti-Defamation League, "Overall, 31 percent of respondents across Europe blame Jews in the financial industry either "a great deal," "a good amount" or "a little" for the current global economic crisis."[203] Although this Europe-wide surge in anti-Semitism springs from different sources, "In Spain, Italy and Greece the Judeophobia feeds off resentment towards the global financial system, which is widely blamed for these countries' economic woes and deep recession."[204]

Anti-foreigner as well as anti-Jewish and anti-Roma sentiment is particularly strong in Hungary. Hungarian philosopher Gaspar Miklos Tamas claimed Hungary has, "a new official state ideology [calling it] a mixture of euro-skeptic nationalism and ethnicism."[205] Hungary's Jobbik party[206], branded by its leader Gabor Vona as "the strongest national radical party" in Europe, won twenty percent of the vote in the 2014 election returning Prime Minister Viktor Orbán to power in a right-wing coalition with Oban's party Fidesz. Jobbik advocated detention camps for Roma "deviants" and has argued that Jews are a "national security risk"[207] One Jobbik MP went so far as to propose national registration lists for Jews.[208] While Orbán tried to downplay Hungarian anti-Semitism before the World Jewish Congress in 2013, *Der Spiegel* reported:

> Orbán also appeared to attribute Hungarian anti-Semitism to the alleged failures of the European Union, which has criticized the Fidesz government on a raft of issues, from a restrictive media law to a controversial new constitution, which Orban [sic] on Sunday called Hungary's "first, democratic Constitution," implying that the country had operated with a

---

203 Anti-Defamation League, "Attitudes Towards Jews in Seven European Countries", February 2009, 16, http://www.adl.org/assets/pdf/israel-international/Public-ADL-Anti-Semitism-Presentation-February-2009-_3_.pdf (accessed 3 August 2015).
204 Anshel Pfeffer, "Anti-Semitism in Europe: A crisis, but not yet a catastrophe" *Haaretz* 12 August 2014, http://www.haaretz.com/jewish-world/jewish-world-features/.premium-1.610089 (accessed 3 August 2015).
205 Deutsche Welle, "Hungary's Orban likes to dislike Brussels" 23 April 2014 http://www.dw.de/hungarys-orban-likes-to-dislike-brussels/a-17587537.
206 The full name is Jobbik: The Movement for a Better Hungary or *Jobbik Magyarországért Mozgalom*.
207 Tony Patterson, "Hungary election: Concerns as neo-Nazi Jobbik party wins 20% of vote" *The Independent* (UK), 7 April 2014. http://www.independent.co.uk/news/world/europe/concerns-as-neonazi-jobbik-party-wins-20-of-hungary-vote-9244541.html (accessed 31 August 2015).
208 Martin Dunai, "Outrage at "Jewish List " call in Hungary parliament" *Reuters* 27 November 2012, http://www.reuters.com/article/2012/11/27/us-hungary-antisemitism-idUSBRE8AQ1BN20121127 (accessed 31 August 2015).

non-democratic Constitution until Fidsez returned to power three years ago. "The economic crisis is shaking Europe to the core, and the unsuccessful crisis management of European leaders is causing increasingly deep frustration, and consuming people's hope," Orbán said[209]

Nevertheless, the Israeli left-of-centre newspaper, *Haaretz*, concluded that although a "crisis", the rise in anti-Semitism is not a "catastrophe" and has not spawned a mass exodus of Jews.[210]

Overall, one could argue that the rise of anti-EU parties reflects the impact of voter alienation that Rodrik's trilemma suggests is inevitable in the EU. Policy during the crisis estranged many voters, particularly those in crisis countries, who had to endure the hardship of their bailouts' austerity conditions. Outside these countries, events of the crisis, particularly political ones, may also have offended the principles of other EU citizens who worry preservation of the Union might undermine sovereignty and democracy in individual countries. To reverse this potential, the EU should create a more integrated, transparent, and accountable form of governance for European voters to preserve support for the Union.

In conclusion, politically, the eurozone crisis seems to have created feelings of 'Europeaness' among more than half of the EU population. That said, it also activated antipathy among the nearly other half. The EU's leaders took advantage of this moment to address major structural reforms to keep the integration process on track, so as to avoid future financial crises. These actions may also have had the effect of improving economic conditions, thereby reducing the power of the anti-EU movement. Nevertheless, the reforms have met with opposition stemming back to the intergovernmentalist/federalist debate, and may yet feed increased resentment and nationalist feelings among non-supporters of such reforms, and the most economically disaffected.

The question now is how economic circumstances will evolve in the EU. If conditions were to remain poor, support could erode for greater integration or for the continued support of the EU, tipping in favour of anti-EU, populist, and/or right-wing nationalist parties. The evolution of political support for the Union could fundamentally change if crisis conditions do not improve – and swiftly – given the high unemployment in Europe, which has improved little since 2012.

---

209 James Kirchick, "Missing the Point: Hungarian Leader Whitewashes Anti-Semitism" *Der Spiegel*, 6 May 2013, http://www.spiegel.de/international/europe/prime-minister-viktor-orban-downplays-rising-anti-semitism-in-hungary-a-898319.html (accessed 31 August 2015).
210 *Haaretz*.

Reforming The Eurozone's Economic Architecture

As stated in chapter three, a perfect currency union should have a banking union, to regulate banks, and a fiscal union, to regulate national spending and budgets. In the case of the EU, each requires that the member state surrender sovereignty to Brussels, in other words, that the member states take a collective step towards political union. Before the crisis, the idea of banking and fiscal unions was a non-starter. The crisis forced the issue, but not without controversy. The continual intergovernmentalist-versus-federalist tensions, in addition to a split and more passionate electorate, means that, despite the necessity for such unions economically, the politicians must tread lightly.

The Banking System

The Eurosystem was designed to preserve sovereign control of each country's banking system and to create a strong and independent central bank, the ECB. The regulation of each national banking system was left to its respective country. The lack of strong oversight in some member states, however, led to significant problems building up in the mid-2000s. Banks both in Ireland and Spain accrued significant portfolios of risky real estate debt that later led to banking crises in both countries. In Cyprus, the banking system accumulated assets greater than eight times the country's GDP, and then found itself undercapitalized when investments in Greek bonds incurred heavy losses, resulting in the need of an eventual bailout. Even in Germany, large international institutions such as Deutsche Bank were allowed to operate with very low levels of capital, allowing the firm to potentially threaten that country's financial system. National banking system crises have been pivotal in the evolution of the eurozone crisis, leading to bailouts being required in Ireland, Spain, and Cyprus.

Breaking the "doom-loop", as the linkage between banking system crises and sovereign debt crises has been called, required several changes to the Eurosystem's structure, specifically, the creation of a European banking union initiated in September 2012.[211] Creation of such a union required three new elements to be instituted in the existing Eurosystem structure: a single common supervisor and set of banking standards across all banks in the EU; a well-defined resolution process to determine how illiquid and insolvent institutions would be dealt with; and a common deposit protection scheme covering all EU deposits.

---

211 See EU (2012) "A roadmap towards a banking union," Communication from the Commission to the European Parliament, 12 September 2012 http://ec.europa.eu/finance/general-policy/docs/committees/reform/20120912-com-2012-510_en.pdf (accessed 3 August 2015).

Before the financial crisis, member states eschewed the idea of a banking union for fear of relinquishing sovereign control of their own banking systems and for fear of being liable for other states' debts, reintroducing the principle of moral hazard. If a common pool were established for bank recapitalization or to finance a single deposit insurance scheme, then the liability for bank failures in a single country could be spread across all currency union members. To reduce that liability and to reduce the moral hazard, a single system-wide regulator could ensure proper bank compliance across the eurozone, but only by having the states give up their sovereign control over their banking systems.

How Would the Banking Union Work?

The first of these new standards would be accomplished by having the ECB take over the regulation of all banking systems in the EU, and imposing a common set of operating standards across each. The common rulebook would ensure that the pressures of bank competition do not result in the worst regulatory practices becoming standard practice, a concern in the past. Further, a single regulator would ensure that similar banking problems in different nations were addressed coherently and consistently, avoiding the build-up of destabilizing problems in some countries and not others. Such a change would reduce uncertainty among regulated banks, and avoid problems seen in the past when domestic political incentives reduced the willingness of national regulators to deal with banking problems.

The second reform, the Single Resolution Mechanism (SRM) created consistency and greater certainty across the eurozone by instituting a common set of practices by which troubled banks would be shut down or recapitalized. Critical to this process is the determination of how such recapitalization might be funded to avoid such actions triggering a national sovereign debt crisis, that is, the "doom loop". One suggestion was to allow the European Stability Mechanism or ESM to inject capital directly into banks, thereby transferring the liability incurred by such actions to the greater EU and not to the country where the problems occurred. This suggestion, however, has been controversial, and opponents to the plan have argued little incentive would be created for careful regulation if someone else's funds were available to finance the costs of a failed bank, again leading to moral hazard. In June 2013, common EU resolution rules were initially agreed upon, which included allowing the official use of ESM funds for bank recapitalization.[212] As a compromise to ensure that nationalist interests did not

---

212 The agreement initially limited such uses of ESM funding to €60 billion, and required that funds in the country requiring aid be exhausted first. Further, it was resolved that for all

interfere with bank regulation, the EU created the Single Supervisory Mechanism (SSM) in November 2014, allowing the ECB to directly oversee the largest banks, while allowing national regulators to oversee the other approximately 6,000 banks in the euro area, or in any other countries that chose to be under this system.

The final reform necessary to create a banking union is a common bank deposit insurance system. In the past, banking insurance guarantees have been the responsibility of individual nations. If, however, a country were perceived as unable to guarantee the deposits due to its sovereign debt position, such fears would lead depositors, in times of financial crisis, to withdraw their funds and transfer them to banks in countries perceived as safer, thereby weakening already troubled banks and exacerbating the situation in troubled countries. A common banking insurance scheme funded by a single pool across all of Europe would undermine such withdrawal incentives. Such a system could be financed by a tax or levy on each bank proportional to their deposit base and guarantee all deposits in the EU up to some limit.[213] The idea of creating a common deposit insurance system, allowing the ESM to be used to recapitalize troubled banking systems directly, and imposing a common regulator over all European banks has been controversial and to date not yet adopted.

The German Constitutional Court has been the site of several of the legal battles against the concept of joint liability. Several reforms made, since the crisis began, have potentially undermined the principle banning joint liability in the Maastricht Treaty. Specifically, the creation of a jointly funded permanent bailout mechanism, the European Stability Mechanism (ESM), the ECB's program to intervene in sovereign debt markets to purchase member state bonds, and the banking union itself, have raised the ire of those who wish the Union to adhere to the original Maastricht principles. In January 2014, the Court in Karlsruhe ruled that the ECB's Outright Monetary Transactions (OTM), or bond buying scheme, violated the German constitution.[214] Peter Gauweiler, the German MP who brought the case, revelled in the ruling: "Karlsruhe has shown ECB President Mario Draghi what a bazooka really is."[215] However, the OTM action, although never put in force, was not cancelled; the Court referred the case to the European Court of Justice. As of

---

banks in all countries, recapitalization would first occur at the expense of bank shareholders and creditors, and then depositors with over €100,000 in deposits. Only after these resources were exhausted would EU taxpayers become liable for the remaining costs of recapitalization through ESM efforts.
213 Currently, this limit is €100,000 across the eurozone.
214 https://www.bundesverfassungsgericht.de/en/decisions/rs20140114_2bvr272813en.html.
215 "Europe or Democracy? What German Court Ruling Means for the Euro" *Der Spiegel* February 10, 2014, http://www.spiegel.de/international/europe/german-court-calls-ecb-bond-buying-into-question-a-952556.html.

publication, the ECJ had not yet ruled. In March 2014, the German Court ruled that the ESM was legal because it did not violate the Bundestag's autonomy over federal budgetary measures.[216] In July 2014, five academics filed a case arguing that the banking union had "no legal basis in the EU treaties and so represents a breach of constitutional rights." Markus Kerber, a finance professor at Berlin Technical University (TUB), and one of the plaintiffs, told reporters that the ECB's supervisory system with the power to oversee and, if necessary, shut down European banks is the "pinnacle of Brussels power-grabbing to date."[217] That said, without power and autonomy, the ECB is useless. *Der Spiegel* summarized the matter as a choice between "Europe or Democracy".[218] Clearly, the politics of the banking union have yet to be resolved.

Fiscal Union

The goal of the fiscal union is to codify budgetary discipline to ensure that member states do not exceed certain levels of debt, so as to avoid similar financial crises in the future. Eurozone members originally signed the Stability and Growth Pact, which entered into force in two stages in 1998 and 1999, requiring that governments keep deficits to three percent of GDP and debt to sixty percent of GDP. However, the pact was viewed as too inflexible and too unenforceable, so much so that European Commission President Romano Prodi called it "stupid".[219] Although Germany insisted on the pact to shield itself from others' poor economic decisions, it, itself, violated the pact in 2002; France did as well soon thereafter. The two major powers insisted on reform in 2005 to loosen the rules.

With the onset of the sovereign debt crisis, the member states set out to revise the rules once again. The EU's new fiscal governance has several parts including the Six-Pack, the Two-Pack, the Fiscal Compact, and the Treaty on Stability, Coordination, and Governance (TSCG). Five regulations and one directive, hence the Six-Pack, came into force on 13 December 2011 providing fiscal and macroeconomic surveillance. Through clearer definitions and a stronger sanction system supported by Reverse Qualified Majority Voting

---

216 Deutsche Welle "Germany's top court upholds legality of ESM rescue fund" 18 March 2014 http://www.dw.de/germanys-top-court-upholds-legality-of-esm-rescue-fund/a-17503069.
217 Honor Mahony, "Banking union faces legal challenge in Germany" *EUObserver* 28 July 2014, http://euobserver.com/economic/125117.
218 "Europe or Democracy? What German Court Ruling Means for the Euro" *Der Spiegel* February 10, 2014, http://www.spiegel.de/international/europe/german-court-calls-ecb-bond-buying-into-question-a-952556.html.
219 *The Economist*, "Charlemagne: Reforming the EU's stability pact" 24 October 2002, http://www.economist.com/node/1403588 (accessed 3 August 2015).

(QMV), where a QMV in the Council must be attained to *stop* such sanctions from occurring, the Six-Pack strengthens the Stability and Growth Pact.

In March 2012, the EU leaders signed the Treaty on Stability, Coordination, and Growth, including the Fiscal Compact, to run alongside both the SGP and the Six-Pack. In May 2013, the Two-Pack came into force providing for budgetary surveillance. At Germany's insistence, the compact enshrined the "golden rule", committing states to balanced budgets. The Compact requires national parliaments to adopt country-specific, medium-term objectives (MTO) to facilitate both convergence and compliance. Its implementation has, in part, accelerated some labour market reforms. The compact, which required countries to submit budgets to the Commission for approval prior to implementation at the national level, allowed exceptions to debt and deficit requirements under specific conditions. For example, as was the case with France in 2013, deficit targets can be relaxed in exchange for competitiveness reforms. However, conditionality imposed by demands from the EU has allowed national governments to obviate responsibility for unpopular reforms by blaming Brussels. In doing so, the governments portray the currency union as a cost to national sovereignty and, therefore, may undermine support for additional economic and political integration.

In the end, all member states signed on to the new reforms except the United Kingdom and newcomer Croatia, but not without some unease. The Czech Republic was the last to sign in 2014, because its previous centre-right government refused to as long as it was in power. France supported the move with reservations. French Socialist, Elisabeth Guigou, head of parliament's foreign affairs committee, explained, "We don't like this pact, it is a Sarkozy legacy. Merkel insisted on it because France has been breaking stability pact rules since 2003."[220] To make the pact more palatable to those in his party, Hollande negotiated a package of European growth measures to be enacted at the same time. Nevertheless, with the UK veto, the treaty must be an extra-EU treaty, that is signed outside the auspices of the EU.

In the end, the post-crisis 'fiscal union' is not so much a fiscal union as an attempt to strengthen the origami of fiscal rules so that they hold more rigorously than they had earlier with the original Stability and Growth Pact. Cynically, one could say that these reforms are "same old, same old": more rules to control what some countries do. While these rules could stabilize the currency somewhat, they are also one-sided regulations coming down on the austerity side of the austerity versus stimulus debate. With reference to Rodrik, without political reform, such policies may further alienate some people. After all, should not the people of Europe decide the austerity/stimulus balance? If the general European public wanted greater debt to stimulate the

---

220 Catherine Bremer and Emmanuel Jarry, "France readies EU fiscal pact for green light" *Reuters*, 19 September 2012.

economies, such a choice could alternatively be accommodated in a stable currency union if joint liability and transfers were allowed, alongside national market reforms. These fiscal reforms are ultimately a straitjacket, but not necessarily a golden one.

Rodrik's trilemma suggests a complete fiscal union must also include a political one that allows voter representation at the supra-national level. A fiscal union would not only allow greater coordination of fiscal policies across member countries, but it would also allow the European electorate the ability to influence these policies and create EU accountability to the entire union, and not only to the domestic electorates each leader now serves.

Conclusions: Economically, the EU Needs Political Union; Politically, EU leaders Cannot Afford It.

The depth and duration of Europe's crisis has primarily occurred for two reasons. One is that the scale of the problem was very large. It has involved the entire financial system of an area defined by seventeen countries whose collective GDP is larger than that of the United States.[221] Second, the policy response has often appeared uncoordinated and slow owing to the significantly more complicated and restricted political and legislative environment of the eurozone, where consensus rules the day. Moreover, policy actions have required coordination of three separate entities, the European Commission, IMF, and ECB, or the "Troika", causing delays due to the multilateral bargaining necessary before a policy could be enacted.

In addition, the governance of the EU is constrained by the demand that the sovereignty of each state be respected. In essence, all important matters must be decided by unanimity. Chief executives, who define eurozone policy through their decisions on the European Council, were elected to represent their countries' own national interests, not those of Europe. They have recognized and acted with this limitation in mind. Moreover, recognizing the delicate politics that exist within each member state, leaders typically refrain from putting other elected leaders in such a position openly. Therefore, the problem of slow policy implementation and limited reform can be traced to the incentives posed by currency union members' narrow self-interest within the EU system of governance, to wit, the lack of a strong Europe-wide federal system.

If domestic concerns dominate the decisions of the European Council, Germany's and France's domestic concerns have dominated it the most. In the EU, not all countries are created equal. Given that the crisis has required

---

221 When the crisis began in 2009, there were only sixteen countries. Estonia joined the currency union in 2011.

significant commitments of resources to support bailouts and credit guarantees, policies have especially required the consent of those who would be the primary paymasters – the largest economies in the monetary union. For this reason, France and Germany, representing almost half of the total funding guarantees to the EFSF and ESM, the two main funds used to administer the crisis bailouts, have dominated the negotiation of all agreements. Combined with incentives to follow national self-interests, this constraint implies that the domestic interests of Germany and France have overall played the greatest role in determining eurozone policy. The failed eurobond proposals are a good example.[222] These proposals, which found backing in several other countries in the eurozone, faced vehement resistance in Germany because the electorate there saw such proposals as violating the prohibition of joint liability and potentially very costly to their own country. For this reason, eurobonds have never been considered seriously as a policy option. It is difficult to imagine that similar concerns in Luxembourg, for example, would have had the same effect on eurobond proposals, had France and Germany been on board.

Figure 6-11 illustrates the reason for France and Germany's significant influence in policymaking during the eurozone crisis. Throughout the negotiations, three blocs often formed. Germany and the northern countries (Austria, The Netherlands, and Finland) formed the first bloc controlling over forty percent of the collective commitment to Europe's bailout funds and financial firewall. Germany alone represented over twenty-seven percent of the commitment. These countries have typically called for the greatest fiscal responsibility in aided countries, resisting joint liability proposals and usually in favour of smaller, less costly aid packages. France and other countries (Belgium, Luxembourg, Cyprus, Malta, Slovakia, Slovenia, and Estonia) composed a second bloc accounting for another 27.7 percent share of commitments, with France by far the largest contributor.[223] This set of countries has often acted as the balance of power between calls for more conservative policymaking and calls for greater action. SPIGI economies represented a third bloc. While, in theory, SPIGI countries have a significant contribution to make to the financial facilities, in practice, they have been the primary recipients of aid, thus their potential contributions have mattered less and their negotiating position weakened. Effectively, it is the credit of the French and German blocs in figure 6-11 that guarantee the financing of both the

---

222 Eurobonds refer to proposals that would allow sovereign debt among eurozone countries to be sold as bonds that were backed directly or indirectly by eurozone or EU member countries as a whole. Such bonds create a specific form of joint liability and have therefore been controversial.
223 Estonia does not have a contribution requirement in the EFSF as it joined the eurozone after this fund was created. It does have a contribution share in the ESM.

EFSF and the ESM, and within these blocs, France and Germany's concerns matter most. The European financial crisis has demonstrated that the EU's monetary union is not one of equals.

Overall, policy response in the eurozone crisis has depended on the speed with which countries were willing to commit to specific actions and, in particular, on the interests of the two countries with the greatest means, i.e., France and Germany. Their willingness, in turn, has depended on their leaders' willingness to act. That readiness has not necessarily been determined by the perception of a threat to Europe's best interests, but instead to threats to the best interests of their own countries. This conflict of interests has slowed the adoption of policies to address sovereign debt market instability and aid programs for troubled nations and often resulted in the scope of policies adopted being compromised once chosen actions are agreed to. Power in the eurozone comes from the pocketbook, and the pocketbook also grants the power to dictate the speed circumstances will be reacted to.

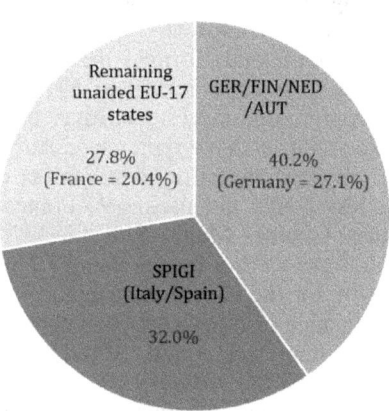

Bailout Resource Shares

Figure 6-11: The share of EFSF/ESM commitments across the, at the time, seventeen countries in the eurozone at the start of the crisis. Northern countries led by Germany were responsible for over forty percent of the funds guaranteed if future bailouts were needed, with Germany representing twenty seven percent of the total. SPIGI countries that had not received a bailout in 2012 (Spain and Italy) accounted for thirty-two percent of resources, and the remaining countries including France accounted for 27.7 percent. Germany and France alone accounted for over forty-seven percent of the liability, thus it is understandable how Merkel and Sarkozy – Merkozy – emerged as the two leading policymakers during the crisis. Source Data: European Union, ESM treaty, Annex 1 adjusted assuming Ireland, Greece and Portugal had responsibilities suspended due to their bailouts.

The influence of national self-interest and the need for compromise have also almost certainly contributed to policy mistakes. The northern European countries strongly supported the implementation of costly austerity programmes, in part, to reduce the contributions they faced in supporting bailout programs. As discussed previously, austerity has likely undermined economic recovery in aided countries and worsened the economic circumstances bailouts were supposed to improve. Similarly, the original lack of EU support to include private sector losses in the first Greek bailout almost certainly stemmed from the fact that French and German banks would have incurred the largest losses in resulting private write-downs and bond haircuts. In hindsight, this unwillingness to allow private sector losses only increased the eventual total cost of the Greek bailouts.[224] Overall, national self-interests have resulted in aid programs that have proven too small, too slow, too costly, or too harsh in their implementation, creating the conditions under which aid has been less effective than it could have been. Further, the potential for policy mistakes and the difficulty in predicting policy outcomes due to the EU's need to achieve political consensus has contributed to greater uncertainty in financial markets during the crisis, which, in turn, has raised bond rates and made finance more difficult in troubled countries.

The clear solution to the eurozone crisis is political union. European Commission president Barosso declared: "Let's not be afraid of the words: we will need to move towards a federation of nation states. This is what we need. This is our political horizon."[225] A currency union is fundamentally as much a political undertaking as it is an economic one, especially if it to be maintained. There are only two ways to achieve political union. One is through convergence. In other words, all member state economies and polities become similar enough in appearance and behavior that they can very easily follow the same policy paths. In this case, political union comes from member states reading from the same page to speak together with a common voice. This process is cumbersome and can lead to cacophony. The second is through explicit federation whereby one entity that represents the whole speaks with a single voice.

---

224 See IMF "Greece: Ex Post Evaluation of Exceptional Access under the 2010 Stand-By Arrangement," IMF Country Report No. 13/156, June 2013 https://www.imf.org/external/pubs/ft/scr/2013/cr13156.pdf (accessed 3 August 2015).
225 *Euractiv*, "Barroso: 'We will need to move towards a federation of nation states'" 13 September 2012 http://www.euractiv.com/priorities/barroso-seeks-public-space-launc-news-514761 (accessed 3 August 2015).

Federalists are often impatient and unhappy with piecemeal unification. They prefer furious negotiation to hammer out differences in order to produce a constitution, but what happens if the people reject the attempt? The Constitutional Convention was called in 2002 "to reinvent the system, and propose a New Europe."[226] Although its goal was a constitutional treaty rather than a constitution per se, the treaty was to address the shortcomings of the Amsterdam and Nice intergovernmental conferences, recognize that the EU had gone beyond the Treaty of Rome with the introduction of foreign and security policy as well as justice and home affairs, and to establish clear rules before enlargement in 2004, when, with ten new members, the process would become ten times more difficult. As Valery Giscard d'Estaing, Convention Chairman, explained in his speech to the College of Europe in Bruges:

> The founding fathers knew that their system, which remains the basis for integration, would have to evolve and transform itself once European construction moved beyond economic integration to address political matters. In his memoirs, Jean Monnet, who was in this sense as much a visionary as a pragmatist, points out that: "The purpose of the Community was confined to the areas of solidarity enshrined in the Treaties, and while we always believed that those areas of solidarity would call forth others, and would gradually result in the broadest integration of human activities, I knew that their progress would halt at the boundaries where political power begins. At that point, it would be necessary to reinvent."[227]

After much fanfare and myriad references to George Washington and Philadelphia, two founding members of the EU, France and The Netherlands, rejected the treaty in 2005 in popular referenda. In 2007, the European Council announced, "The constitutional concept, which consisted in repealing all existing Treaties and replacing them by a single text called "Constitution", is abandoned."[228] The political support for federation was insufficient.

Where is the boundary between economic integration and political power? Perhaps, there is none. Margaret Thatcher recognized the link and refused to cross the line: "this Government has no intention of agreeing to the imposition of a single currency. That would be entering a federal Europe through the back-Delors. Any such proposal involves a loss of sovereignty

---

226 Speech By Valery Giscard D'Estaing, Chairman of the European Convention, Opening of the academic year at the College of Europe, Bruges, 2 October 2002, 4 http://european-convention.europa.eu/docs/speeches/3314.pdf (accessed 3 August 2015). Underlining used for emphasis in original text.
227 Ibid., 6.
228 Council of the European Union, Brussels, 26 June 2007 POLGEN 74 11218/07, http://register.consilium.europa.eu/doc/srv?l=EN&f=ST%2011218%202007%20INIT (accessed 3 August 2015).

which Parliament would not accept."[229] This position was, in fact, an echo of Winston Churchill's 1946 speech calling for a United States of Europe, one that he had no intention of seeing Britain join for exactly the same reason. Elsewhere in Europe, Denmark also rejected the euro, for similar reasons. The Annual Report of the Deutsche Bundesbank also recognized the link between currency and national sovereignty, but rather than opposing the euro, embraced it: "As a monetary union represents a lasting commitment to integration which encroaches on the core area of national sovereignty, the EMU participants must also be prepared to take further steps towards a more comprehensive political union."[230]

Without political backing for federation, the only other option for political union is to limp along, working towards convergence until the public support can be found. That said, Thatcher was correct in saying a common currency would lead to federalism. The euro is arguably a more successful political tool than economic tool. In public opinion polls, all countries that use the euro report feeling more 'European' and are more supportive of 'Europe' than non-participanting populations. Federalist/intergovernmentalist tensions will remain until European citizens feel 'less tense' about federation. Time may be on the federalists' side. Opinion polls demonstrate that the more educated an individual and the more he or she interacts with the EU, the more supportive he/she will be of integration. European history is characterized by fits and starts. Just as the eurozone crisis spawned a banking and fiscal union heretofore unimaginable, a limping European Union can still move forward.

At the same time, perhaps that conclusion is too optimistic. *The Economist* cover from 25 October 2014 depicted a dead parrot representing Europe's economy. Alluding to the famous Monty Python skit, The Parrot Sketch, Angela Merkel responds "It's only resting".[231] Limping along may not be enough to deal with the continuing economic crisis. After the deployment of Draghi's Big Bazooka, the pressure of the immediate financial crisis in Europe seemed to subside. The eurozone economy improved, and Europe continued with its bitter medicine of austerity measures. Not surprisingly, the austerity measures in aid-recipient countries reduced demand in those countries for goods from the north, especially from Germany. Growth and growth forecasts for Europe have generally been anemic since 2012 despite the end of the financial crisis. The ensuing lack of growth has not only failed to re-

---

229 Margaret Thatcher, Speech to the Conservative Party Conference in Bournemouth, 12 October 1990, http://www.margaretthatcher.org/document/108217 (accessed 3 August 2015).
230 Annual Report of the Deutsche Bundesbank, 1995.
231 *The Economist* "Europe's Economy", 25 October 2014. The joke referred to a famous skit by the British comedy troupe Monty Python, in which a pet-store owner attempts to sell a dead parrot to a suspicious customer, claiming the parrot "is only resting" https://www.youtube.com/watch?v=npjOSLCR2hE (accessed 5 September 2015).

duce unemployment significantly in most countries, it has also led to a period of little inflation, causing many economists and the ECB itself to recognize the potential threat of general economic stagnation and even deflation within the eurozone. Deflation is particularly worrisome as a general fall in prices would not only reduce incentives for increased economic activity, but such pressures could cause debt burdens to increase, possibly leading to the break-up of the euro. Charlemagne writing in the *Economist* concludes, "Europe did well to hold together during the crisis years, but its failures are apparent: a jobless army 25 million strong; millions more underemployed. Such numbers do not seem to galvanise politicians the same way bond yields at 7% do."[232]

Throughout the European financial crisis, EU leaders have only been able to agree to policy when severe crisis conditions demanded action be taken. The structure of the EU has left leaders 'between a rock and a hard place'. If the currency union failed, blame for the outcomes would be theirs. At the same time, reforms to avoid such a failure are taken only at the last possible moment with the least resource commitment possible because subordinating national interests to European interests undermines political support at home. Under such conditions, leaders face an incentive to delay any decision, hoping circumstances will change in the interim. The result is weak leadership and actions that seem too little, too late.

Given these incentives, it is possible that only a new crisis will spur the necessary reforms needed to move forward. Discomfort spurs cooperation. In just three years between 2009 and 2012, the financial crisis forced greater integration than had been achieved in the previous decade. Ironically, success in averting an ultimate breakup during the crisis may have allowed leaders to avoid finishing the process in a way that could have led to more permanent stability in the monetary union. The final lesson learned may be that only through the crucible of crisis will Churchill's "United States of Europe" become reality.

---

232 Charlemagne, "Gummed up" *Economist*, 25 October 2014, 58.

Index

Anti-Semitism 189-90
Austerity 5, 17-18, 52, 66, 73-75, 79, 106, 110, 115, 120, 126, 127, 130-136, 140, 142-159, 164, 166, 171-176, 187-190, 195, 199, 201
Austria 14, 37, 51, 54, 75, 78-81, 86-89, 94-95, 136, 165, 167, 170-174, 181
Banking union 26, 39, 41, 48, 59, 60-62, 67-68, 121, 146-148, 163, 191-194
Barroso, José Manuel 28, 187, 199
Belgium 22, 30, 37, 54, 56, 81-82, 86, 131, 165, 167-168, 171, 181, 197
Berlusconi, Silvio 111-112, 133, 135
Bretton Woods Agreement 64
Bundesbank 36, 41, 78, 130, 131, 137, 201
Cameron, David 173, 188
Captain Euro 33-34
Croatia 195
Cyprus 38, 59, 81, 83, 96, 100-103, 112-114, 143-144, 147-148, 157, 162, 167-168, 171, 186, 191, 197,
Czech Republic 195
De Gaulle, Charles 23-24, 41
Delors, Jacques 24, 30, 36-38, 186, 200,
Denmark 14, 23-24, 29, 80-81, 85-86, 201
Draghi, Mario 18, 56, 68, 74, 115, 117, 139, 145, 162, 193, 201
Estonia 38, 167, 170-171, 196-197

Eurobond 47, 131-132, 197
European Central Bank 8, 18, 19, 28, 32-34, 37, 62, 65, 68, 74, 157
European Coal and Steel Community (ECSC) 22-23, 38, 110
European Commission 10-11, 22, 25-27, 32, 36, 42, 51, 58, 66, 101, 103, 111, 122, 131, 140, 146, 157, 194, 199
European Council 14, 24, 27, 35, 36, 37, 52, 75, 78, 185-186, 196
European Court of Justice 23, 25, 27, 28, 193
European Economic and Financial Affairs Council (ECOFIN) 10-11, 28, 37, 101
European Financial Stability Facility (EFSF) 124-127, 140-141, 162, 197-198
European Monetary Institute (EMI) 37-38, 55
European Monetary System (EMS) 35, 44
European Monetary Union (EMU) 13, 37, 42, 48, 61, 68, 117, 172, 201
European Parliament 12, 22, 24, 26-31, 34, 66, 107, 164, 180, 188, 191
European Stability Mechanism 193
European System of Central Banks (ESCB) 56
Eurosystem 55-57, 59-62, 68, 122, 191
Exchange Rate Mechanism (ERM) 55, 65
Federalism 26, 34, 41, 66, 201

Finland 37, 51, 54, 75, 78-81, 83, 86-89, 94-95, 112, 136, 140, 165, 167, 170-171, 173
Fiscal Compact 55, 140, 149, 170, 177, 194, 195
France 10, 14, 22-23, 29-30, 33-34, 37, 52-54, 56, 62-63, 74, 81-83, 86, 109, 111, 123, 129, 131, 141-142, 144, 149, 155, 162, 165, 167-171, 177, 181, 187, 194, 195, 196-200
General Agreement on Tariffs and Trade (GATT) 64
German Constitutional Court 128, 193
Germany 7, 10, 13, 19, 22, 30, 34, 37-38, 42, 44, 47-49, 52-54, 58, 62-63, 73-83, 86-90, 93-95, 106, 110-111, 118, 123, 125, 128-132, 136-137, 141, 148, 162, 165, 167, 169-173, 177, 180-181, 187-191, 194-198, 201
Greece 9, 10, 11, 15-19, 37-38, 47, 52-55, 58-59, 62, 66, 69-73, 78-79, 81-115, 118-120
Greek Referendum of 2015 158
Grexit 129, 142, 154
Hollande, François 141, 149, 195
Housing bubble 87, 104, 106, 108, 110-114, 118
Hungary 14, 189-190
International Monetary Fund (IMF) 34, 42, 67, 95-96, 104-108, 118, 120-121, 123-128, 133, 155-157, 167, 169, 174-175, 186, 196, 199
Ireland 18, 23-224, 37, 54-55, 59-60, 71-72, 78-79, 81-87, 90-91, 102-106, 108-114, 120, 123, 125-128, 133-134, 136, 138, 143, 149, 161-162, 165, 167-171, 174, 181, 191, 199

Italy 13, 18, 22, 30, 36-37, 44, 54, 56, 59, 62, 66, 72, 78-83, 85-87, 91, 102-103, 110-115, 133-138, 142-145, 147, 162, 165-171, 174, 181, 188-189, 198
Karamanlis, Kostas 9
Keynesianism 17, 77-78, 172, 175
Latvia 38, 167-168, 170-171
Lehman Brothers 111, 117, 124
Lisbon Treaty 24, 28
Lithuania 38
Long Term Refinancing Operation (LTRO) 138-140, 161
Luxembourg 22-23, 30, 35, 37, 54, 56, 81, 90, 105, 165, 167, 171, 197
Maastricht Treaty 26, 29, 37-38, 41, 48-49, 54, 56, 62, 111, 114, 123, 128, 131, 170-171, 193
Malta 38, 167-168, 170-171, 197
Merkel, Angela 11, 15, 34, 75, 125, 131-132, 141, 144, 173, 178-179, 195, 198, 201
Merkozy 34, 141, 198
Monnet, Jean 21-22, 41, 200
Monti, Mario 112, 135, 147
Moral hazard 49, 58, 73-74, 76-77, 123, 126, 129, 131, 133, 145, 151, 192
Netherlands 13-14, 22, 30, 37, 54, 75, 78-79, 81, 84, 86-87, 89, 94-95, 162, 165, 167-168, 171, 173-174, 187, 197, 200
Optimal Currency Area 45-46, 48, 178
Orbán, Viktor 189-190
Ordnungspolitik 77
Outright Monetary Transactions (OMT) 74, 145
Papandreou, George 73, 101, 133

Portugal 18, 28, 37, 52, 54-55, 59-60, 72, 79, 81-83, 85-87, 91, 102-103, 107-109, 111-112, 114-115, 120, 123, 126, 127, 133-134, 136, 138, 143, 147, 149, 161-162, 165, 167-171, 174, 179, 181, 199
Prodi, Romano 110-111, 194
Renzi, Matteo 147
Rodrik, Dani 42, 63-66, 150-152, 160, 190, 196
Sarkozy, Nicholas 34, 141-142, 195, 198
Schuman, Robert 22, 38, 41, 163-164
Single European Act (SEA) 24, 139
Single Resolution Mechanism (SRM) 192
Single Supervisory Mechanism (SSM) 193
Slovakia 38, 167-168, 170-171, 197
Slovenia 38, 167-168, 170-171, 197
Sovereign debt 10-11, 55, 58-60, 76, 92, 101, 104-105, 110-111, 118-119, 122-123, 125-126, 130-133, 138, 140, 142-146, 149, 151, 161, 164, 176, 187, 191-194, 198
Spain 16, 18, 28, 37, 54, 59, 66, 72, 78-79, 81-83, 85-87, 91, 102-103, 107-115, 133, 135-138, 142-147, 149, 161-162, 165-171, 174, 179, 181, 189, 191, 198
Stability and Growth Pact (SGP) 38, 49, 52-55, 62, 67, 74, 96, 107, 195
Sweden 29, 81, 85-86
Treaty on Stability, Coordination, and Governance (TSCG) 194

Treaty(ies) of Rome 23, 26, 51, 163, 200
Troika 121, 124, 127-128, 130, 134-136, 140, 145, 147-148, 150-153, 155-160, 162, 168, 196
Tsipras, Alexis 101, 152, 154, 156-157, 159
United Kingdom 23-24, 29, 81, 85-86, 104, 113, 148, 188, 189, 195
Van Rompuy, Herman 14
Varoufakis, Yanis 153, 159
Werner Plan 35, 38
World Trade Organization (WTO) 64

Trouble spots

Anton Bebler (ed.)

"Frozen conflicts" in Europe

2015. 215 pp. Hc. A5. 49,90 € (D),
51,30 € (A), US$75.95, GBP 46.95
ISBN 978-3-8474-0133-9
eISBN 978-3-8474-0428-6

Oft forgotten but simmering "frozen conflicts" continuously mark the political map of Europe. All located in South Eastern Europe, the Black Sea area and Transcaucasia, these conflicts run along ethnic, national, cultural and linguistic lines, separating communities. The analytical chapters and comments in this volume present different viewpoints on the cases of Northern Cyprus, Transnistria, Abkhazia, South Ossetia, Nagorny Karabakh, Kosovo, and Crimea.

Order now:

Verlag Barbara Budrich
Barbara Budrich Publishers
Stauffenbergstr. 7
51379 Leverkusen-Opladen

Tel +49 (0)2171.344.594
Fax +49 (0)2171.344.693
info@budrich.de

shop.budrich-academic.de

Anticorruption Report | vol. 3

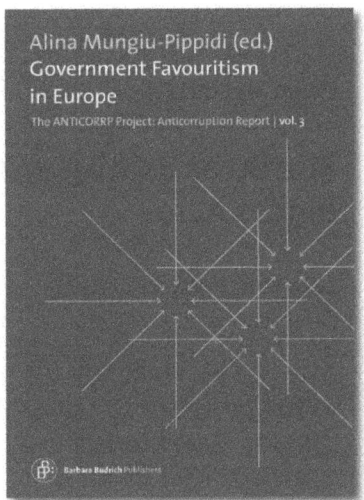

Alina Mungiu-Pippidi (ed.)

Government Favouritism in Europe

The ANTICORRP Project:
Anticorruption Report, vol. 3

2015. 128 pp. Pb.19,90 € (D),
20,50 € (A), US$29.95, GBP 17.95
ISBN 978-3-8474-0795-9
eISBN 978-3-8474-0921-2

This volume is entirely based on objective indicators and offers both quantitative and qualitative assessments of the linkage between political corruption and organised crime using statistics on spending, procurement contract data and judicial data. The methodology used in the analysis of particularism of public resource distribution is applicable to any other country where procurement data can be made available and opens the door to a better understanding and control of both systemic corruption and political finance.

Order now:

Verlag Barbara Budrich
Barbara Budrich Publishers
Stauffenbergstr. 7
51379 Leverkusen-Opladen

Tel +49 (0)2171.344.594
Fax +49 (0)2171.344.693
info@budrich.de

shop.budrich-academic.de

The EU and Children's Rights

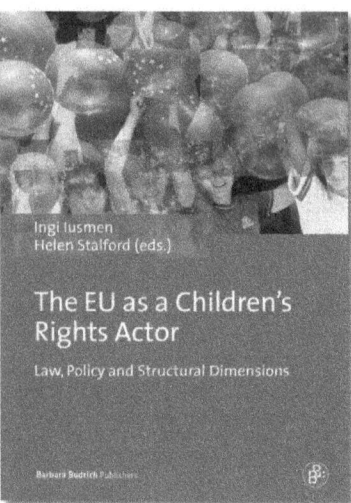

Ingi Iusmen
Helen Stalford (eds.)

The EU as a Children's Rights Actor

Law, Policy and Structural Dimensions

2016. 331 pp. Pb. 42,00 € (D),
43,20 € (A), US$58.00, GBP 36.95
ISBN 978-3-8474-0193-3
eISBN 978-3-8474-0412-5

This edited collection critiques, from an interdisciplinary perspective, the growing body of EU children's rights activities in the light of broader global political, economic and legal processes. Specifically, it interrogates whether EU intervention effectively responds to what are perceived as global violations of children's rights; the extent to which EU efforts to uphold children's rights complement and reinforce parallel national and international pursuits.

Order now:

Verlag Barbara Budrich
Barbara Budrich Publishers
Stauffenbergstr. 7
51379 Leverkusen-Opladen

Tel +49 (0)2171.344.594
Fax +49 (0)2171.344.693
info@budrich.de

shop.budrich-academic.de

GPSR Authorized Representative: Easy Access System Europe, Mustamäe tee 50, 10621 Tallinn, Estonia, gpsr.requests@easproject.com